MIRACLE IN THE MOUNTAINS

BOOKS BY HARNETT T. KANE

LOUISIANA HAYRIDE—
The American Rehearsal for Dictatorship

THE BAYOUS OF LOUISIANA

DEEP DELTA COUNTRY
(American Folkways Series)

PLANTATION PARADE

NATCHEZ ON THE MISSISSIPPI

NEW ORLEANS WOMAN
Biographical novel of Myra Clark Gaines

BRIDE OF FORTUNE
Novel based on the life of Mrs. Jefferson Davis

QUEEN NEW ORLEANS:
City by the River

PATHWAY TO THE STARS
Novel based on the life of John McDonogh

GENTLEMEN, SWORDS AND PISTOLS

THE SCANDALOUS MRS. BLACKFORD
Novel based on the life of Harriet Blackford, with Victor LeClerc

DEAR DOROTHY DIX
With Ella Bentley Arthur

THE LADY OF ARLINGTON
Novel based on the life of Mrs. Robert E. Lee

SPIES FOR THE BLUE AND GRAY

THE SMILING REBEL
Novel based on the life of Belle Boyd

MIRACLE IN THE MOUNTAINS
The Story of Martha Berry, with Inez Henry

MIRACLE

IN THE

MOUNTAINS

BY

HARNETT T. KANE

WITH

INEZ HENRY

DOUBLEDAY & COMPANY, INC.

Garden City, New York

371.1092
B534b
1956

CONTENTS

PART ONE
STEEPLES ON THE CHICKEN HOUSES

PART TWO
EVERYBODY MUST BE GOING SOMEWHERE

PART THREE
"SOMETHING WONDERFUL AROUND THE CORNER"

EPILOGUE
"BUT TO MINISTER"

PART ONE

Steeples on the

Chicken Houses

CHAPTER I

SOME KNOCKS,
SOME BUFFETINGS

MARTHA BERRY stood one day in her later years beside a young student, admiring an oak tree that towered over them. "All the buffetings it's had," she mused, "all the knocks . . . But it was the knocks that made it grow." This was one of her favorite themes: "The troubles you've had—they're what make you."

At first glance it might appear that the young Martha Berry knew few difficulties. Hers was a lively childhood, filled with more sun than shadow. The heavy Ionic columns of Oak Hill had an air of solidity, the façade of a crowded, many-roomed house in which a youthful wife and older husband looked after eleven children, eight their own, three those of a dead brother.

In a way the young Berrys were highly favored, with a governess, shining carriages of ornamented woods and glass, dark servants, and other marks of the cotton gentry. The family never lost its stately white house, as did others around it. Yet

9

Martha was born in 1866, the first year after the crushing end of the war with the North, during which Sherman's army had marched by, laying a scourge on the red earth. Disaster brushed close to Oak Hill as Captain Thomas Berry applied himself furiously to keep himself and his neighbors going. As the second oldest child Martha necessarily knew more of the family's problems than did most of the others. As a girl she also became the one who "looked after the rest" when need arose.

In a time of rapidly changing conditions she had before her the example of not one but two parents of strong personality. Her father, big-framed, hard-working, was an entrepreneur who saw a great deal of his world before he hitched his star to a cotton wagon. In the 1600s the first Berry reached Virginia from England, moved to Maryland, and became an assemblyman with indentured servants and lands granted by patent. Born in Rockbridge County, Virginia, Thomas was the son of a gentle and scholarly individual who, as one of the family phrased it, "had the practical sense of a rabbit." The father signed a large note for a relative who disappeared, leaving him bankrupt and burdened with the care of the man's wife and five children.

At thirteen Tom left school to help support the family, and for a time his mother tried to run a boardinghouse. The boy had a warm heart, and when his father's slaves were eventually put up for sale he asked a sister what would happen to a beloved older servant. "If we pray, God won't let them take her." Inside the house they knelt together, but when they emerged they saw attendants pull the weeping woman away. Years later the episode still haunted him.

The adolescent Tom showed signs of developing into a good businessman, one who could make much out of little. Several years later his father moved down to the strategically situated Tennessee town of Chattanooga, where he re-established himself and became its first mayor. After a while the twenty-year-old Thomas Berry heard of an area beyond the state line in

Georgia, which had begun to thrive as a cotton center. Only a short time earlier the whites had forced the Cherokees to migrate to the West and had started a dusty, straggling town at the junction of two rivers, the Etowah and the Oostanaula, which combined to form the Coosa. The settlers called the place Rome, because, like that other spot across the sea, it had seven hills.

Having scant capital, Thomas Berry went to Rome and found a storekeeper willing to take him on as an apprentice. He began by sweeping the floor and quickly worked his way up to becoming a partner in the business. People were pleased with the alert, good-looking young man, and eventually he had his own store. His enthusiasm matched his ambition, and Georgians recall him as a salesman par excellence. One "old Roman," as the locality described its citizens, explained that she often took the opposite sidewalk, "because he always brought out things I 'had to have' or couldn't resist."

But adventure called, and he rode off at the outbreak of the Mexican War to fight at Vera Cruz. Back in Rome, he bought a fertile tract of land some miles out of town, and then was away again on a quest for more excitement, the California gold rush. He returned with only a handful of nuggets of little value and a lively tale or two.

By this time the rich Georgia earth poured out its cotton. The white gold of the fields, forced labor to draw it forth, and boats to take it to the world. . . . The pattern had been set. The bachelor Thomas, now thirty, saw his acres spread and opened a cotton factor's office in town. "Father's idea," one of his daughters said, "was to buy land at fifty cents an acre, grow cotton, buy cotton, and ship cotton." By means of agility, concentration, and perspiration he made the Berry name grow steadily in importance.

Almost midway between Atlanta and Chattanooga, the countryside of Rome lay partly on the flat river bed, partly in the foothills of the long ranges that reach a thousand miles

11

across the South. Mountain settlers and cotton families lived within easy distance of one another, and Thomas had friends among both groups. In his office along Cotton Row he arranged deals with the big growers, and gave advice and occasional loans to the highlanders.

Contemporaries called him a kind as well as canny man. Going to a ball, he saw a girl who sat timidly in the corner, a wallflower. The personable planter sought her out, to dance with her until the end, and "gave her a wonderful time. It was the kind of thing he often did." . . . Then in the late 1850s an itinerant photographer showed him samples of daguerreotypes, and Thomas' finger pointed to the likeness of a bright young girl. "Who's that? I'd like to meet *her*."

She was Frances Rhea, whose father owned the big Turkey Town plantation near Gadsden over in Alabama. Before long Thomas Berry made the trip there and liked the girl even more than he had her picture. At eighteen Frances was small, dark-eyed, intent. In time the forty-year-old Thomas brought her back to preside over the house he built up at Oak Hill. Both went to work to develop their joint estate.

By 1860 the differences dividing North and South had crystallized. Thomas Berry looked with distrust at the hothead orators on both sides; like others he said that if war came it would be a politicians' fight. The politicians had their way, and in April of '61, her first child within her, Frances heard the echoes of the firing at Fort Sumter. Sadly Thomas Berry waited until Georgia seceded, and then volunteered.

As a veteran of the Mexican War, he formed his own infantry company, gathering a band of county residents, including gaunt-cheeked highlanders of the adjoining Lavendar Mountain. Other merchants were repudiating their debts in Northern cities; let the Yankees whistle for their damned money! To Thomas Berry this was dishonest; totaling his accounts, he sent payments in full to his Northern creditors.

Before going to war, he took his wife and infant daughter

Jennie to one of her family's Alabama plantations. There the sturdy Frances nursed her Confederate spirit at the same time she did her baby. When she heard that "Yankees are comin'," the young wife sent all horses and cows across the river and stuffed pillows with meal and flour, sugar and coffee. On rode the invaders, East Tennesseeans who had gone Unionist—"traitors," Frances called them, her eyes flashing. She stared helplessly as the soldiers killed chickens, ducks, and animals and ran through the house, pilfering, wrecking. When they discovered the pillows they set fire to the precious supplies.

As soon as the marauders departed Frances raced to the Union encampment with a demand to see the commander. "I'm not afraid of real Yankees, but I am of Southerners in blue," she cried to him. "And I demand protection!" Amused by her spirit, the officer provided her with a guard. For the rest of the war Frances Berry ran a half-ruined property and nursed her resentment. Once, finding a Unionist on one of her missing horses, she seized the bridle and would not let go until higher officers gave it back to her. Let them kill her first. "The Confederacy may have surrendered at Appomattox," in the words of a daughter, "but she never did."

Back at Oak Hill, Frances welcomed her returning husband to a shabby house set in seared and yellowed fields. Neither of these firm-minded individuals intended to give up. The now gray-bearded Captain Berry put his fieldworkers, freed by the war, to the planting and restoring; Frances Berry directed several Negro women at the spinning wheels and in the vegetable gardens. When Captain Berry canvassed his financial situation, she gave him her watch, a bracelet, and whatever other items of jewelry she owned. The small cash they might net would be the Berrys' only capital.

Captain Berry decided to call on his Eastern financial friends. Before he left, Frances worked over an old suit of clothes and gave him a knitted shawl. Thus costumed, Captain Berry sought out his former Philadelphia associates, and they arranged a small dinner at a leading restaurant. When he entered in his strange, unfashionable garb, many eyebrows were raised.

That evening Thomas Berry told his story simply. Some of the men here had known him over the years, he reminded them. If they had trust in him, he would work day and night to re-establish himself. He described his property, the plight of the farmers in his area, and the highland people, who lacked even seeds to start again. All that he had to offer, he said, were his name and reputation.

He left the East with an advance of $50,000. On the way home, concerned for the safety of the funds in his money belt, he was afraid to sleep in well-known inns, but traveled by back roads and slept in the woods, the money under his head, a gun in his hand. At Oak Hill, Thomas and Frances Berry began to rebuild their fortune. On a fall day of the next year, 1866, Martha was born; brothers and sisters followed until there were six girls and two boys.

The first postwar decade or so had hard, often painful hours. As Thomas Berry labored to pay off debts, keep crops going and staff fed, he saw more and more of the highlanders who had fought beside him at Vicksburg. Hearing stories of their need, he gave them money and other help. At times he rode the highland trails and took the young Martha with him. Between the girl and her father the bond was close from the start.

She had her father's gray-blue eyes, a firm nose, cheeks that flushed quickly in excitement, and it became evident that she had also inherited his generosity. The placid older sister Jennie and others of the household shook their heads when Martha returned from the mountains without her hair ribbon or a coat that she had left with one of the families.

Martha's mother had no leisure for trips or gifts. In these tense years the necessities of each day made Mrs. Berry, in the words of one of the Berrys, a "real general." She ran household finances "when such things called for hard management." She supervised vegetable gardens whose produce could be sold in

14

town. During the isolated war times Mrs. Berry had learned to treat a variety of sicknesses, "and we thought her the best doctor in the county." She collected much-thumbed books on home medicine, dressed wounds, repaired smashed fingers, and coped with other plantation ills. From her the serious daughter Martha had early lessons in care for the ailing.

The practical Mrs. Berry kept a large bottle of castor oil for instant dosages. "Whenever she saw Martha and the rest leave the orchard," another daughter adds, "she didn't take time to find out if the fruit had been ripe or not. We got the oil." Mrs. Berry made herself a specialist in handling pneumonia and related ailments. Covering the victim with a liniment of lard, turpentine, and camphor, she sewed him into red flannel pieces and left him inside, perspiring and groaning, until he recovered.

Meanwhile Captain Berry headed back toward financial security, though money threats still alarmed Martha and the others. He managed always to provide a good teacher for his brood. Most memorable of the governesses was Miss Ida McCullough, frail, slightly humped, less than five feet tall. "We never realized that a saint walked among us until we were old enough to see the halo over her head." A South Carolinian, daughter of an Episcopal minister, Miss Ida gave patient attention to the large band. (When Thomas Berry's brother and sister-in-law died in the "fever country," he took in their children.) She fostered a romantic ambition to have Martha, her favorite, presented at Charleston's elite St. Cecilia ball, but the hope never materialized.

Miss Ida taught her charges in a small white cottage, then in an unpretentious log cabin on a nearby rise. After one of their mountain trips, Martha asked her father if she and her brothers and sisters might have a cabin for play and study. He agreed, and in time they had the tiny pine place with its plastering of mud and big fireplace. Eventually it became Martha's special, more or less private retreat. Brothers Tom and Ike occasionally avoided classes by locking the door from inside and climbing through the chimney.

There was love in this household, a busy, unsentimental love, shown in impulsive acts rather than declarations. Family life was sprawling, informal. The children played some of the usual pranks; when a pompous English cotton agent visited Oak Hill they put a goat into his bed, and young Tom made a lady caller faint by slipping a frog into a bowl of cherries. Martha joined the rest in making sleds of barrel staves and scattering pine needles along the hill, to serve in place of snow.

With the other girls Martha rode horseback and joined her father and her brothers for fishing expeditions. In the evenings the Berrys gathered around the fire or paid visits about the neighborhood. Daily hospitality was the rule, and at most meals an extra plate waited on the table "for the drop company."

The home atmosphere was unrigid. Though Episcopalians, the Berrys entertained Catholic bishops, Methodists, Baptists, and freethinkers. "If a Hindu had wandered over the Georgia countryside, I'm sure Papa would have welcomed him," one of the younger daughters says in fond recollection.

Visitors saw a household of casual comfort rather than marked elegance, a house with a big front parlor, library, sitting room downstairs, and crowded bedchambers above. Oak Hill's terraced grounds had several gardens and arbors, a separated kitchen, dairy, and servants' quarters. A long tree-lined path led to the turnpike at the front; behind the house a silent river threaded its way through the flatlands which it enriched. It was a region of sun-warmed greenery, of softly flowering bushes in the early spring.

The poetic-minded governess, Miss McCullough, taught the Berry children to appreciate lines of sentinel-like trees at the hilltop, and the hazy loveliness of distant valleys. Under Miss Ida's direction they rode or walked to places like Hickory Nut Grove and Mossy Dell, to hunt "Indian pipes, lady-slippers and heartleaves with the little brown 'jugs' at their roots." Whatever new plants they found she identified, took apart, and used for lessons in botany. The eager Martha acquired a magnifying glass under which she studied the leaves and stems, and for the rest of her days she talked of the natural world that Miss McCullough opened to them.

In social matters the leader was the handsome, first-born Jennie. Reaching her teens, Jennie took semiannual trips East for clothes and "polishing." Soon Captain Berry agreed to send Jennie to Europe; the family had connections there, and she developed friends of her own abroad. After several years in France and Germany, Jennie returned with a command of tongues and a glow that kept her juniors, Laura and Frances, Bessie and Leila, in awe of her.

Jennie had her own saddle horse and a high-wheeled cart, black-bodied, maroon-wheeled, and gleaming. As she swept through town the natives gaped and called her "that foreign Berry girl." Leaving on a trip, Jennie sometimes had Uncle Enoch, the coachman, remove the wheels and lock them away so that the younger Berrys could not damage her treasure. In time she was to marry an Italian prince and move to that other Rome across the Atlantic.

Less lustrous, more domestic in her tastes, Martha remained generally in the background but took responsibilities and intervened in juvenile disputes. "She did the hard things, without being asked, and still she never took the front seat," one of the younger sisters notes. "She had something the rest of us lacked, I suppose—a certain feeling of duty and with it an inquisitive mind. Martha was forever asking things, 'poking around' in matters that didn't interest us. At heart she must have been much more serious than we were, but she smiled a lot and she had a good, healthy laugh. . . . Martha organized things, boat rides and walks and especially trips to the woods. If we didn't want to go she went alone."

The junior Berrys seldom accompanied Martha when her

father took her to the mountains. Ultimately she acquired
Roanie, a bright-colored, spirited colt on which she rode to the
distant reaches. There she shook hands with dark-visaged men
who had served beside her father in the war. Years later she
spoke of the discreet help that he gave them, and also the way
he occasionally frowned over their methods. Many struggled
endlessly, yet without skill. "Work, hard work—that's the
thing, but not the only thing," her father told Martha. "We
have to use our heads too. If we don't apply intelligence, all our
work won't matter." For decades she was to quote his words.

Learning of mountaineers' troubles, Martha did more than
talk. One morning she heard of a family who had bought a set
of furniture on credit. The highlanders had managed to pay all
except the last installment; now the company was about to take
the furniture back. "Well, they didn't take it. Martha met the
man and laid him out. She let him know what she thought of
anybody who'd do a thing like that! When Martha wanted to
carry a point, she carried it. The fellow backed away, and the
family kept its things."

In another case, coming upon a mountain child who lay desperately ill, Martha brought her home and put her to bed. The
startled family could hear the girl's cries: "I'm not going to die,
Miss Martha? You're not going to let me die. . . ." Martha
remained with the child to the end.

Looking on then and at all other times was another woman,
whose influence over the Berrys was exceeded only by their
mother's. She was "Aunt Marth" Freeman, the Negro who
served as cook, household aide, and assistant arbiter of affairs.
Years earlier Aunt Marth had married Uncle Enoch; after her
two boys died she turned upon the Berry family a fierce energy,
an encompassing love, and a strong sense of the fitness of
things. Anyone who violated her sense of the proprieties was
told about it and in scalding terms.

Lean, middle-sized, and turbaned, Aunt Marth had a sharp

hand, a sharp mind, and a sharp tongue. In understatement, Martha Berry once called her "a truly authoritative member of the family"; again, gently, "my next of kin." Martha added: "I cannot remember when I have not known her and when her kind and capable hands have not cared for me. She thinks she owns me. . . ." Often it appeared to others that Aunt Marth did.

In the kitchen the dark family assistant reigned jealously; those who entered did so on sufferance only. Mrs. Berry herself had never been one for cooking, and if she intervened at the back of the house Aunt Marth reprimanded her: "Miss, you know you don't belong 'ere. Ef the food ain' right, den you kin complain."

One of the younger Berrys recalled: "If we did wrong, Aunt Marth came at us, hands flying at our backs and bottoms, screaming: 'You fiends, you fiends!' And we ran. We loved her but we obeyed out of a fine healthy fear. When Mother came back from a trip we always told her 'Aunt Marth's been too strict.' Mother would nod, and Aunt Marth would go right on as before. She ruled the other servants, too, with a big stick. When we heard her call a lazy housemaid a 'Hessian' we shivered at the mysterious, sinister sound. Only when Miss Ida's class reached the American Revolution and we learned about mercenaries used against the colonists did we finally understand the word. But even then 'Hessian' never lost its black meaning."

For all Berrys, Aunt Marth had lofty hopes and standards. "A Berry don' ack like dat." "You behavin' like trash." Newcomers must prove their worth; often she maintained a long neutrality, then grunted a "Humph." The "Humph" told more than a long discourse. When aroused she might add: "That man a fool, an' you a fool if you pays 'im any mind." In some of Aunt Marth's devastating judgments the Berrys found shrewd estimates of human character.

Her Berry partisanship was matched only by her piety. Of a

simple Baptist faith, Aunt Marth prayed steadily, talked of her God, and quoted her Bible. Though she never learned to read and counted only to ten, she made adept use of everything she knew. When she tabulated sales of eggs and vegetables, she scratched thin lines on the wall, "and was never, never wrong."

Above all Aunt Marth hated shams, such as lady visitors who smirked and gushed. One such woman spoke to her of the Civil War times. "Well, you've seen a whole lot in your day, haven't you? Tell me some of the things you've seen." The lean Negro woman stood silent, arms folded, and her eyes surveyed the questioner from head to foot. Then she said quietly: "What *Ah* sees, Ah keeps to myself," and left with the dignity of a queen.

For Martha Berry a change approached. The family had plans for its second daughter—specifically Madame LeFebvre's Edgeworth Finishing School in Baltimore. Martha resisted: "Father, must I be 'finished'?" Nevertheless she had to go. At once she found herself harshly unhappy among the glossy city girls, who sniffed at her "country" clothes and forthright manner. As she said later, costumes that Oak Hill considered sensible looked dowdy or ridiculous to the young sophisticates. Writing home to tell of her misery, she announced that she intended to leave.

Captain Berry promptly informed his daughter that if she returned he would send her right back again. At the same time he addressed a note to Madame LeFebvre with a check enclosed. When the next Saturday came the sympathetic headmistress took the country girl on a shopping spree. Martha reappeared with a complete outfit which even the shining sister Jennie might have worn. But the new coat had to be altered; unwilling to wear her old one, she went without either, contracted a bad chest cold, and stayed in bed for days. So much for fashion!

The rest of the year went better, yet not altogether well. While she made two or three good friends, she had no feeling of kinship with the other girls, and she never grew to like the "finishing" process. She dressed more smartly, "but I'll never be the city type," she said. Later she often spoke understandingly of the highlanders' embarrassment when placed in a new environment.

Before the term ended, Captain Berry suffered a stroke and the anxious Martha returned home at once. He made a partial recovery and, despite difficulties, continued to operate his plantation and his cotton office. The smaller Berrys knew their father only as a friendly, bearded man in a wheel chair. Sadly he asked: "Who's going to take care of the little ones if I go?"

The doctors suggested trips to one health resort after another; Martha accompanied him, and at home she stayed close to his chair. She never went back to the Baltimore school, and in the bustling household she served as her father's helper. About this time he summoned her for a talk. Referring to her habit of distributing her belongings to the mountain children, he told her: "Martha, you have 'giving hands.' You must be more careful or you'll have nothing for yourself."

As his daughter reported the conversation, Thomas Berry added: "When I die you'll get the tract of land across the road. Land and trees . . . They'll never lose their worth. Look after them, and when I'm no longer here they'll support you." His next words Martha would always remember:

"The people around us so often need help, child. But how to give it the wise way—that's the question. If you simply hand things to somebody you destroy his pride, and when you do that you destroy him. Let him take charity and he comes to expect charity. If he gets a bag of flour the first time, you have to give him another on the second visit, and the third time he'll look for more than that. But if you can lend him seed and tools and let him make his own crop, he'll keep his self-respect. . . ."

Martha did not remain always, of course, with the captain. The young bloods of the neighborhood were noticing her. She had a fair, fresh skin, candid light eyes, blue-black hair, and an

21

attractive brightness of manner. Her figure, slightly rounded, made the boys turn as she passed.

One young man spoke admiringly of "her beautiful arms and shoulders"; in the reticent style of the '80s and '90s he ended his catalogue there. Others referred to her quick movements— "nimble as a sand crab, going four ways at once when she was in a hurry"; "she seemed to have springs in her heels." The women talked of Martha's expressive hands, and always of those small flying feet and the animation of her look when she grew interested in a subject.

She had a series of what the Southerners called *beaus;* the younger brothers and sisters peeped through the curtains and sometimes chuckled at what they heard. On one evening, hilarious to them, a suitor banged out in a huff, to find his carriage delayed. The Berry dogs leaped at him, and he sat in a tree until Martha rescued him.

One visitor in particular gained her interest—a Virginian five years her senior, who served for a time in her father's cotton warehouse. He was a connection, a member of his family having married one of the Berrys; he came of one of the Old Dominion dynasties. Calling at first on business, he stayed for parties, for weekends, and gradually word spread of an "understanding" between him and Martha. The families approved, and Thomas Berry considered the purchase of a neat house in East Rome, with a shaded lawn and garden. In the words of one of the sisters, "There was one love in her life, and he was it."

But the "understanding" was to become a long one, with many interruptions. Captain Berry's health grew worse, and toward the end he lost his voice and sat in his wheel chair, paralyzed, trying painfully to communicate with those around him. When Martha was still in her early '20s, he died. In those dark hours three women took up the assorted burdens at Oak Hill— the indefatigable mother, the fierce-eyed Aunt Marth, and, in her own way, young Martha.

22

After the funeral Mrs. Berry assumed the reins. If she had been a "general" before, Frances Berry now rose to commander in chief, "a female Napoleon," in the words of a daughter. A caller at Oak Hill told how he saw her late at night, bending over her account books; before five he woke to hear her marshal the labor force and give orders for the planting in the corn patch, the clearing of a creek, the building of a fence.

Graying but sturdy and still keen, Frances Berry taught herself a good deal about finances. She bought the New York papers, she studied market pages, called business friends, and asked questions. "She could correct me when we talked about the market, and she knew the costs of food, of timber, and anything else you mentioned," the same family friend reported. And while her Virginian waited, young Martha lent her hand wherever needed.

She helped look after all of the younger ones, but three in particular drew her special care, the good-tempered, religious little Frances, high-spirited Laura, and the sympathetic Tom. Later Tom became a successful businessman; then he was a kindhearted brother with bright eye and easy humor.

With its several rivers, the Rome area was frequently in danger of floods. One year the waters rose higher than ever, and when heavy rains threatened, Frances Berry appealed to her family: "Tonight, pray that the floods don't come. If they do our crops are ruined." Remembering other years when floods made it possible for them to ride joyously into town in boats, the younger children prayed hard for a cloudburst. It arrived, and the next few days were ones of roaring fun but also of near disaster for the plantation.

Oak Hill survived, and Martha gave increasing attention to her younger sisters. Still the Virginian stood on the sidelines, waiting. But soon there began a development which settled the course of her life, and also his.

CHAPTER II

TEARS IN THE NIGHT

NOT LONG AFTER her father's death, Martha Berry received an invitation to spend part of a summer with an old friend, a girl whose family had a vacation place in the mountains. Accepting promptly, she lived for the first time among the settlers of the far-distant regions. She learned from close experience of the richnesses of the forests, the craggy heights against the sky—and also of the people themselves.

Daily Martha and her friend Emma passed bleak huts half hidden in weeds and undergrowth. Crudely built of logs and clay, the houses had "cracks and crevices large enough for a dog of fair size to leap through," as she said. Many of the one-roomed cabins sat in small clearings of heavily trodden ground, treeless settings for quarters that had no less barren an air.

At first the men and women in the narrow doorways stared at her with a suspicion that approached sullen hostility. Grimy children peered out, then ran to hide like frightened animals. What did this stranger want? Only after a time did Emma's assurances lessen their resentment. Allowing Martha to enter their dim living places, they watched warily as she strove to win their good will.

Inside the heavily smoked huts she found muskets on the wall, with strings of red and green peppers. From the rafters hung dried herbs, and pots and pans were stacked in the corner. In open fireplaces Martha made out pots of greasy meat and beans, beside cold slabs of corn pone. Corn and hogback. . . . It was the unvarying diet that produced pellagra and hookworm and other associated diseases of the region. And in the pale faces and dulled eyes she read a listlessness, an apathy beyond anything she had ever known.

Here was the heart of the mountains, more primitive than anything she had seen at her father's side. She talked with women of thirty who looked fifty, their teeth gone, their hair straggling. "No, miss," they told her, "the chil'ren ain' never had no shoes. No, ain't been to school neither. Nearest school ten mile' off, an' it jes' ain' possible to sen' 'em afoot two ways to the day."

The girl from Oak Hill discovered the real isolation of these people. A member of a large family had married and gone to live ten miles away. A decade later she had still not returned to see the old folks; the distance was too far, the dim paths too hard to follow. In another case a post office stood only four miles from a family which never used it. The members could not write and knew none who could write or would want to write to them.

As Martha glanced about the clearings she found signs of the most hopeless of farming methods—patches of fields long overused, ancient plows, rusty rakes, a neglected fruit tree. Yet soon her eye halted at surprising objects in the shadowed chambers—a once-fine chair, an ornamented trunk, a handsomely embossed Bible whose words the owners could not decipher.

"Gran'maw brought the trunk when she fust come over the mountin'. . . ." "This be Gran'pa's name, I think." Here was the tragedy of a people pushed steadily backward through the years. And yet Martha Berry recognized something more: the clear intelligence that shone in the eyes of the awkward, timid children, and the look of tired women who were strongly concerned over the future of those children. The highlanders were beginning to respond to her efforts, to talk more easily, in meetings that Martha would never forget.

With her friend Emma she spent weeks in traveling up the valleys and over trails that led to misty falls in the distance. Emma had a gentle voice and a taste for poetry; together they enjoyed the sunny beauty of the region, the kindness and occasional humor of the mountaineers. More and more often Martha heard the friendly invitation: "You 'uns must light and come in ter dinner." Once, when she had accepted, the old highlander took his long gun from a forked hickory-stick holder and, without stirring a foot, shot a chicken in the yard. Before she thought it possible the chicken lay fried on a plate before her!

Toward the end of her stay Martha noticed that Emma seemed strongly interested in Jim, their part-time mountaineer-guide. The trim, darkly handsome youth asked dozens of questions about the outer world and talked of his wish to "git book larnin'." Jim and Emma were together more and more often. While Martha considered him pleasant, she wondered about the two of them. With such different backgrounds, could they have hope for a life together?

Back at Oak Hill she received word that when Emma's parents objected strongly the girl had run off with Jim, and they were married in the light of a torch by a minister who peddled chickens on weekdays. More than ever Martha puzzled over the couple. Some months later she had an opportunity to revisit the area and rode out to the place where Jim's family lived.

At the one-room cabin, empty at the moment, cowpeas simmered in an ancient pot and corn bread browned in an oven. Looking further, the caller spotted books of Emma's favorite poems on a rude shelf, with a second reader and arithmetic.

Clearly the girl had been teaching her husband—surely a helpful sign.

Jim's mother arrived, smoking a long pipe, her bonnet hanging over the back of her homespun dress. "Jes' foller ther trail through them bushes and over ther foot-log at ther creek, and you'll fin' that-ther woman a-helpin' Jim on ther new house."

A short way off Emma stood on top of the building, holding shingles which her husband nailed into place. Against the sky the girl's figure appeared much leaner, her skin deeply browned. Emma's hair, plaited down her back, was bleached by the sun. Calling out to Martha, she cried at her approach while Jim grinned awkwardly and rubbed his hands together. On the way back to the family cabin Martha learned more of their story.

Although Emma talked with good cheer, she admitted after a few minutes that things had not worked out quite as she had hoped. When they first set up housekeeping, Jim had been very attentive, bringing her water daily from a spring at the bottom of the steep hill. Soon, however, neighbors laughed, and Emma learned that mountain men were not supposed to wait on their women. Besides, the others had "never knowed a woman to use so much water."

After another week Emma carried her own buckets, and now she did her washing at the spring, with a big pot for boiling and a stick to beat the clothes on a "battling bench." At the house Martha noticed that her own wedding gift of a knife and fork was the only silver Emma owned.

While his wife knelt at the fireplace, Jim washed before a mirror on a tree in the back yard. He joined them, his hair slicked down with a strong-smelling grease, and sat silently eating with his knife. Emma managed to speak with a certain brightness as she explained how she helped her husband in the field and shared other labor. After a while, however, her friend's shoulders drooped "as if she had been carrying heavy weights," and yet Martha thought she detected indications of some hope

27

for the couple. Once they settled in their own house, matters might be better.

Pressing on them a loan of a hundred dollars to finish the building, Martha Berry left. After long, difficult months the couple repaid the money, and about a year later Emma urged Martha to visit her again. This time she seemed almost broken in health, but she "worked harder than ever." At her side toddled a child with her mother's dreamy eyes.

As for Jim, Martha quickly observed that he had regressed. He studied no more books; he had "gotten in" with moonshiners and was drinking heavily. Now, she wrote later, she began to realize the effect of environment. If Jim had been removed from the influence of old associations, old customs, things might have gone differently for him and Emma.

Martha was to stay for several more days, and she made up her mind to learn more about the mountain life. Could she see a still? she asked Emma. Her friend hesitated; she would want to think before she answered. Hesitantly Emma pointed out a man who rode up with a meal bag supposedly holding vegetables; under the beans lay a jug of corn whisky. Jeb, the moonshiner, stopped in for dinner, and Martha began to talk to him about his children. He smiled as he described his Waverline, "the purtiest gal on yan side o' the mountin'." Reaching into her valise, Martha drew out a gift for Waverline, which pleased Jeb a great deal. But when she said she would like to ride over and look at the still, he showed his astonishment. No'm, it couldn't be done. To let a stranger like her see what they were doing would be right risky for her and him, too.

Martha continued her appeal, "and when she once set out to get something, not many people kept on saying no," in a friend's words. After an hour or so Jeb relented. Leaving their little girl with relatives, Emma and Jim joined them as they took a steep bluffside trail over Hog-back Mountain to a one-room cabin lost in pines and laurels. There Martha discovered the haggard wife, ten children, and six hounds that comprised

Jeb's family. During the next twenty-four hours she met several other mountaineers, recognized their deep love for their families, and heard of their troubles. They earned so little with their farm produce that selling whisky, they said, was their only way to make a bare living.

The still sat in a deep ravine. With her friends Martha descended a dangerously sharp trail, to come upon a half dozen "wild-looking men" working with tubes and coils. Seeing her, they jumped up in a fury. After a few minutes, however, Jeb calmed them and they accepted Martha's presence. Before long they were telling her of the risks of their work, of the way Jeb's mother had been shot through the shoulder by a revenue officer; and then they spoke of their wives and the "young 'uns."

That evening Martha tried to sleep on the rude bed provided for her and Emma. All of Jeb's little girls used the other bed, and their mother stretched out on a quilt before the fire with her six-month-old baby, while the men occupied a lean-to. During the long, unnerving night Martha reflected on this hard life and on the waste she saw all around her—"the worst kind of all, human waste."

For the older ones there was small hope, she realized; only through the young could any real changes be made. One need appeared obvious: schools. Yet repeatedly the mountain people had explained to her: "Neares' school is miles off, miss, and when weather's bad you cain't get there a-tall." Distances seemed endless, and cabins were scattered everywhere. And when she came upon an occasional school it proved to be rickety, dirty, with an old man as tired as the building itself, trying to teach classic subjects for which the mountaineers had no use. What would happen to Emma's little girl? Martha thought of her often during the next few years.

In Atlanta she consulted a lawyer friend. "Have you ever been out in the mountains?" she asked. He admitted that he had visited some of the fringes of the area. "You have no conception of what it's like!" Martha persisted, and she talked of the eroded land, the vast needs of the people, and begged him: "Can't we get laws passed?"

"Martha, to do anything at all would cost millions, and where would we get the money?" The lawyer reminded her that there were whole counties in Georgia without rural schools. Her spirit low, Martha left him.

Not long afterward, on a Sunday afternoon in spring, she sat alone in her old log-cabin playhouse near Oak Hill. Of late the little building had become a den in which she kept her reading matter. Today the family expected her in a half hour to meet guests. Skimming through a book, she was enjoying the soft air and quiet when she became slowly aware that someone was watching her.

Turning, Martha caught sight of three small faces in the window. "They were bright faces, and the unspoken longing that I saw in them caused me to throw aside my book, to go forward and speak to them." The barefoot boys stood before her in patched, dusty shirts and overalls. They wore the wide straw hats, raveled at the edges, of mountain children. Timidly they lowered their eyes and were about to run off when she held out apples and persuaded them to enter.

Where were they from? "*We*'s brothers, and lives in Trapp Holler at the foot o' Lavendar Mountain, and *he*'s from over in Possum Trot. No'm, ain' got no church, 'cause the roof fell in."

Where did they go to school? "Ain' got no school. They has one o' t'other side the ridge, but it's fer boys livin' thetaway, beyon' the gap."

Martha went on with her questioning. "Don't you go to Sunday school, either?"

The tallest boy stared. "What *kin'* of school?"

"Where they teach you about God and Jesus."

The three were more surprised than ever. "They's somethin' to learn about 'em?"

"They tell you Bible stories, too."

"Oh, we 'uns got a Bible, on'y Pa cain't read it." The tall one stepped forward. "They has stories in it?"

"Yes. Would you want to hear some?"

Nodding, the boys settled down. As one friend put it later, Martha was a storyteller with an imagination that "made her characters leave the pages and walk around the room with you." When she pictured David, Samuel, and Abraham, the grimy faces shone in wonder.

"Give some more," they begged, and she proceeded to Jonah and the whale, to Jesus and his love for people everywhere, in mountains and in plains. The time passed swiftly, until Martha realized that dusk had come. Yet her guests were reluctant to leave, and the tallest went on and on about "that feller Jonah and his whale. That's the all-timedest whopper I ever heerd!"

Martha asked if they would like to return next Sunday and bring their brothers or sisters. The eager eyes gave their answer. Handing them some of Aunt Marth's ginger cakes, she watched them start the long trip to the hills, before she raced up the pathway to her home.

Her sisters and their guests wanted to know what had happened. As she explained, the other Berrys nodded. It was sad, yes, but what could anyone do about it? When the talk turned to a boating trip planned for the following weekend, Martha said quietly that she would be with those children again. Mrs. Berry made it clear that she had her doubts about the wisdom of all this, but Martha's face set, "and when she took on a look of that kind, you didn't talk about it any more."

During the week she spent considerable time at the cabin, rehearsing her Bible stories, remembering the way the boys had absorbed whatever she said. On Sunday she expected her callers by afternoon; that morning Aunt Marth rustled in with a frown on her face: "White trash chillin wantin' to see yer."

There were the boys with several new recruits, including three girls. "We brang us some sisters." The sisters shyly eyed the ground, and Martha realized that they were even more be-

31

grimed than the boys. Joining them at the cabin with food and books, she also brought along her old magnifying glass.

She had decided on a bit of strategy. Filling a cedar bucket with water, she took out soap, a gourd and wash pan. "Look at your fingernails through this glass." Their eyes widened: "Real quair, ma'am." "Who'd think things'd take on sich a fashion!" While young ones worked over their hands and arms, Martha lectured them about germs, and offered a proposition: If they promised to scrub themselves this way every day, there would be lemonade as well as cakes and Bible stories the next time.

The following Sunday saw more new arrivals, the one after that a doubling of attendance. To the children's delight Martha played an old rosewood melodeon from her earlier days for a session of hymn singing. The instrument had suffered with the years, and one boy had to hold its broken pedal, while another supported the wobbly frame. At each class, several scrambled for these posts of honor.

She told the children of her liking for walks in the woods. "You go fer huntin'?" "No, I like birds and animals too much to kill them." "Then why?" So she went out with them, magnifying glass and basket in hand, explaining the varieties of plants, mosses, ferns. When she caught a butterfly they studied the trembling wonder of its wings and released it; they examined birds' nests from a distance and looked at furry caterpillars under the glass. Their bright interest, their eager intelligence led her on. They arrived at class with odd leaves, wasp nests and fragments of colored stone. "Why don't you decorate the cabin?" she asked, and smiled as they ornamented the fireplace and walls.

One Sunday a girl lingered behind to ask, "Be it all right ef Maw and Paw come too?" Martha nodded but wondered if the parents would be interested. Everybody told her that highland people were very lethargic. At home she said little of this project of hers; now and then her mother or Aunt Marth asked a question about it, then usually lapsed into silence with a sigh.

Her sisters accepted the fact that they seldom saw her on Sunday; her suitor no longer visited on that day. By common consent the family passed over the matter of her Sunday classes. Martha would soon have her fill of them, they indicated.

The aloof Jennie had only an uncomprehending stare for such activities. Young Frances, the devout and warmhearted one, looked on Martha's interest with a somewhat sympathetic eye. "But even I," Frances remembered later, "wondered why Martha had to behave in quite so 'different' a fashion." And Tom, the brother for whom she had a particular affection, did not hide his puzzlement.

The next Sunday, a good fall morning, Martha lay drowsing in bed when she heard a rumbling, a grinding of wheels. From her window she saw a sight that made her jump to her feet. The highland people were rolling up in ox carts and wagons and on muleback. In the grove men were hitching up horses and oxen; children ran about and family dogs barked.

Hastily she got into her clothes, to be confronted by an irate Aunt Marth. "You sure don' 'spect *me* to feed that passel!" The tiny Mrs. Berry stood in the doorway, her lips pressed sternly together. Sweeping by, Martha went to the kitchen where, under Aunt Marth's baleful stare, she gathered bread, meat, and anything else she could commandeer. Soon afterward she was finding places for the crowd in the cabin, settling women with four or five children around them, taking white-haired grandfathers to the front.

For Martha Berry, and for these people as well, it was an important hour. She nodded to two of the boys, and they darted to her "aged and infirm" melodeon; when she opened the songbook her voice trembled. Practically no one else could read, and therefore she "lined out" each hymn until its words grew familiar. At first the strangeness of the atmosphere made the highlanders shy; then their voices rang out, deepening, strengthening, and she knew she had won them.

The next weekend brought more wagons, more dogs, more

people. The cabin filled to the doorsill, and a dozen or so stood outside or at the window. Soon they carried their own chairs or substitutes for them, soapboxes, animal skins, and "shuck mats." Their meeting place was getting much too cramped, and Martha also had to consider the annoyance at Oak Hill. Aunt Marth scowled at the topless buggies, wagons with broken sides, and children who tumbled over the lawns. "A crazy picnic groun', dat what we are. Never had anythin' to shame us like dis."

Another beloved face showed its dismay and concern. Her fiancé had frequently asked her to set the date for their marriage. First her father's illness had delayed it, and now this Sunday school absorbed her. Each time she told him: Soon, soon. . . . Once she finished the work she would be ready. Unhappily he bided his time.

It was obviously necessary to get more space for the classes, and Martha remembered the neglected churches she had seen in the mountains. Why not use them? She spent a week in riding about the area, and found them in even worse condition than she expected. Steps collapsed under her; she discovered that dogs had stayed in them for months, and one man drawled out that on his last visit "the fleas fair took us off the benches." Nevertheless they were going to "make do," she said, and chose Possum Trot, a settlement eight miles from Oak Hill. The place had a battered building leaning slightly awry toward the red clay of its neglected grounds.

On an overcast Sunday Martha rode up to meet a fair crowd, huddled in the dingy old church. For the occasion she had put on her best ruffled muslin dress, with a big hat held by pins on the crest of her dark hair. Someone had swept the building, she saw, but it still had layers of long-accumulated grime, and the floor near the front had a gaping hole. But in a moment dirt and holes became minor worries. Martha had hardly advanced to the front when a gust of wind rose and rain beat suddenly down upon Possum Trot.

At once water poured from a dozen cracks in the roof. Some held up papers for protection, while others retreated to dry spots in the corners. Martha tried to go on, wiping away the water that rolled down her face, but her muslin dress was soaked through, and now she stopped. "We just can't go on until we get a roof and fix up the whole place. Let's have a church working—two or three days from now, to make sure the building's finished by next Sunday. Who'll volunteer?"

No one replied, and her heart hurt. She wanted these people to do things for themselves, to share in whatever she did. After a long pause one of the elders called to her: "Miss Marthy, hit's jis' like a woman, gittin' in a powerful hurry. Ef hit's a-rainin' this week we cain't kivver hit, and if hit ain't rainin' we don' need hit kivvered. And hit moughtn't rain fer a month."

Several others nodded in agreement, and hesitantly Martha answered him. "Yes, it moughtn't, but again it mought!" When she heard a good-humored response she felt better and announced: "I'm declaring a working, for eight o'clock *Wednesday morning*, with meats, a barrel of lemonade, and cakes. You men cut down a big tree, saw boards, and we'll do it."

Would anyone appear? On Wednesday, to her great relief, she met a crowd. Almost at once, however, she heard several murmur that they had come only to watch the goings on. Martha surveyed the men and informed them: "Anybody that won't work won't eat." Soon she found no onlookers as men sawed, hammered, paused for refreshments, and then resumed their labors. Finishing the roof ahead of schedule, they pressed on to mend the steps and floor and fix the walls. By dusk Martha gave approval to the last bit of repair, and the ancient objector of the previous Sunday added an oblique commendation: "I seed a lot in my time, but hit's the fust time I ever seed a woman a-bossin' a house-kivverin'."

Martha smiled sweetly through the dust that coated her. "No, you good men did it." Years later an old friend said fondly: "That was one of her best tricks. You worked like fury just as

35

she told you. Then she thanked you and said you'd managed everything, and you almost believed it."

By Sunday, with the aid of the older boys, Martha had cut out cardboard signs and painted them in large block letters. "God is Love" went over the doorway. Above the pulpit she placed another: "Suffer the Little Children to Come unto Me." At the opposite side she set a third one: "The Eyes of the Lord Are in Every Place, Beholding the Good and the Evil." Her class went well, and yet she noticed that few of the children took seats near the last quotation. When she asked she received a ready explanation. Their mothers had been reprimanding them: "I shore hate for you to be a-settin' under the Lord's eyes and have him a-beholdin' all the meanness you been into this week." They wished therefore to "git fur away from thim eyes"!

The Possum Trot venture had gone so well that she decided to follow it with classes in other former church buildings. Riding again over the area, she located one at Mount Alto, another at Foster's Bend, a third at Pleasant Valley. She tried to stagger the hours so that she could go from one to the other, but at the same time she looked about for neighborhood assistants to handle the work. Somewhat to her surprise, her younger sister Frances showed a growing interest. "Can't I help?" the girl asked. Thereafter Frances took over Sunday chores at her side.

Martha's buggy was constantly rocking up hill roads, hurtling down steep slopes for visits to the country people. "I would ride my pony for miles through a zigzag path in the resinous woods, leading up to some isolated little cabin. The whole family would come out to welcome us. And these words grew quite familiar: 'Yonder comes the Sunday lady! Hitch yo' nag and 'light—'light and come in. We-uns be pow'ful glad to see you.'" The Sunday lady . . . She accepted the title with pride, and smiled as she heard the name applied to Roanie, her high-spirited steed, "the Sunday horse." With the children Roanie became a petted favorite.

Into her work Martha turned all of the energy that her father had once demonstrated. She was also revealing something of her father's own skill in organizing and, though tentatively, in promoting an enterprise. She came to know, she said, every house, every child, cat, and dog for many miles. She recognized scores of one- or two-room cabins, the doorways filled with dogs, chickens, and babies asleep in wooden boxes which served as cradles.

As she approached the mountain houses, Martha frequently saw something that pleased her. The children rushed to the well, dipped hands, arms, and head into a tin basin, and stumbled out again, moist and beaming. They had not forgotten that primary lesson of hers.

She would sit for a time with the family and soon move on to the next cabin, with the children behind her and the "Sunday horse." Before long she formulated one of her principal rules for dealing with highlanders and others as well. "We all like a little praise," she told an aide with a smile, "especially when we deserve it." Systematically she noted the good things these people did and let them realize how much she admired them. "What a beautiful coverlet; did your grandmother give you the pattern?" "You're doing some mighty fine planting these days."

Martha was letting them see that she understood the way they lived their lives and also, of course, putting them in a receptive mood to do the things she wished. She knew more and more names, the children's, the old people's; locations of remote settlements; ailments of the mountain folk. "How is Esty, and Joe, the one with the smile?" "Is your earache better?" "You know, I heard of a remedy for that foot condition, Mrs. Johnson. . . ."

On one occasion Martha wrote: "During one of these visits my simple desire to do something . . . became a determined resolution to devote my entire time and means to teaching them a way to help themselves." Soon afterward she was visited again by her fiancé, and one of the family has recalled that

37

they were together for an hour. The young Berrys stared from the windows when he left, his step quick and angry. The family learned that he had delivered no ultimatum but made a simple request. Even now he would wait a while longer—if she would only fix the date. She was then thirty, he thirty-five, and they had been engaged a long time.

At their meeting Martha had argued that she could not leave her work, at least right away. Couldn't he see that? Why must he have some specific time? He still insisted that he must know. After a time she asked if he could not fit his interests to this work of hers; couldn't each of them have his work, each in his own way? The Virginian's reply was no. . . . Here was an issue which many other women have faced, particularly in America. In Martha's case, however, the period was the 1890s, when few men wanted a wife to have a "career" or even understood just what the term meant.

After a last few sharp words together, Martha turned away from her fiancé, and he said good-by and did not return. Certain of her friends have said that Martha Berry must not have wanted to marry him, or not have wanted very much to do so, or she would have given up her other interests. Some have suggested, however, that she hoped to the final moment to have both him and those interests. Then, required to make a choice, she could not surrender her work.

That night and for some time afterward, Martha cried in the silence of her room. Little privacy was possible in so crowded a household; she thought she protected herself by leaning out of an upper window. Those who heard her sobbing in the night did not forget.

For a time she seemed pensive, subdued, and then she smiled again. Much later she hinted to the mountain girls that she had once planned her own marriage, and she let them understand that she sympathized when they wanted a festive wedding. Many times she dropped other labors to arrange a ceremony, smooth the way, and plan details.

Nevertheless she maintained a close silence about her own love. "She had so many friends, North and South and other places," a woman close to her said. "But in that respect nobody ever really knew her. There was a curtain, ready to be dropped. You reached a certain point, and down it went—a fast curtain." Another explained: "Even though she might deliberately have chosen her school instead of the man, the situation left scars; now and then I thought I caught glimpses of the scars."

The Virginian returned to his native state, and after a time he married, had several children and a successful career. He and Martha met again years later, after each had achieved recognition in his own way. They spoke in friendly style, and yet, when she went back to Georgia, Martha said little to anyone about him. The door stayed closed.

A member of her board of trustees declared later: "There was nothing of the spinster about her. Few men who met her failed to realize that here was a woman who could be very desirable if she wished. She liked men; she did not play coy the way some old maids do. From almost our first meeting, I had the feeling that she had been strongly in love. A woman as delicate as she was in her perception of other people's hurts— she herself must once have been badly hurt. To know so much of life, you must have lived it."

And at times, the board member added with a laugh, she would turn to him and mention someone she had heard of. "You know him, don't you? What's he like; is he really as handsome as they claim?"

Often she said: "My five sisters were married in the drawing room of our home. Five times I came down the steps as a bridesmaid . . . and thought that one day I would have the most beautiful wedding of all." Instead, she concluded, she eventually "stepped across the road and married my schools." The day of that wedding was approaching.

39

CHAPTER III

CHRISTMAS—
AND THE PLUNGE

TOWARD CHRISTMAS, Martha received a tempting invitation to a holiday party in Atlanta. It would be her first such event in a long time, and the family urged her to go. Whatever the Berrys thought about the broken engagement, they accepted the situation. Now, as she might have expected, they regarded the Atlanta visit as one which might produce another romance.

For weeks Martha had been admiring a blue silk dress in a store window in Rome. She started out to buy it when, she said, "I thought of those mountain children." She had been talking on Sundays about the Christmas spirit, and they had cried to her excitedly about it. "We never had a Chris'mas tree. What is they like?" The season of good will, the time of happy cheer. . . . Shouldn't she let them see that spirit in action?

And so Martha Berry took the money she had set aside for the new silk dress and used it to give her highland people a "sure enough tree" and a small present for each. She announced to her Sunday groups that all who could make the trip to the cabin near her home would be welcome. "It's going to be a wonderful Christmas," she promised.

During the last few days before the holidays her family did not hide its annoyance over the change in her plans. One member, however, gave her approval—the serious young Frances, who said that she wanted to help, as she had in other cases. She and Martha went to town to buy dolls, knives, candy, nuts, oranges, and popcorn. They had learned that a number of the elders would attend, too, and for them she added handkerchiefs, shawls, and neckties.

For the highlanders the Christmas mood gained momentum. For days, with Frances' assistance, Martha drilled the children in carol singing, and meanwhile she sent a few older boys to the woods for a big pine. There was only one place for the tree —the center of the log cabin. The stove had to be removed, "but we'll be moving around so much that we won't miss the heat." Behind closed doors Martha and her helpers made up bags of nuts and sweets, filled several barrels and boxes with presents, and decked the tree with cotton tufts and strings of popcorn.

Everywhere they attached cotton, because Martha wished to demonstrate how they could use whatever lay at hand. On the mantel shelf Martha printed "Kyndle Friendship" in Old English lettering; from the pine pole rafters they hung strings of red pepper and ears of yellow and red corn. On the tree they fixed tall candles and set a single star which shimmered at the top. Tired and depleted, the small band of workers went to bed on Christmas Eve.

Two o'clock in the afternoon had been set for the party. About nine in the morning Martha was startled by a sight for which nothing that had previously happened had prepared her. People were streaming toward the cabin from every direction in vehicles of all sizes and ages. Running out, she recognized

41

dozens of familiar faces, but also those of many that she did not know. A smiling farm wife explained that she had sent word to Uncle Bill's folks, twenty-five miles up the mountain. " 'Pears like they never seed any sich tree. They thought they'd come and bring all their young 'uns, and 'lowed they'd all git a fine present."

Another farm wife took her pipe from her mouth and told Martha: "Ol' Sal thar's from a right smart ways off. Started day 'fore yesterday and walked all the way." Someone introduced Grandpa Dye, who claimed to be a hundred years old. He sat with a benign air, his face shriveled as a dried crabapple, his withered hands folded in his lap.

Martha felt a moment of panic; she did not have half enough gifts. She ran back to Oak Hill, where she opened her top bureau drawer and dumped ribbons and handkerchiefs into her apron. Happily she found her brothers away, and in their rooms she searched for socks and handkerchiefs. Her sister Frances contributed some of her own Christmas presents.

Martha glanced toward the cabin again. More wagons, more people, more dogs; but at least she didn't have to think of gifts for the dogs. In the kitchen she added cups and saucers to her loot, and stray bits of crockery from the sideboard. A moment later she gazed into Aunt Marth's unblinking eyes. "Yer cain't git nothin' more—none o' *my* things." Soon afterward she heard the housekeeper complaining to Mrs. Berry: "Ol' miss, she gone plumb crazy. Efn we don' lock up ever'thing, it'll all go."

Martha herself had gone. Loaded with packages, she edged her way through the throng and explained that they must wait until the cabin was ready. Inside she and several adult helpers worked for a long time. Nobody must be forgotten. . . . At last the presents had all been set out, and she held a whispered conference with her two-boy "fire crew." A well-filled rain barrel sat just outside the window, and they understood exactly what to do in an emergency, didn't they? she asked.

In crept an elderly, bearded country man, Mr. Joe Barnes,

the day's Santa Claus. He wore a long-tailed black coat and trousers, "so old they had turned green," Martha noted. A paper bag ornamented with cotton bolls became his hat; bits of cotton had been attached to the suit, and assistants disguised him by adding a mask with glittering fringes. Here was a homemade Santa.

Miss Berry lifted a taper to the candles and signaled to Santa to hide. He did, but a moment later ran out again, crying hoarsely, "Fire, fire!" The cotton in his whiskers had touched a flame, and a blaze was spreading over his costume. Martha called to the boy aides: "The barrel!" The fire crew threw up the window, caught Santa, and dropped him headfirst into the barrel, so that only his trouser legs and brogans kicked in the air. With a hiss and a trail of smoke Santa went out.

A few seconds afterward Mr. Barnes had been pulled up, gasping but grateful. Throwing blankets around him, Martha went to work to calm the excited crowd. "Let's all get back to Christmas." The candles gave the room a ruddy glow; sitting at the melodeon with her helpers to pump and steady it, she began the program. The children pushed in, and Martha struck a chord for the carol that they were to sing; but no voices were raised.

"I looked up," she wrote. "They weren't hearing the music nor seeing me. They stood wide-eyed, openmouthed, paralyzed with joy. Their first Christmas tree! It stood before their eyes, a thing of beauty beyond their expectations, so tall it touched the ceiling of the cabin, gleaming with lights and loaded with gifts. It was the revelation of a lifetime. . . ."

One child cried in excitement, and others pressed forward, staring at the lights, the loops of popcorn, and murmured to one another.

"Oh, I wants that sol'jer."

"Hit pears I *must* git that-thar doll; hits dress is set on same as a butterfly's wings!"

"Histe me clean up, Pap, so I kin see thet blue and red tootin' horn."

The elders merely gaped. As one of Martha's aides noted: "These people did not express their pleasure in words; they could only look their joy."

Without the assistance of the retired Santa Claus, Martha and her friends distributed presents. There were cries of delight and one or two whimpers that produced substitutions. At least one mistake ended happily. When an elderly man received a tiny mirror and a helper proposed an exchange he protested: "No, I ain' seed one o' these in a long time, and I ruther likes what's in it." He sat for the rest of the party, smiling into the glass.

The festivities went on. Miss Berry asked for songs and recitations, and for the first time many mountain mothers and fathers watched their children "rise up and talk right out, like thet." In the rapt faces she read a new wonder, a new pride. As dusk fell the party closed. Awkwardly the older people made their good-bys, and the children grinned their thanks as they clutched the gifts in their arms. Outside some sank to the muddy clay roads to make sure that the tin cart wheels worked and that the dolls' cradles really rocked.

Martha saw the crowd trudge off in the dark, holding blazing torches to light the path. She had given up her holiday in Atlanta, her old friends' welcome, and the evening dress. She had spent all the money she had, including what she saved for some of the family gifts. But, she said, it was the finest Christmas she had ever known. And she made up her mind that as long as she stayed here, there would be such a Christmas for these people.

Martha made another decision. Her Sunday school classes were not enough. The children asked so much about other matters—how to write their names, how to "figger numbers"—that she was going to try a small day school. Half a mile from the cabin, on part of the land her father had left her, she picked a spot and spent a hundred dollars for lumber. Hiring one or two workmen, she called in several of the larger mountain boys as helpers and supervised the erection of a one-room rough-board schoolhouse.

She was starting from scratch to demonstrate how a country school building should look. "Let's put our best foot forward," she said. She could not spend much, but she wanted the high-landers to see how bright a one-roomer could be. After a thorough whitewashing she planted flowers and shrubs around the building. She used planks between soapboxes for benches, and her "desk" was a big dry-goods packing case.

Her first classes proved agonizing, for she had to teach "by ear." She had had no formal training, no instruction in methods, and she knew no rules of classroom procedure. Miss Ida McCullough's kindly instruction and her own part-term at finishing school were hardly calculated to prepare her for handling backwoods boys. Nevertheless she bought a few books, questioned more experienced people, and plunged ahead.

In the neighborhood she sought several women friends. They agreed to help, though they warned that they could give only limited time. "Fair enough," Martha nodded. Promptly they discovered that they were working far longer than they had anticipated. "Still," one said, "Martha worked so much longer than *that*, that we didn't have the heart to quit." They were learning, as would others after them, that a Martha Berry project was a hard thing to leave!

Sister Frances came in to teach the boys to recite and even debate, after first explaining what the latter term meant. Frances also labored to instruct the country girls in the arts of sewing. In all too many families the old crafts were being forgotten. At times discipline was hard. Older pupils became bored or restless; several played jokes, splattered ink, and guffawed at their more earnest fellows, until Martha caught them by the ear and led them out. She had a healthy temper, as the difficult

45

ones learned. "She could scorch you with a word," a contemporary observed, "and when she did you stayed scorched a long time."

In spite of such troubles things went happily, so that Martha soon increased the size of the tiny building—a room added to one side, a second one which did not quite match it on the other, a bigger one at the back. She put in crude folding doors, and by opening them had space for a chapel. After an inspection from the outside, she frowned. "It needs something else—a spire." That week there rose a steeple, also whitewashed, with a bell.

"Cruciform," someone called the structure, and it was that in a way; others termed it, out of kindness, a "unique kind of architecture." "But to me," said Martha Berry, "it looked beautiful." The pupils agreed; as they gazed at the minute spire they clearly found it as impressive as if it had been the national Capitol in Washington.

That suggested something else. Why not use those old highland church buildings for branches of the day school? She tried one, then another, and before long she had urgent need of additional helpers. After some thought she called on the head of the county school board. Could he provide one or two teachers? If he wanted to see how she conducted her classes . . . The chairman stopped her. He had heard about Miss Martha's work, and she could have her teachers.

But simply to hold classes was not enough. Martha and her aides had to call on parents, urge them first to send the children and then to enforce attendance. Many times the older people insisted that they saw no need for "book larnin' or sich." "A-studyin' letters—whut fer?" "A plumb waste o' time." After she won grudging consent Martha had to provide books, pencils, slates, and also protection against rain. When a mother or father protested about the difficulties in rainy weather she gave out umbrellas and wraps.

Before long Martha was paying the young school-board assistants extra amounts to make regular visits to the parents, "just to keep things going." The regular Georgia school term lasted only five months; to continue hers beyond that limit she hired the helpers for additional weeks. And still she received emergency messages: "Come to the Bend, quick; we're losing ten pupils from one family!" Martha would saddle Roanie, ride to the cabin, and reason with the parents. "That-there gal's jus' too young and onserious." "We 'uns want a nice, settled 'un like you, Miss Marthy." More often she had to arbitrate disputes, arguments between families, claims of favoritism.

More and more Martha felt the need of experienced aid. A friend heard of a Miss Elizabeth Brewster, possessor of an impressive diploma from Leland Stanford in California, and Martha wrote her in the next mail. Tentatively she asked if Miss Brewster would consider joining her, even though she could pay very little.

That brought a forthright answer, in which Elizabeth Brewster brushed aside any discussion of money. The work sounded more than interesting, and she would come for nothing or practically nothing. As Martha rode out to meet the train, however, she experienced slight misgivings. For a complete stranger, unused to Georgia ways, would the whole situation be an impossibility?

Her first sight of Miss Brewster, Martha said, convinced her that her invitation had been a wise one. Tall, slender, and erect, with dark hair puffed neatly at the front of her head, the newcomer might have appeared severe, except for the hint of humor in her eyes. Elizabeth Brewster had a rich voice, a direct look, an energetic manner; many times the two women would differ, and although Martha usually carried her point, her assistant seldom withheld her frank opinions. Elizabeth was to stay, except for brief interruptions, for nearly twenty years.

Another day school was scheduled to open at Mount Alto soon after the assistant's arrival. "Let's not lose any time," she told Martha, and they commandeered a youth with an ancient

47

mule and no less ancient buggy, tied her trunk to the back and rode off. Only one place seemed available—a gloomy hut in which someone had murdered a woman; the mountaineers considered it, of course, to be "hanted." But neither Martha nor Miss Brewster had time for a lady ghost, and they ignored her to make the school work.

Another year passed, and another. By the early 1900s Martha had four day schools, and she might have been content. Slowly, however, she had begun to feel that what she did was not enough, "still not what I desired." Vacations were so long that the students forgot a great deal of what they learned. For six months or so, during part of each day, they were taught new facts, new habits. During the other half year they forgot the facts and relapsed into old, careless ways.

A boy who finished a term with a hundred new words and a knowledge of simple arithmetic returned to school to stare blankly when Martha gave him a test. Others had to be re-taught tasks that they had previously mastered. Attendance fluctuated badly, for no matter how many umbrellas she made available in rainy weather, roads could turn to lakes and isolate the schools for days at a time. Worst of all was the matter of lost weeks or months when the children stayed out of class to work on the land.

The parents had ready explanations: "Me an' Jim is allays needin' of the young 'uns ter dig the 'taters and pick the bolls." "I got nothin' 'gin larnin', but it sure seems like I needs all my boys." When the school term ended and Miss Brewster went North for the summer, Martha mulled over the situation. Somehow she had to bring the young highlanders into another environment and keep them there long enough to make the experience count for something. She thought again, as she did from time to time, of her friend Emma and the girl's young husband, who had lapsed into his mountain lethargy. If it had been possible to take Jim from those old associations . . .

Then one day it came to Martha: a school in which the highland boys would live, month in, month out, and learn things that would benefit them—not Latin and the classics, but subjects that would help them to cope directly with the life around them. A phrase suggested itself: education of hand and mind, in which one would not be a stranger to the other.

Yet she recalled her father's words about charity and the way it destroyed pride and the recipient himself. Somehow she had to reconcile what she hoped to do and the precaution her father had impressed upon her. She went to bed very late that night, but not before she had reached another decision.

After breakfast Martha drove Roanie into town, where she went first to the bank, unlocked her safety box, and removed the deed to the property her father had left her. A little later she hitched the buggy before the office of the young Judge Moses Wright. The burly, big-chested Wright had been a close friend of the family's; now he was courting her sister Bessie. He had a reputation for interest in the mountain people, for concern with the troubles of those who appeared in his court.

Taking a seat in the judge's office, Martha explained that she wished to consult him about her schools. They were working well, she thought, but not well enough. As she spoke Moses Wright looked relieved; as a matter of fact, he told her in a slow, deliberate voice, her family had just been asking if he would talk to her, ask her to give up "this school business." Certainly her experience had taught her a lesson by now.

Martha put out her hand to interrupt her friend. "Yes, I've learned several lessons. I see that I have to go further than I've ever gone." When she hurriedly explained her boarding school plan, Judge Wright stared: "Don't you know what it would cost to board boys?"

"I have an idea, and I want to start in a small way, with a dozen or so of them, and a little two-story dormitory." Bending forward, Martha took out the deed in her purse. "I want to transfer my land to the new school, for a place where they can learn and also earn their way at the same time. They'll all work,

49

and pay back the costs of their board and education, or part of them. Don't you see?"

Pausing for breath, she heard the judge explode in protest. "Martha, you don't understand what you're doing. It's the most valuable thing you have, this property. Once it's deeded, neither you nor your heirs could ever reclaim it. Suppose you realize you've been wrong and change your mind?"

Martha Berry shook her head. "I won't change my mind. I'm going to give the land to the mountain children, and they'll be my heirs."

This time Judge Wright shook his head. "You don't realize the things you'll have to do, the trouble you're starting for yourself. And when you're through you'll be just as poor as you want to be."

"You may be right," she smiled. "But meanwhile I'll be raising a sight better crop than you can get out of those acres now." Briskly she added: "I want you to be the first trustee, and I'd like your help as I go along. Still, if you can't draw up the papers I'll have to find somebody else."

Hesitantly the judge nodded. "I can do it, Martha."

The reaction at Oak Hill was swift and stormy. Had she taken all leave of her senses? "Girl, those day classes are one thing, but something like that! You'll kill yourself." "Anyway, what do *you* know about any kind of school?"

As always Martha's mother and sisters reverted to another old argument. They realized that her engagement was over, and they would not talk about it. But didn't Martha ever expect to be married? They could name five or six men who would need little urging. If she would only be sensible . . .

While the family talked on, Martha figured busily. The boys could cultivate the fields, sell their produce, start a dairy, put up buildings. As they worked they would learn about good farming, improved dairy methods, craftsmanship of a dozen kinds. After further thought she set a figure of $50 a boy, the smallest amount it should take to educate him for eight months or so. If the students could pay this tuition, that would be fine; if not, she hoped they could work out the amount between terms. As for their board during the school year, they would labor several hours a week to make that up. And no one would attend without contributing some kind of work; she would make it her cardinal rule.

That reminded her of the college-trained Elizabeth Brewster, still on vacation. A letter went off; surely her friend and assistant would like the boarding school project? The reply surprised Martha, for Elizabeth was strongly pessimistic. The costs would be high, she pointed out, and the problems enormous; if the matter were left to her, she would much prefer plain day classes.

If Martha suffered discouragement, she concealed her feeling when she wrote to Elizabeth to return, and went on to commit herself more thoroughly than ever to the new undertaking. For years she had known and respected a plump and white-bearded family friend, Captain John Gibbs Barnwell. A former Charlestonian, a member of a clan which contributed leading ministers to the Episcopal Church, he had followed two usually unrelated professions. After a time as a sea captain, John Barnwell had become an architect.

Then several years earlier Captain Barnwell had turned his back on the world to spend his last days, as he said, in reading and sober contemplation. He was now a leader of the Plymouth Brethren, a sect without regular ministers. Martha described the captain as "a man of large soul and white life"; he also had, she said, the spirit of an artist, and she meant to use that spirit for her school.

Going to Mount Alto, where Captain Barnwell lived alone in a simple, vine-grown house, she found him under the giant sycamore trees in his front yard, a Bible open in his lap. She talked in a rush, giving him no chance to interrupt as she sketched her hopes and her determination to go ahead. She was

51

going to help the mountaineers catch step with the world, join the procession that now moved past them.

At last the captain spoke quietly. "So. It is for the poor, and it will be Christian education, I trust."

"It will be Christian education." Martha mentioned no sect, for already she had decided that this would be a completely nondenominational school. "I hope you'll help, sir; we'll need a beautiful dormitory building. You know, so many schools look as if they'd been put together on a dark night. I want the boys surrounded by fine things so that they can absorb them and become part of them."

The captain glanced away; he was interested, yet apparently not enough. "I cannot take on such work, my child. I'm not a rich man, but I've saved enough to meet my plain wants for the rest of my life, and I plan to devote my time to meditation."

Martha caught his arm. "Ah, then you're just the man I'm hunting for! You can meditate under these sycamores and design our buildings. You don't need the money, and in any case I have none to offer you." For instance, she said, she hoped for a striking entrance which she would call "the Gate of Opportunity." It would open two ways, "for those coming in to learn and those going out to give the world what they've learned."

The saintly Captain Barnwell looked grave. "Martha, I warn you to keep the gate narrow, lest it let the world into your school." Though Martha nodded, the gate that went up eventually was wide enough to admit thousands. She talked on, her enthusiasm soaring, and finally the captain agreed: "I think it is the Lord's work, and I promise to help, Martha." Another battle had been won, and until his death Martha would have the services of a man who, out of goodness of heart and a true skill, set a pattern of construction as simple as it was impressive.

Before the captain had settled back with his Holy Book, she was riding through the mountains with a new light in her eyes. Whenever she saw a likely (or even an unlikely) farm she stopped Roanie and went in. Wouldn't the family like to send its older son to live and study at her new school? It would be for boys of fourteen and over, and entrance requirements would not be too rigid at first.

Objections developed quickly. "A long time like that, Miss Marthy, months and months!" "Our boy's sixteen, but we need 'im more than the young 'uns." Other highlanders were even more frank. They just didn't see the need for *that* much book business; it sure wouldn't help 'em on the farm.

Martha insisted that the school would benefit the boys in a hundred ways, and she cited facts and figures, tried argument after argument, with scant success as far as she could discover. "Well," they told her, "we'll think 'bout it. Cain't promise, but we'll think some more."

She hunted for the young men themselves, explained, and left written descriptions with them. She found several tired youths already trying to study at musty little "academies" in country towns. They listened but, like others, they appeared dubious. "You're sure, miss, it's going to open like you say?"

"I pledge it." Her determination shone through any temporary discouragement.

"Well, I might could do it, maybe."

"I'll see and let yer know."

Going farther and farther afield, Martha reached the Tennessee border and rode about the Lookout Mountain area and its environs. Even then she could not count one definite acquisition. As the family continued to assure her that she would fail, she might have been depressed. If even the mountain people themselves had no interest, why should she go through with the venture?

Nevertheless young Frances and her other sisters saw again what they called "that look" about Martha's jaw. She was going to get students if she had to steal them!

CHAPTER IV

BRAVE NEW YEAR

RAIN OR SUN, cloudburst or forest fire, Martha had determined to open the boarding-school doors on January 13, 1902. Even if nothing were ready she would ring a bell and begin proceedings.

More than ever before, her operations would be a gamble—curriculum, discipline, faculty rules. She had a small collection of new classbooks, but much of their contents would mean little to mountain residents and she would have to improvise and improve on them as she went along. As for the handling of the highlanders, the thought already made her tremble.

Martha knew well that mountaineers were independent, set in their ways. The boys in their teens were "rangy," hardly inclined to remain cooped up simply because Martha Berry wanted it like that. She had to win their good will or there would be no school, and yet she must let them know that she, not they, would run the place. For all her ebullient manner, she found herself biting her lips at times.

Miss Brewster was delayed in the North. One or two assistants in the day classes, which would continue with the boarding school boys attending beside the others, would help out, and Martha had sent inquiries to teachers in other towns. But all at once it looked as if they would meet any new students without even a place to house them. The prospective architect, old Captain Barnwell, obviously believed in the contemplative process which he had praised to her. Several weeks after her first interview she found him under his sycamores again with a Bible in one hand, a fan in the other.

Martha extended her hand. "Captain, you're so calm and cool, I know you've finished my plans!"

"No, Martha. I'll have them in God's time." Like Captain Barnwell himself, the fan moved slowly.

"Why, Captain, God built the world in six days, and you've had weeks on one building."

The captain fingered his beard. "You go too quickly, Martha. Take time to pray."

"I do pray, and hard, and then I get off my knees and go to work."

It required two or three more visits before she could prod him into action. The day he handed her the blueprints for a neat ten-room building she did not return to Oak Hill, but drove young Roanie on to Rome to make arrangements. Construction must begin within a few days at the latest. Long ago she had gone over her land and settled on a slightly elevated site across from Oak Hill, where she had played in girlhood. As she beat her way through the underbrush, she considered means of developing the grounds. However, first things first.

The dormitory would require practically all of her available money, $2500; the figure seemed very high. Though she did not argue, she made certain that she obtained full value. When the first men from the Sunday schools arrived, they discovered Martha on hand, and she remained there while they labored.

55

She brought lunch, shared it with them, and nobody shirked on the job.

In the meantime she made careful plans for the interior. She could not afford to spend a dollar on furnishings. From her room at Oak Hill she took a sofa and bed; from the hall and living room she confiscated other items. Foraging in the attic, she pulled out a broken divan, chairs without seats, chairs without backs, a dulled mirror. When she began to "borrow" side tables and dressers, Mrs. Berry and Aunt Marth intervened: no more! Two of the sisters, about to go East on vacation, took their own precautions. All of their possessions that might be removed went into two heavy trunks, which they padlocked.

At the homes of friends Martha stopped to chat, and the conversation sooner or later veered to the school and her need of supplies, "anything you'd like to get rid of." Into her net fell an undersized cooking stove, pots, pieces of china that had lost their mates, and other items. Finding castoff lumber and dry-goods boxes, she called boys from her Sunday schools, and they turned out crude wardrobes, bookcases, and washstands. Her sister Frances brought a sewing machine and whipped up chintz coverings and curtains, pillowcases and sheets.

A windfall came when a woman asked if the school would like an upright piano, well scratched but usable. Before she could change her mind, Martha sent the Berry coachman for it. Someone pointed to a Chattanooga newspaper advertisement—an auction of army goods. Taking a train to Chattanooga, Martha made a bid on a good lot of cots and returned flushed with her achievement.

The day the carpenters left, Martha stood before a white building with green trimmings and shingled roof. "Our wonderful first dormitory," she wrote under a photograph of it. Now, overcome by joy, she did a thing that made her chuckle long afterward. Going to the newly installed bell, "I started to yank on its rope. I rang and rang and rang it."

At the peals her family went running over the road, with

Aunt Marth in the lead. When they arrived they stared in disbelief. "Dis thing a-burnin', or what's de matter wid yer?" demanded Aunt Marth, and the other servants gaped.

"I looked at that crowd following her from the house, back at Aunt Marth, and then at my sisters," Martha reported later. "And I said 'I was thinking—thinking that this new bell is going to ring out the old devils of ignorance in the Southern highlands. It means the beginning of a new day. Somehow I got so excited as I thought of what a school I intended building that I just began ringing that bell!' "

The incident did not improve the family's attitude toward Martha and her schools. Someone else was not greatly impressed. Arriving late from the North, Miss Brewster followed Martha on an inspection of the dormitory with its improvised furnishings. She would work for the project, but she had yet to be won over to it. Outside the building Martha asked: "I wonder if you know what I'm going to name it?"

Elizabeth Brewster smiled: "The Castle of Remnants?"

"This will be Brewster Hall," Martha told her, and it kept the name as long as it stood. Soon afterward she advised the Berrys that she thought it best for her to live in the dormitory with Miss Brewster, one or two other staff members, and the students. She could not expect them to endure primitive conditions which she did not share. Her mother objected: "Martha, it doesn't sound right for you to leave your comfortable house. People will ask why you're behaving so peculiarly. . . ." Her voice trailed off in dismay.

"I have to be on hand to help with the quarters and the food, too." At that the family hooted. For Martha's survival, and also the boys', they said they hoped nobody would try *her* cooking. Aunt Marth contributed her own complaint. "Other folks' chil'ren! Git married and git your own, and stop runnin' after strangers' young'uns." More than ever the sisters asked one another why Martha could not behave like other people. . . .

57

As opening day, a Saturday, approached, she tried to make certain she would have at least a handful of beginners. At each of her day schools she picked an especially bright older student and pleaded hard with him and his parents. "I know you can't afford $50 tuition," she explained, "but you can make it up by extra work and also earn your board as you go along."

Using every bit of her Berry salesmanship, she made a counterargument to every negative response. "If you don't like it you can always leave." "Of course, your father can come see how you're getting along." When several at last agreed she nodded in relief. Each boy's success would provide good propaganda for the school; she had only to make sure that they *were* successes! A few days before opening, the first two of these "specials" arrived, and she set them to raking the lawn. The great day dawned with nearly everything in readiness—for what?

Morning passed in silence, and afternoon started. Then there was a creak of wheels and Martha, Miss Brewster, and the two boys ran out. A small fellow, who appeared younger than the supposed entrance age of fourteen, climbed down from a wagon with a trunk in his hands. Martha stared at Elizabeth, and the boys grinned. Glory be to God, they had themselves a "volunteer," whom nobody had had to dragoon! Everybody shook hands, and the name of Pinckney Dean went down in big letters on the books.

Martha hoped that Sunday would produce an addition or two; though they listened hard they heard no more grinding of wheels and their spirits lowered. With Monday she sent the three over to the "cruciform" building to study with the day pupils. That afternoon, she made clear, they would launch the work schedule, which must be followed as rigorously as classes. For the time being it would consist mainly of whacking at the brush that engulfed them, cutting wood, and rooting out tree stumps.

But Monday saw the arrival of another "hand-picked" recruit

from the mountains and then, joyously, another "volunteer." Later that week came three more; soon the student body reached twelve, and before the year ended, a glorious eighteen. They rode up with ancient satchels held together by ropes or with bulging boxes of belongings. In Martha's words, "We had boys of all ages, sizes, and conditions." As to their scholastic accomplishments she felt occasional doubts. Nevertheless she *had* them, and that was what counted.

The first week brought realization of one error, for the superb army cots had a small defect. They were all for extremely short men and, whatever her mountain boys' deficiencies, they were usually long. To each cot she had to add a box to hold a pair of feet.

Cooking for the school became a matter of agony. At first she tried several women from the neighborhood, who proved to be incompetent. Often Martha and Elizabeth assumed the duties. Martha had learned at least to make good corn muffins, and her colleague recalled her, "a towel around her head, with a very flushed face, taking the muffins from the oven and hurrying to get them on the table for a crowd of hungry boys."

The dining room seemed cavernous for the tiny band, and they ate in the kitchen. But the gift stove was too small, and they had pots of potatoes and beans boiling constantly over the open fire. To feed the boys there never appeared to be enough of anything. Looking back lightly to this period, Martha several times declared: "I started with boys because they were so good-looking and I thought boys could do more than girls. I didn't know how much boys could eat or I might have begun the other way." One morning she remarked to a youth who sat near her: "I know you're going to develop into a worthwhile citizen." Puffing up, he asked why, and she replied: "You've eaten too many good muffins, and I know all those muffins can't go to waste." (They did not, for he became a senator.)

During these first few days discipline offered no difficulties. Martha labored to keep the boys so busy that they had no chance to grow fidgety or rebellious. Long hours of class and hours of work were followed by short hours of night study. And, without special permission, the boys could leave the campus only on certain evenings a month. For each infraction of various kinds, so many demerits, and long sessions of destumping of trees. Too many demerits, and the student left. Today these former rules seem rigid indeed.

"I learned a great deal about boys in a very short time, and not from books," Martha said. "I found that they might want to be improved, but not too fast." She discovered this fact with the school's first crisis. It had no money for laundresses, housemaids, or other servants; in any case she wanted the boys to do the work. One morning, soon after the opening, she announced: "Monday's going to be wash day," and told them to bring down their soiled garments. Two of the youths sawed barrels in half to make tubs in a clearing beside an iron kettle. Calling the band there, Martha produced soap and several corrugated scrubbing boards and faced them. "Everybody will do his own clothes."

The mountain boys stared, and patiently Martha repeated: "Go to the tubs, and I'll show you how to do it so that they'll be clean."

Again no one moved, until a tall youth mumbled: "We don' do no women's work. I ain' never seen no mankind do no washin'." Another seconded him: "Washin' clothes is somethin' we ain't got to do."

"These things have to be washed," Martha pointed out.

"By somebody else, ma'am." When Martha saw the glint in the eyes, the tightening of the folded arms, she understood that they meant what they said.

"Very well." It was a turning point; Martha had a sick feeling, and yet she had to go through with this test. Suddenly she rolled up her sleeves, showing smooth white arms. "Then I'll have to do it for you. There's shade under those trees, and you can sit there in comfort."

Martha caught up an armful of the clothes, dropped them in; a minute or two later she was scrubbing and splashing, wiping at her wet face. The boys had not moved. As they watched, cheeks reddened, arms dropped to their sides, and they shifted weight from one foot to the other.

The oldest went toward her. "Ma'am, please." His voice had a choked sound. "I'll take over."

Martha put a tired hand to her head. "Still, if you really think you shouldn't . . ."

"No'm, I don't think that way." He went to her side, pulled up his sleeves, and thrust his arms into the soapy water. One by one the others followed, and Miss Berry left them with a smiling good-by. Out of sight in her room she cried. She had scored a hard victory.

Only a few days later she faced a new showdown. Of this incident Martha Berry herself never spoke, for it rankled too deeply. She was working in the dormitory while a group of boys cut a new path outside the building. A buggy rolled up, and out stepped several women from a town beyond Rome. Having heard of the odd doings, they had to see for themselves.

What they saw made their hackles rise. One of the visitors cried out, "You poor things! She has you working like prisoners in a chain gang." Her companions clucked in agreement: "I never . . ." "Just like field hands!"

One boy dropped his shovel and another lowered his rake in dismay and shame. The words had touched an old prejudice among the hill people. Then a small hurricane of ginghamed wrath descended upon them. Overhearing part of the comment, Martha had caught the significance of the scene. "Look here" —she shook a trembling finger—"if you women would go around encouraging people to work, the South wouldn't have the poorest farms in America! We wouldn't be crawling with sickness, and we'd have decent farms and taxes paid so we'd have better schools!"

She advanced upon the invaders, and sparks seemed to flash

from her eyes. "Work never hurt anybody; laziness has." With that Martha faced the students: "All right, when you finish that last stretch we'll go to supper. Good-by, ladies." The ladies twitched back to their carriages and rode off in a huff. Martha felt suddenly afraid; what would the boys do now?

One scratched his head. "Whew. You told 'em off right." Another snickered, and after a moment the whole group roared. Lifting shovels, they returned to their chores, and Martha resumed her fight with another devil, the budget. . . . Could they cut out that store-bought meat, or do with a pound less of meal?

Meanwhile, she had to watch always for troubles among the students and guard especially against loneliness and longing for home. Several times she put everything else aside to concentrate upon a highlander who sat with shoulders hunched at his desk, eyes swollen with tears. Martha enlisted assistants in campaigns to revive lagging spirits, to get the saddened one interested in the school. "I never exerted myself to entertain my beaux when I was a girl," she declared, "as I did to charm those first big mountain boys . . . into forgetfulness of their homesickness."

Her watch had to be a general one. "I was afraid to leave the place for even a few minutes at a time. It was like a fire that broke out in a new spot every time you turned your head." The evenings called for a special guard against restlessness. After supper the boys washed dishes and deposited them on rough shelves, then took places about the brisk fire. It was study hour, with help provided when needed (and almost always it was needed) in preparing the next day's lessons.

After that, shoving the books aside, the students and staff gathered again before the fireplace, sang songs, and spoke together. Lifetimes of isolation in the mountains often produced dour, taciturn men. "Tell us about your settlement," she would say in drawing out a new arrival. "What's farming like in your valley?"

Earnestly Martha went on to tell them of her hopes, of the way she wanted the school to grow and the highlanders to improve. "We're just beginning something that can be very big," she would explain, and the youths beside her would stir with the ambitions that she worked to plant inside them. Surroundings were bleak, the dormitory and schoolhouse draughty and badly lighted, the grounds thus far unplanted. A rainy day meant mud tracks everywhere, and a cold spell brought blue lips and quivering fingers. Nevertheless they were on their way. . . . After the evening's talks came Bible reading, a short prayer, bed at nine—morning call at five.

A hopeful entrant appeared. On one of her boy-hunting trips Martha had met Clayton Henson, who yearned to become a lawyer. As Martha rattled off promises of her great school, Clayton had cocked his head in doubt and asked: "How high can you carry me?" Her answer was prompt: "As high as you can go—through the roof and up to the sky." After some hesitation Clayton arrived, and she and her helpers put their heads together. A future lawyer! They would have to work hard over their books to keep just ahead of him, and somehow they did.

Then, overnight, a near disaster. After dark on a chilly day Martha met a boy and a pig attached to him by a rope. "Please, ma'am," the boy said, "I'm Willie Jackson and this is my pig, and we 'uns is come to school. I done carried him here for my larnin'. He's powerful lean now, but he'll pick up tolable quick."

Willie himself looked "powerful lean"; Martha said he was one of the saddest objects she had ever beheld. A pair of broken shoes had almost fallen off his feet, and his ravelled clothes seemed older than the child himself. She drew him inside and after he had caught his breath Willie went on: "I come thirty miles—on foot, yes'm. Hadn't no other way."

Willie explained that he was an orphan and had been working in a factory when he decided that anything else would be better. How long had he had a job there? Ma'am, practically as long as he could remember. Touched, Martha turned to the pioneer student, Pinckney Dean. "Pink, you're a Christian. Won't you show your practical Christianity by taking this boy and giving him a good bath? And burn those clothes."

Pinckney agreed and later reappeared. "I got him well scraped off, Miss Berry. But he won't come in now."

"Why not?"

"I burned his things, like you wanted, and he ain't got nothin' on."

Martha and the others scurried to locate trousers, a coat, shoes, and Miss Brewster contributed one of her shirtwaists, which fitted Willie approximately. He went to bed smiling and tired. In the morning, however, he could not get to his feet and, feeling his brow, Martha's assistant said that he had a fever. Looking closer, she saw a "peculiar eruption" on his face.

Martha called the only available doctor, a young one from Rome, who made a quick analysis: "I'd say it's smallpox." In Miss Brewster's words, "we had no time to be panic-stricken, but we had to get him away from the other boys." Heavily wrapped, Willie was taken to Martha's old playroom-cabin, while Martha herself rode about trying to find someone to nurse him. Though she promised good pay, none would run the chance of death or disfigurement.

What was to be done? She was needed at the school, but she was also needed here. She chose the boy and stayed with him hour after hour, taking his pulse, giving him liquids. Learning of the situation, a kindly Negro attendant at Oak Hill trudged over to assist from time to time; for the most part Martha herself carried the burden at the side of the frightened child. A day or so later the Berry family doctor arrived and said there had been a mistake. Willie had measles and also pneumonia.

Relief was short-lived, for while the case was less serious than they feared, Willie remained quite ill, and soon two other boys had the measles. Within a week every student who had not previously caught measles also had them. Martha and her helpers had to drop everything to concentrate on their patients. It was only the beginning; the young boarders passed their measles to the day students and through them to the Sunday-school boys and girls. Had Willie not looked so helpless, they might have blamed him for it all.

Again unknowingly, the boy produced a problem. Martha was confronted by a six-year-old child in what appeared to be his father's costume. He was Willie's younger brother. He had followed Willie's trail here, he said, and a kind countrywoman had given him a night's shelter and her husband's overalls.

For the time, at least, they could not turn the boy away. Clutching his trouser legs to hold them up, he walked around the grounds behind the others. To help in the "industrial work," he picked up chips for the stove. Still, he was far too young to be a boarder, and eventually Martha placed him in an orphan's home. Brother Willie stayed on at the school and thrived.

In these first days the institution bore the name of the Boys' Industrial School; repeating the letters B.I.S., the youths of Rome called the students "the Biscuit Eaters." Before long Martha made up her mind to send her charges to town in a body for Sunday services. Let the Romans see how neat and sturdy they were! To maintain the school's nonsectarian policy, they would attend one church one week, another the next.

On the first Sunday she herself could not go, and Miss Brewster lined the boys up to make certain that all buttons were on, coats brushed, shoes shined. The buggy had room only for Elizabeth and one student; the rest necessarily would walk the two miles or more. The day was dry and dusty, and when the marchers reached the First Presbyterian Church they were grimy and dispirited. Miss Brewster brushed away some of the dust and whispered encouragement as they reached the church.

The congregation gaped, and an usher showed them to a back corner. Growing more cheerful, the boys demonstrated an audible interest, for most of them had never been in a town church, and the pews, people, and above all the pipe organ made them nudge one another. One confided loudly that the organ's reverberations made his head "like to sing." The music and the sermon had another effect on several others; they went to sleep.

On their return Martha inquired brightly: How many people had they met, and had the minister known they were there? "I replied that I rather hoped our presence had been unnoticed," Miss Brewster reported. Nevertheless they went Sunday after Sunday to the churches; nobody was going to overlook the B.I.S. if Martha Berry could help it.

A brief spring vacation permitted a few, who could afford it or who lived nearby, to go home, and their absence made Martha fret. Suppose they didn't come back? One by one all returned. "We told the home folks how good we was gettin' along, ma'am." "We sure glad to get back, Miss Martha." She could breathe easily again.

With warm weather the boys set out fields, cut drainage ditches, plowed, reaped, put up side buildings. The B.I.S. acquired a cow, and the months that followed brought more applicants for admission and more stock, now and then in unexpected combinations. An expert-looking youth drove slowly in with a yoke of magnificent oxen. He was Emory Alexander, and he had come nearly forty miles with yonder animals. "They're broke for plowin', Miss Berry, and they're the fee for larnin' me."

Martha hesitated, realized how much the oxen must mean to the boy's family. Then she accepted, silently promising to work very hard with Emory, to make the sacrifice worth while to him. The boy had a request; his animals were "used to him," so could he keep on handling them? Martha assured him that he could. A little later she felt even more touched when another boy applied with a big cow beside him. After discreet inquiry she discovered that his mother had saved for years to buy the animal, the only cow the family ever owned. Now she had chosen to give it up for her boy's education.

For Emory and the boy with the cow and the others like them, Martha told herself, this school *had* to succeed. . . .

For months she had been thinking of an old family friend, John Eagan of Atlanta, a businessman of high conscience and broad concern for the well-being of his fellow men. His interest in his workers led him eventually to leave his large pipeline company to them. One day Martha went to him and spoke for a long time about her boys, her plans, and her food bills. She knew he believed in people; did he know of a better way to show it than to become chairman of her board?

If John Eagan had any reservations on the subject, Martha soon ended them. Calling at the school, he looked around and quickly consented. For about twenty years he gave her the benefit of unpaid guidance in a hundred ways. Mr. Eagan surrendered other duties on several days of each month to go to the campus, working like any other member of the staff over finances and related matters. As in many other cases, she spurred his interest, then left him alone to do his work. The result was a highly efficient business system, so economical that, as Martha put it, "we spent both sides of the dollar."

It was time to plan new buildings, and she conferred once more with Captain Barnwell. They agreed that all should be simple, rustic structures in log-cabin pattern. When her saintly friend drew blueprints for a barn, Martha looked up. "Captain, I want to make one change—a spire."

Captain Barnwell was disturbed. "On a barn? That would not be proper."

She lowered the sheet of paper. "Why do we put spires on churches?"

"We go there to worship. We are in a respectful mood, and they are appropriate."

Martha nodded. "Captain, it's easy to have our best thoughts on Sunday. But through the week these boys will be doing hard, hot work, work that has to be done day after day. They'll need cheer and courage. If they have a steeple it will catch their eye now and then, and they'll think of God's blessings, including the blessing of having work to do."

Stroking his white beard, Captain Barnwell agreed. "I never thought of that, Martha; you will have the steeple." From then on the architect put spires even on chicken houses at the school. He also assisted in planning a project that caused the raising of other eyebrows. When Martha's friend, Judge Wright, made a visit to the campus, he was surprised to see a long double line of newly planted elms, running from the outer road to a sizable knoll.

"What good is a thing like that, leading to nowhere?" The judge frowned. "You're simply taking space from a pretty good field."

"No, I'm preparing," Martha assured him. "Before long those trees will grow into a fine approach for a great big building up there." She pointed, but Judge Wright shook his head dubiously, and for some years others did the same thing as they passed. Less than a decade later the recitation hall went up, and the trees provided an impressive entranceway as she had predicted.

After another year it became clear that the school would be able to hold its first commencement with a graduating class of one—Clayton Henson, the hard-working boy who would leave to carry on studies for the law. It was mid-May of 1904, and the exercises would demonstrate the things being done at B.I.S. A staff member offered ten dollars for the winner of a grand oratorical contest, and Martha arranged dialogues, recitations with "gestures," and, as an aesthetic climax, a "Delsarte drill with music." For that spectacular episode, older day school girls would be draped in pale cheesecloth gowns with wings and "angel sleeves" trailing gloriously about them.

Tragedy threatened, however, and Clayton was almost cheated of his honors because of a mild Lothario of a fellow student. The latter, a hill-country ladies' man, was the general favorite to win the declamation award until he disappeared of an evening to call on one of the girls. This violated a regulation, and Martha and her aides ruled that the offender could not take part in the contest.

The girls walked out of rehearsal, angel sleeves and all. If he did not appear, they would wave no wings at the audience. Martha summoned Judge Wright, Captain Barnwell, and others, conferred for a long time, and a Solomon-like decision resulted. The boy could speak but would not be eligible for the prize. Everybody was satisfied, and the Delsarte girls floated back.

Martha announced that the evening's speaker would be the Honorable Hoke Smith, former President Cleveland's Secretary of the Interior, later governor of Georgia and a believer in conservation of natural resources. Boys were natural resources, Martha said, and she worked hard to get Hoke Smith to come. At the last minute a telephone call arrived from Atlanta; Mr. Smith said he was in the midst of a heavy traveling schedule and regretted that he would not be able to reach the B.I.S. after all.

"That fellow never heard a plea like the one he got from Martha Berry," a friend has reported. "She said she could not believe a man like Hoke would go back on his word. She'd told everybody he'd be there, and it would look real bad, wouldn't it? She was afraid her school could never recover from the blow, and so on. Smith didn't have a chance; he came."

The exhausted official, who went without sleep to keep his promise, was met by a chipper Miss Berry. "Where is the school?" he asked wearily.

Martha extended her arm. "Here."

"Where, Miss Berry?"

She indicated the dormitory and the school building in the distance. Mr. Smith cleared his throat. "How many receive diplomas tonight, Miss Berry?"

"One, and oh, he's a fine boy." She went on blithefully, as if she were describing a great pageant. "Clayton's the class valedictorian and the honor graduate as well." Hoke Smith said little more but followed her noncommittally. But he could not conceal his astonishment as he approached the school hall to hear a blaring town band, and found greens and streamers everywhere and a crowd of men, women, and children who filled the school, sat on the stairs, and stood outside. It had been weeks since he had seen so large a throng.

As Miss Brewster pictured the evening, Martha rose to a roaring applause. Clayton, king for a night, won shouts and whistles and tears, and Mr. Smith received one of the ovations of his life. The ceremonies went on for a long time, with wings flapping, hands thrust oratorically into the air, and a moment of high emotion when Clayton received the school's first certificate. He was crying, and so were his parents, his brothers and sisters, and Miss Berry herself. Hoke Smith admitted that he had never known anything to match that evening.

Many in the crowd had come from long distances and could not hope to get home that night. Somehow accommodations were found; students surrendered their beds and Mr. Smith drew a prize—the dormitory guest chamber. Just over his head, however, he quickly discovered that twenty boys were sleeping, or about to sleep, on mattresses. The excited young men talked and laughed for hours; through the thin planks he heard every word, every turn, every chuckle.

Repeatedly the guest began to doze, only to sit up at the sound of a thump from above. He grunted, groaned, and cursed to himself. At last, completely spent, he slipped off, but after what felt like only a few minutes he opened his tired eyes again. The students were rising early for their journeys home.

Hoke Smith heard them dragging tin trunks, bump, bump, bump, down each step. Nearby Martha was sleeping, or perhaps not sleeping, since one by one the boys knocked at her door to make their farewells with cheerful, noisy thanks. One mountain mother called to another outside, a child fell from a porch, and two babies cried lustily. And at the same time student janitors, dairy attendants, and farm workers pounded their way through the dawn.

Soon afterward Martha appeared. "Mr. Smith, you've left your room so early, and you've needed your rest!" she exclaimed. The guest explained wryly that he had hoped to get more rest outdoors than in. A moment later he grinned. Actually, he'd had time for a good day's electioneering among these mountain farmers.

Somewhat pointedly Smith added that he was much impressed with the school's need of dormitories. He wanted to give a check for this purpose, and he made it out immediately. Martha Berry used the money to complete what became known as the Hoke Smith Cottage. And, like many others who showed a flicker of interest in her school, Mr. Smith ended as a member of her board.

CHAPTER V

"LADIES,

PICK UP YOUR BABIES"

HER SCHOOL WAS succeeding, Martha assured herself ironically—if only she could keep it from going bankrupt. Her students had reached thirty, then gone beyond that number, as newcomers arrived from Tennessee, Alabama, Georgia, the Carolinas. But each addition increased the costs, and almost every day produced a new demand, a new and usually imperative need.

She dropped hints to friends, wrote letters to people in Atlanta and Chattanooga, Nashville, and Montgomery. Paying visits to merchants, lawyers, doctors, and professional men, she let them know that her school would accept any kind of help. Her childhood friends complained. Whenever you talked to Martha these days, somehow the conversation got around to that school. If they were not interested Martha left them, to spend an hour helping the boys cut at the underbrush, then work over bills and ponder at night over educational journals, trying to make up for her lack of formal school training.

At the end of a term she and her aides scoured walls, gathered dormitory sheets for mending, collected leftovers. Once she located a skilled mountain woman and brought her to the B.I.S. to show them how to make soap from kitchen fat. That same week, sunbonnet on her head, she stood beside a steaming pot when a pompous book agent arrived and demanded that she take him to "the person in charge of the school's literary needs." He gasped when he learned who she was. A few hours later, doffing her bonnet, Martha was off to Chautauqua, New York, and Northfield, Massachusetts, where she attended institutes "to learn how wrong we've been in the way we do things."

One thing she could not learn—how to run a school without money. For all her labor, for all of Chairman John Eagan's skill in finances, funds reached a new low. One of her sisters has told of an evening when Martha visited Oak Hill and sat at the fireplace with several bits of paper in her hand. Getting up, she absent-mindedly threw the scraps into the fire, only to realize that she had accidentally tossed away a ten-dollar bill.

"I saw her face turn white. After so much effort to raise the money . . ." Martha said very little, but went upstairs and took out a locket given to her by a former beau. The next day she rode into Rome and sold it. Yet she would need much more than lockets. She had drawn on every source open to her, and still a heavy deficit was on the B.I.S. The faculty watched in silence, and so did the boys. In the air hung the phrase so common to mountain communities—"breaking up the school."

And the school might well have broken up, except for a prayer. One night, as Martha went into the dormitory, she heard a boy's earnest words at the evening assembly. "Lord, Miss Berry told us we ought not to ask You to send things, but jes' let You know we'll do what we kin if You'll show the way. Now, Lord, you know the dishpans, the washtubs, and might' nigh ever'thing we got is wearin' out." His voice became more plaintive. "The big pan has three holes now, and even with all the mendin' we do it won't last much longer. And them plow-lines ain't good for another season."

Martha stood in the doorway as the solemn plea continued. "I'm wonderin', Lord, whether You ain't showin' the way right now. I read in the paper about some New York people givin' money to schools. Dear God," he finished, "give Miss Berry strength to get up there and tell them folks how much we need things. Amen."

She felt "almost petrified." To go among strangers with her hand out—that was what it meant. "But when somebody prays for you, you just have to do something." That night she went to her room, sat for a long time in the dark, and later in the week she saw her family and Judge Wright, then had Roanie hitched up to take her to the train. She was heading North.

On her way Martha realized too late that she had neglected to gather letters of introduction, or written information, or photographs of her schools. Did she know anyone up there, anyway? Only two or three names occurred to her, those of her former Baltimore schoolmates, now married and living in New York. Her spirits sagged steadily. On leaving Georgia, she had imagined herself almost a heroine; by the time the ferry carried her across the river to Manhattan she felt "like a bag of jelly."

She had arrived in bleak, snowy weather. Blowing on her fingers as she left the gray station, a single bag in her hand, Martha was "ready to sell out for two cents." She would have to watch every nickel she owned; after shaking her head at the hansom-cab drivers who reached for her luggage, she looked into a nearby dry-goods store and saw a telephone. When she called her first friend, a startled voice cried: "How nice, Martha! You must come to lunch."

Accepting the invitation, she asked several women clerks in the store to recommend an inexpensive boardinghouse and took the name of a respectable place, for women only, near Thirty-eighth Street. There she rented a dim upstairs bedroom. She should feel at home, she thought; it was almost as cramped as her school quarters.

Martha rose early the next day. New York of the early 1900s appeared far more brusque, far more frenzied than the city she had visited a few times before. Faces were either harassed or bored, and the elegance of the women's dresses made her ashamed of her own costume. At the windows of the great shops she paused, then forced her thoughts back to her errand.

At a cheerful apartment the former schoolmate gave her a warm greeting, but sat silent as Martha talked of her school, of the boys and their needs. Slowly her friend shook her head. "Martha, let some frump do things like that. You get yourself some new clothes, hunt up an old beau, and marry him."

Strongly disappointed, Martha left soon after the meal. At the first store she discovered she telephoned a second friend, to receive the same eager invitation. "Please don't ask me to have a meal," she answered. "Just let me come talk quietly about something that's very close to me."

In a gray apprehension she approached the second woman, who listened and responded pointedly. "My dear, New York is crowded with petitioners and fund raisers, some noble, others complete frauds. It's something I don't know much about, anyway." Nevertheless, at the sight of Martha's face she thought for a moment and went on. "Still, I might get my old pastor in Brooklyn to let you talk at prayer meeting. When I lived there we had much more time for such things."

That was better. Two evenings later, on a Sunday, Martha left her room with an invitation to talk at a Presbyterian church in Brooklyn. Heavy snow began to fall, and she had never set foot in the distant borough, yet she could not afford a cab. At the corner a friendly news vendor motioned to a boy, who said he would guide her there in return for a quarter. They took a streetcar, rode a long time to the bridge, and there the youth confessed that he himself had never been in Brooklyn.

75

By this time the snow piled inches deep. Martha again asked directions, changed cars, and arrived at the church just as services ended. Panting, brushing flakes from her hat and coat, she went uncertainly up the long aisle. About to pronounce the benediction, the minister inquired: "Miss Berry?" After hearing her breathless apology, he bowed: "Won't you tell us of your work—in a few words?"

It was the first time that Martha had ever appeared before an audience of strangers; at Chautauqua and the other institutes she had spoken briefly to people who had been interested in advance. "In a few words . . ." What could she say? As she steadied herself with icy hands against the pulpit, she prayed that she would not disgrace herself, the school, the South, and women in general.

Hesitantly Martha began, and then caught the eye of an elderly man. In a moment she was talking to him, telling him about the boy who had begged God that she be guided to call on Northerners; the young one who had brought his pig on a rope, the boy whose family gave up its cow. "They want only the chance that others have, that boys in New York get every day," she finished, all her troubles and all her hopes in her voice.

When she stepped down from the platform she needed no one to tell her that she had stirred her listeners with her simplicity and the warmth of her words. A group crowded around her, asking questions, writing down her address.

"You say $50 will provide a scholarship?"

"Will you take books and clothes?"

"My wife and I would like to send a set of kitchen utensils."

At the last words her heart beat faster. So the boys would have their new pots and pans!

Martha heard a small woman whisper to her husband: "Couldn't we give her the name of that Wall Street man you know—the one that's helped a lot of people?" The husband handed Martha an address but cautioned her not to mention his name. "We've sent so many to him."

In a daze Martha left the church, and long after midnight she lay awake in her chilly room, optimistic for the first time in weeks. The Wall Street reference had certainly been oblique, but still she would chance it. The next day, following her land-lady's instructions, she arrived at the impressive office door of R. Fulton Cutting. Vaguely she recalled the name as that of a man active in political reform, a contributor to many move-ments.

In the big reception room several people waited, including one or two whose crisp efficiency awed her. An hour passed and, nervously folding and refolding her gloves, Martha tried to organize her appeal. A door opened and a secretary called her name. Her hands shaking, she met a pleasant-looking man, stumbled through her opening words. Then, as she had the previous night, she forgot everything else when she described a mountain home with three boys old enough to enter the school. In a few years they would have lost their chance. If only she could get a $50 scholarship for one of them. . . .

Mr. Cutting interrupted. "I hope you won't mind this, but how much salary do you make?"

"Salary?" She had been taken by surprise. "I don't make any salary. I've given my property, I pay the bills and my expenses too."

"Still, what do you get out of this?"

Martha gazed thoughtfully at him. "I get a great deal. I see boys come with only the clothes on their backs, and go home to change the life around them. I watch them develop. . . ."

R. Fulton Cutting's eyes softened as he listened. After a few minutes Martha got to her feet: "I mustn't take more of your time. If you decide that we're doing good work, I hope you can help a boy with a scholarship."

"Wait." He smiled, went out, and returned with a folded

check. "I'll be interested to keep in touch with you, and when you're up East again, let me know."

So Mr. Cutting was giving her something without further quibbling. Beaming, afraid to speak, Martha left him. In the crowded elevator and outside in the biting air, she clung to the check; only when she reached the Broadway corner to wait for her streetcar could she open the paper. It was for $500, enough for scholarships for ten boys!

Dazed and tearful, Martha boarded the wrong car; people were staring, and she realized that she must be radiant with happiness. Changing cars, she tried to appear as blasé as her fellow passengers and failed. In the boardinghouse she sank to her knees to thank God, and then sent the school the good news and also word that she would be home soon.

A few days later came an answer which must have been written within an hour after her letter arrived. It said: "Don't return yet. We are sending a list of needs." Before the list reached New York, Martha had gone on with fresh energy. Getting suggestions from the interested landlady, names from the telephone book and elsewhere, she wrote a stream of letters on the table beside her bed. How could she say what was in her heart? Anxiously she tried to fit each explanation to the interests of the person she addressed—a lawyer, a woman from New Orleans, a Texan of whom she had heard.

Many ignored her notes. Some who saw her made contributions, a few large ones, most of them small. All too often she heard the most discouraging of excuses: "Your school is too new to know how it's going to work." But if she didn't get some kind of support for it, nobody would ever know how it could work! She set and kept appointments, regardless of icy streets, slush, a near blizzard.

After several days the landlady, hearing no sound from the room for hours, knocked and found Martha flushed and voiceless. The exposure of the past few weeks had had its effect. Later Martha explained lightly: "I was just wondering whether to hang on to the interests of this world or turn all my thoughts to the next."

A doctor pronounced her case pneumonia and prescribed hospital care or a trained nurse. In a feeble voice she objected that she could pay for neither. Nevertheless he summoned a nurse, and for days Martha fought for recovery. The first morning she could get up she wrote letters of appreciation and totaled her funds. She had gathered more than $1700, enough to make certain that the school would last until summer. As she settled back, pale and drawn, in the train for home, she knew that she had achieved something else: she had begun to bring the story of her mountain people to the men and women of the country.

Her staff and several boys welcomed her. At their first glimpse they bundled her up and the driver cracked his whip to speed her to the school. Sitting before a great open fire, she told of her Northern visit and led a service of thanksgiving. Her family arrived, and when Aunt Marth saw her worn face she lectured her fiercely: "You killin' yo'self, and dese people aroun' here helpin' you do it!" Thereafter for weeks Aunt Marth sent over soups and custards, tender inquiries and roaring messages: "You tell Martha Berry she nothin' but a fool."

Wherever she turned, Martha discovered that she was needed. There was, for instance, the matter of big John Wesley Cooper. One day two young giants stopped before the school and she gave them a special welcome, because the last few applicants had been so much underage that Miss Brewster announced they were running a kindergarten. While both of the new boys did well, Martha quickly decided that the school had a true acquisition in the pleasant-mannered, deep-voiced Cooper.

"Don't you sing?" she asked, and almost immediately a magnificent baritone rang through the living room. That day Martha started to plan. "You have a voice for grand opera," she told Cooper, "and you're going to use it. Remember that."

79

The others liked John Wesley Cooper's good will, the way he assumed his share of the work. Classroom effort, however, proved more than John Wesley had bargained for; he stared glumly at pages he could not follow, and gradually it became evident that he was yearning for his old life in nearby Texas Valley. One night poor John Wesley's tears fell steadily into his uneaten food.

Martha reasoned and cajoled, but to all her words he had a single answer: "I'm just not satisfied." When she joked, John Wesley smiled, but not for long. Then one morning a wagon pulled up, driven by Mr. Cooper, who was there to see how his boy progressed. Promptly John Wesley told Pa he had had enough of the academic life; he wanted desperately to go home and take a good drink of mountain spring water. "You pack," said the father, and John Wesley began to throw his possessions into a tin trunk.

Martha came out and saw that the older Cooper had hitched his mule to one of her most treasured dogwood trees, and that the animal was nibbling at the bark. Could she ask that he be moved? No, highland people could be very sensitive, and it was more important to save the boy than the tree.

Inviting the father onto the porch to wait, Martha launched into her arguments: John Wesley had real musical talent, and he could train his voice while he trained his mind. Someday, perhaps, even the Metropolitan! Pa made it clear that thet-there Metropolitan place meant nothing to him. Like his son, he had one reply to everything: "John Wesley ain't satisfied."

As they talked, the mule continued to bite into her dogwood. Moreover she could hear the bumping of the boy's trunk down the steps, and with each crunch of bark, each plop of the trunk, Martha said she felt as if a nail were being driven into her casket. Excusing herself, she hurried to the kitchen, where they were now using one of the students as cook. She had an inspiration and she told him: "Make some big fat biscuits. Use the best streak-ed meat that we've cured, and put on plenty of coffee, three times stronger than usual. And hurry!"

John Wesley had lifted the trunk into the wagon when she stepped up. "Mr. Cooper, you two must stay to dinner."

"No'm, we got to hurry back."

"Now, Mr. Cooper, if I were at your house and you had dinner and asked me to stay, I'd stay."

That did the trick, and before long John Wesley and his father were consuming bulging biscuits, juicy streak-ed meat, and coffee. The mule chewed harder than ever, too, but Martha concentrated on John Wesley, still arguing as she plied him. John Wesley ate and ate; some said he ate more that day than he had during all of his previous stay. Finally he pushed back his chair and stretched.

"Pa," he murmured dreamily, "them biscuits are prett' near as good as Ma makes. This coffee beats the grain-to-a-gallon kind we sometimes has, and I never dreamed meat could be so fine. Pa, I think I'll stay a spell longer." He stayed a spell (four years in all), and though he never reached the Metropolitan, Martha made him a choir soloist with Rome's Baptist, Methodist, and Presbyterian congregations. He also sang in Atlanta and became a well-known businessman.

An even more stately pupil was Mr. J. Andrew Bird. He had taught for several years in a remote country school before he decided that he himself needed a good education. At Miss Berry's school he served as janitor, giving his full services for his tuition. He cleaned erasers and blackboards, kept fires going, and swung the ax with a book open near him at all times. To staff and fellow students he remained always "Mr. Bird."

With the coming of another spring Martha and Captain Barnwell bent over plans for a two-storied "rustic cabin," to be built by the boys as a place to house guests and, though the students did not know it yet, to indoctrinate them as well. In Miss Brewster's words, it would demonstrate to the highlanders that "a home may be simple and inexpensive and at the same

81

time in good taste and even beautiful." Furnishings were in keeping with a log-cabin style of architecture, and the boys made chairs and sofas of untrimmed logs.

Above the fireplace hung another print of Martha's favorite phrase: "Kyndle Friendship." In this room the boys would meet with school guests and staff, to kindle good feeling and companionship. More than ever Martha insisted that the students "speak up and speak out." She would challenge the inarticulate ones: "Give us a little talk, about anything you want." As they sweated in anguish, some of them found the room a place of trial and torment.

But shyness or no shyness, Martha said, "we can't have any mutes here." She taught toast-making, with water or coffee. A reserved teacher, if he wished to stay, must lose some of his reserve. And guests promptly discovered that they also had to join in conversation and the making of little speeches. Not only did everybody work at B.I.S.; everybody talked.

With Captain Barnwell's assistance Martha now began gradually to landscape the grounds with winding paths, lines of trees, vines at the doors. She "tagged" fine trees, tying red cloth around the most promising ones she spotted in the woods, instructing the boys to uproot them and bring them to the campus. As one graduate said: "I used to think I'd lifted and moved every big tree within five miles. That wasn't true; we must have done it with only half of them!"

Over and over again she impressed on them the value of a plain natural beauty. "Once she asked me if I knew what a 'vista' was," a former student said. "When I told her it must be something to eat, she laughed and made me help in making a vista." She instructed them in the framing of views with pairs or groups of trees, and in the building of bridges over campus streams. "I want this place to look as if somebody cared enough to sit up with it at night," she smiled.

One week the boys labored to build a bathhouse, and bath times were rigidly scheduled. "If you are not here at the stated

time, you will miss your bath. And cleanliness is next to God-
liness." Competition became heavy for the preferred hours; the
tank provided warm water for only limited periods.

Mules were needed for the farm, and the school got them
when a friend sang for the B.I.S. Sarah McDonald Sheridan,
a Roman with a voice, gave a recital which netted funds for
an animal and a half. The boys pledged themselves to provide
the other half mule and christened the pair Nip and Tuck.
When Mrs. Sheridan visited there, the paper said her mule
pulled the buggy with obvious pride in its connection.

That winter brought a valuable new friend. Martha received
a message signed with a name that she did not place at once.
Miss Leila Laughlin would be passing through on her way to
Florida, and could she see the school? Sending a wire, Martha
prepared to receive the newcomer. Florida for the winter . . .
She must be an elderly lady, and Martha went out with heavy
blankets and a foot warmer.

Off the train, "practically floating down," came a graceful,
good-looking girl. She had heard Martha speak in New York,
and now she wanted to find out what the place was really like.
For days the energetic Miss Laughlin stayed there, putting
questions, nodding briskly at the answers. On one "blue Monday" she watched the boys groan over the washboards, and
after a time drew Martha aside. "I know that boys like machinery. Would you mind if I gave them a steam laundry?"

"Would I *mind*?" Martha almost cried, the boys roared in
delight, and there followed a chapel meeting at which the students got up, one by one, to speak of their gratitude. "I was so
glad I wouldn't have to scrub my shirts any more, I guess I
prett' near wept myself," a class officer explained. They had
acquired a warm partisan; for a half century, eventually as Mrs.
G. Lister Carlisle, the visitor proved her faith in Martha Berry's
work.

In the spring of 1905 the B.I.S. prepared for a true commencement, for there would be five graduates this time. Word traveled far, with an invitation: Everybody just come. A few weeks before graduation, staff and students retired as usual one night. Soon afterward a bell rang furiously and someone yelled: "Fire, fire!" Pulling on her shoes and a coat, Martha dashed downstairs. The schoolhouse, center of so many of their activities, was ablaze. Boys tumbled from the dormitory, yanking up overalls, racing to the scene.

"Hurry, please hurry!" she cried to them. Almost at once, when she saw the size of the flames, she realized that the building could not be saved. But the students ran through flame and smoke, retrieving desks and chairs, books and supplies; some pulled blackboards from the walls, while others ripped off doors and succeeded in snatching out shutters. All too well they understood the cost of everything on the campus, and the work and effort that had been needed to acquire it.

Shielding their faces, dodging charred sections, the boys carried off practically all the portable pieces before collapsing walls forced them out. Then, while sparks crackled around them, small groups picked up the woodhouse and rescued the fences.

Martha watched through reddened eyes. So much of their history had gone up with the peculiarly shaped building, and so many of their assets! She summoned the students to the dormitory, helped put grease on their blisters (several had serious burns), and called a night staff session. Promptly they decided their course: school would resume as usual in the morning, and they would use the dining room, library, sitting room, and any other space that lay empty. The first session was only ten minutes late in starting.

The boys volunteered to work extra hours to repair a two-room cabin on the edge of the campus. They added several extra rooms, and there, without desks or blackboards, some of the classes went on for the final six weeks of the term. The weather turned frigid, and they had no heat. Teachers and pupils threw on heavy coats and moved outside in the sun. "Not one boy left the school, and not a boy or a teacher complained."

But what of the commencement? Martha heard of a Baptist evangelist who was holding a revival in a tent at Rome. She found it shabby and badly worn; still it would be a covering for a crowd. The evangelist required a great deal of persuading to convince him that a graduation had the same importance as his own soul-saving, but finally he surrendered it for several days.

The boys pitched the tent but did not stretch it properly. When the chorus rehearsed, the acoustics were abominable; the music ran out in all directions. An Atlanta voice teacher suggested that the canvas be repitched and raised; that helped, though the sound was still a bit peculiar. At this point Martha had to start for Columbia, South Carolina, where she had agreed to attend an educational meeting. She was to bring back their baccalaureate speaker.

Due Saturday night for the Sunday afternoon service, Martha and the guest were delayed by a wreck in their path. After a long wait and several changes of coaches they arrived twelve hours late, raced to the campus, and there the speaker was pressed into the pulpit with only a change of shirt.

That night one of the graduates rose to make a talk. He was Mr. Bird, who had just decided to become a minister; as he moved forward a silence fell, for everyone wanted to hear what J. Andrew Bird would say. He began confidently and then, after a sentence or two, his voice cracked with emotion and he could not continue. Closing the meeting, one of the trustees called it a fine one, "but Mr. Bird's talk was the best of all."

The great events were to last for days, and each hour brought more friends and families. At class-day exercises feeling again ran high when a young man of farm background, the gaunt and handsome Gordon Keown, gave the valedictory address. His subject was what the school meant to him, and, like Andrew Bird, he started in a brave voice, only to be interrupted by his own tears. Keown would not give up; three times his voice thickened and tears wet his cheeks. On the stage near him sat Martha, who had forgotten her handkerchief. She leaned toward another woman and asked: "Will you lend me yours?" The answer was muffled: "I can't; I'm using it."

The climax was the grand commencement. Faculty and students worked over the dilapidated tent, adding class banners, pinning up red, white, and blue bunting, arranging boxes of plants and clusters of flowers. On the big afternoon the skies darkened, and shortly before commencement hour rain began. The main speaker was Luther Rosser, then perhaps the leading attorney of Georgia. He rode in late, to find Miss Berry waiting calmly for him at the head of a file of boys, all carrying umbrellas. By then the shower had become a downpour; large areas had flooded, and the speaker had to be brought part of the way by flatboat.

In the tent children screamed, farm wives peered around restlessly, and a drummer boy pounded on and on in an effort to keep up the crowd's spirits. The umbrellaed official procession moved over the last stretch of soggy ground while oxen bellowed, mules brayed, and dogs ran out to bark at the strange sight.

Entering the tent, Mr. Rosser caught a splash of rain from the flapping edge. "You see," Martha smiled brightly, "it's a Baptist tent." A moment later the grand march halted of necessity; the aisle had been blocked by children, playing in the grass. Martha spoke as calmly as if she were ordering tea at Oak Hill:

"Ladies, please pick up your babies."

Babies removed, the procession continued toward the platform to shouts and applause. People rose, benches tipped over, thunder broke. By then the tent leaked at nearly every seam, and as discreetly as possible the board president, John Eagan, used a handkerchief to wipe his face more or less dry.

A student lifted an umbrella over Mrs. Patton, the pianist, as she sat at her bench. Another held a second one above her own head as she moved forward to sing. By the time the quartette chanted, "Don' You Cry, My Honey," water poured from a hundred widening holes in the saturated canvas.

Once more the serious, good-looking Gordon Keown spoke, clutching at the handle of his umbrella. His high moment arrived when he raised his free hand and gestured with the words he had memorized: "And today we go forth from these stately walls of our alma mater. . . ." As Gordon sat down to a wave of hand clapping, Martha's usual brightness left her and she looked shamefacedly at her orator, Mr. Rosser. These stately walls!

At that the perceptive guest bent toward her. "Miss Berry, you have a wonderful school. A wonderful school."

Stepping to the edge of the platform, Luther Rosser told the five graduates that they were indeed leaving great walls, "the walls of the greatest school I know." And there was no doubt that, despite the puddles beneath their feet and showers from above, they and the crowd agreed.

Shortly afterward, pinning a prize on one of the graduates, Martha caught sight of a woman who a few minutes before had been homely, dark, and wrinkled. Now hers was "one of the most beautiful faces I ever saw," the face of the boy's proud mother.

When the program ended Martha hurried behind the mother. "We'll provide a bed, and I hope you'll rest well."

"Bed?" The highland woman scoffed. "Miss Marthy, I want to sit up all night and rejoice and thank the good God. My boy's gittin' his chanct." Her look changed to one of determination. "And I got twelve more at home, and they're all goin' to git sent to you."

PART TWO

Everybody Must Be

Going Somewhere

CHAPTER VI

ATLANTA TO WASHINGTON
TO NEW YORK...

ROME TO ATLANTA to Washington and back to Rome; Philadelphia to Baltimore and Hartford; New York to Chicago and St. Louis. The next few years were crisscrossed with travel, and, as Martha Berry said, she came to know every porter and conductor in half the United States. When she grew weary she told herself that all she had wanted to do was train highland people, and here she went, traipsing one way and another. But if she did not swing far and wide for support, there would be no school.

The mountain people and others of small means did what they could to help. One after another sent envelopes, sometimes crudely homemade ones, with quarters and fifty-cent pieces and dollar bills. Then a custom began; in many valleys and settlements every family forwarded a dollar as the school term opened. Martha accepted in the knowledge that "each such gift represented a sacrifice." The total reached 800 families, and

91

it was an amount on which she could depend, year after year. But much more was needed.

Each time she prepared for one of her trips the students saw how seriously Martha took the effort. "This is so important for us," she would confide, and then she called the students together. "I'm going out to get money so that we can carry on," she would say. "Behave while I'm gone, and pray for me." An early alumnus remembers: "I prayed so hard I'm sure it helped some."

Martha's reports after these campaigns were always optimistic. Watching her closely, however, sharp-eyed associates sensed now and then that she had had no great success. After a day or two of smiles she would be alone for hours, and those who came upon her found her staring out of the window. "She would move slowly, as if she didn't know where to turn," a former student recalls. "Then I'd see her slipping off to her room to kneel for a long time. When she joined us again her spirit seemed much better." Once or twice she told him: "Yes, we're having a hard time, but we'll make it. You stay on and see."

In such hours of tension Mrs. Berry at Oak Hill would not hide her feelings. "Why don't you give up that school and stay home where you belong?" she would ask in exasperation.

"I'm not discouraged at all."

"No, you're too mad for that. You've always had a head of your own, and I'm not going to say anything more to you." But Mrs. Berry generally did say more, a great deal more. The sisters at home, their number thinning by marriage, agreed in varying degree. And meanwhile, more trips. Though Martha never enjoyed these "begging expeditions," her manner concealed her fears. A woman who traveled several times with her said: "The people she met thought her the soul of calm, and so might I, had I not known otherwise. There was one sign that could betray her. Each time at the outset I saw a slight flush at her throat, at the back of her neck. After a few minutes it went; until then she was fighting with herself."

She could stand rejections, Martha declared. Harder to bear was a vague reaction which she often received. "I find it hard to say, 'Give me something.' I may talk and talk of case after case, and then the man or woman will say: 'My, you're doing fascinating work,' and that will be all!"

Often Martha departed suddenly after a wire from New York or Richmond or Boston. Few at the school knew precisely where she was, and she herself let events determine that. Eventually she would communicate with the staff, perhaps from a place that astonished them. Her plans shifted in a moment. Frequently she had already packed to leave for Georgia when a call indicated that someone had shown a flicker of interest; after a hasty change in a railroad reservation she would be off on a new tack. Or there would be a telephone message: "Martha, this is pretty tentative, but if you'd be willing to stay over . . ." "When do we start?" Sometimes she repacked six times before she eventually went home.

There she let everyone understand how much she appreciated Northern help. When an older student did a bit of Yankee-cursing, she rebuked him. "The Yankees have been real friends to us, my boy, fine people with hearts and a wish to do good things. You and I mightn't be here today if it weren't for Yankees." Unreconstructed Southerners stared hard at a picture over her desk—a likeness of Abraham Lincoln. And when she went out in search of good student material she had a favorite saying: "Let's go find ourselves another Lincoln!" If they located one, it would be worth all they ever did.

Each time Martha returned to the campus, she said, she expected to see a new staff member or a change in the line-up. Some fitted themselves wholeheartedly to conditions; others said bleakly that they had never known anything like this, and left in dismay. They had to learn, above all, adaptability, for a classics teacher was hurried into service as a nurse, a man who specialized in dairying was called on to supervise cooking, and a woman who believed she had been hired to teach music took on the debating classes. Miss Annie Manning Churchill Jones, a member of one of the traditional First Families of Virginia, arrived to serve for a time as Martha's secretary. When she inadvertently revealed a gift for music, she found herself taking over the duties of musical director and—in a way she never quite understood—the management of four or five very young boys of the neighborhood.

The school had added the first of a line of male staff members. The boys welcomed them, Martha explained, "because a woman never knows when a man's done enough work." Though she smiled at the comment, she made sure that the men kept up the work standards she had set. The male teachers also enforced the rules against evenings off campus. A new helper placed flypaper along the stairs to trap violators. Another, making the rounds, discovered an empty bed and made sure he would trap the habitual offender. He took the boy's place; when the student slipped back, a hand reached out to him. It was then three-thirty in the morning, and the boy left on the eight-thirty train.

Martha and Elizabeth Brewster had transferred to the log-cabin demonstration building, leaving more room for boys in the dormitory. Miss Jones was given part of the downstairs bedroom with Elizabeth, but when visitors came Martha's upstairs chamber became a guest room and she moved down. On such evenings the three women drew straws to decide who would sleep on the floor. Preparing the straws one night, Miss Brewster shook her head. "The poorhouse isn't over the hills and far away. It's here, and we're living in it."

Whenever she settled a guest upstairs Martha would ask: "Is there anything more you'd wish?" Several times the practical Elizabeth whispered: "Please don't say that. Everything we own is up there now." As Elizabeth predicted, the question eventually brought an embarrassing response. A caller from

Boston replied: "If you please, I'd like a larger bathtub," emphasizing a broad *a* in "bath."

Martha said afterward that the visitor might almost as well have asked for the moon. Nevertheless she smiled and nodded, and collared a boy outside. "Go over to Oak Hill, fast as you can. Ask my mother for the sitz-bath tub. Don't stop to talk, but put the tub on your head and run back."

She beckoned another. "Make a fire under the iron pot in the yard and fill it with water." Meanwhile, reaching Oak Hill, the first boy forgot to knock. As he burst in Mrs. Berry inquired: "What now? Has the whole place blown down?" He gave a breathless answer: "No, ma'am, got a woman from Boston and we got to give her a bath." He lugged the tub off, and eventually the school received a satisfying donation from Boston.

The boys had their own bathing troubles. The much-prized bathhouse burned, and Martha lacked funds to do anything about it. For months the students shivered in a makeshift, cold-water substitute. When she brought news that a new one would be constructed, they shouted their approval. And with that something happened, of a sort that would be repeated many times afterward.

A committee called on Martha. In return for her concern, ma'am, they were going to put up another building, anything she liked, with their own hands. They would organize schedules so that they could contribute their labor at odd hours, and scout around to find the timber. The "Berry spirit" was deepening.

Another phase of the spirit she implanted revealed itself after she accepted an invitation to attend a Sunday program some miles from Rome. One of the boys asked if she would take dinner with his mother, who lived in that neighborhood. "Of course I will," Martha replied. On Saturday he inquired if he could go home for the day; he had written Ma to have everything cleaned up but was afraid she would not have it just as Miss Martha liked.

On Saturday, Martha learned that "Ben had scrubbed with

so much vigor that the floors were quite damp." And his mother informed her that since Ben had been going to the school "he'd ruther scrub than eat." Of that choice Martha expressed tacit approval.

Word came back of the deeds of early graduates. In Tennessee a Berry alumnus named Jim had a dairy job. Early on a Fourth of July morning he reported for duty. Six hundred gallons of milk and cream were scheduled to go off on the mid-morning train, but Jim discovered that the boilers were cold, the separators, churns, and other machinery silent. The other four workers had chosen to take the Fourth off.

Rolling back his sleeves, firing the boilers, Jim bottled everything and, with the help of two small boys who did odd jobs, got the shipment away on time, then cleaned up the place afterward. When the employer arrived he found Jim hot and tired. "Where's the fireman?" he asked.

"Didn't come this morning."

"Who did his work?"

"I did."

"Where's the others?"

"They haven't arrived yet."

"You mean the milk didn't get off?"

"No, sir. It went as usual."

He received three days off and a raise, and the school's reputation went still higher.

On the B.I.S. campus changes were increasing. The boys' clothes, ranging from bishops' suits to overalls, proved altogether too varied. Pride was hurt when one student appeared dressed far better than the others. After some thought Martha chose uniforms of blue denim shirts and overalls, which became a trade-mark of the school.

She had never liked the killing of birds and animals, and now she made another rule: no shooting on the school grounds. The campus became a kind of game and bird sanctuary. Older students who were hunters gazed longingly at coveys of quail and flights of wild duck; the few who brought up the subject with Martha reported that she "gave us a singeing."

When it snowed she drew the boys together. "Think of the birds," she would say, and lead them out to sprinkle bread crumbs. As long as the snow lasted it was a daily rite. In time she ordered the planting of small fields of oats and grain, to be left for the birds. A number of local sportsmen fumed; so many fine meals going to waste, they complained as their fingers itched. She let them go right on fuming and itching.

She and her school were beginning to receive serious recognition at home. Georgia's county superintendents met on the campus in 1906 to study her methods. Within a few months a bill came before the state legislature to provide for a system of "agricultural and mechanical schools," and the measure's author declared that "Miss Berry's establishment was largely the model in my mind." Soon school after school went up in Georgia. Here was a reproof to the ladies who had murmured hostile things about "convict labor."

In the same year a new honor loomed, and with it a new opportunity to spread the story. Robert C. Ogden, nationally known for his role in education, brought to the South a large party of fifty or more officials—a kind of Who's Who of the field. They wanted to see her school. Putting down the date in early April, Martha made full plans for conferences, assemblies, and trips over the campus.

Ten days or so before the time, a message arrived from an Eastern group with an interest in the work. Without hesitation she accepted the new invitation and arranged to be back two full days ahead of the Ogden party. Finishing a visit in New York, she boarded the train for Chattanooga on schedule, and slept half exhausted for hours. When she woke the train was motionless and stayed motionless for a long time. Ringing for the porter, she received irritating word. "Landslide in the mountains, ma'am, and the men's working ahead of us."

Only long afterward did the train move slowly ahead. In the Tennessee city she had missed the daily train to Rome. By going the next day, she would still have twenty-four hours or so before the Ogden group reached there. As she settled in her Chattanooga hotel a bellboy knocked with a telegram. Mr. Ogden had changed his schedule, and they were all there now! Martha froze, then broke into action.

A few minutes later she sat in the railroad office. "I know you don't have any more trains today, but I *have* to be there. Whatever it costs, get me there." Two officials conferred over routing schedules, talked with a yard superintendent. "We have one engine on a siding—a mighty old one, and we might scrape up a foreman and an engineer. But a lady like you wouldn't want to go that way." Not only would this lady want it; she demanded it, and also the cutting of all red tape to put her swiftly aboard the engine.

On the campus, affairs were going as badly as Martha feared. None of the staff had her flair, her art in dramatizing the work. While Miss Brewster ushered guests to the platform, someone whispered: "Have you read the morning paper? A terrible earthquake in San Francisco—the whole place on fire, and people dying everywhere." She had relatives in the area, and her heart missed several beats. Yet she could not halt; "the program had to go on, even if the earth should open and swallow everything dear to us."

Somehow the staff stumbled through the morning meeting and an awkward luncheon. The occasion was like a fallen soufflé, but what could they do? Then they heard a stir in the yard, and in came Martha—a Martha such as they had never seen, face and arms black with soot, cinders clinging to her hair and coat. She beamed and turned the incident into a light-hearted comedy. "You can tell how anxious I was to get to you!"

After a brief explanation she took the reins with a sure hand;

she told stories, she gave moving examples. Only when things were going at a quick tempo did she slip off to wash her face at the nearest basin. And she carried the day. While she had to spend nearly $200 of badly needed funds, the result far outweighed the expense.

Suddenly the year 1907 brought a national economic panic which hit the campus hard. The school's wants grew steadily, while much of its support crumbled. Everywhere she looked the demands piled up, and she was feeling more than a touch of personal depression on the day of the school's fifth anniversary. Ceremonies, brave and high-minded, went according to schedule. Then, as the audience prepared to leave, Walter Weaver of the senior class jumped up. He announced that the students had voted to present Miss Berry with a purse of a dollar from each boy. In chucklesome detail he told how every one of them had labored during the Christmas holidays, and he gave her seventy-one crisp envelopes.

As she took the gifts Martha did not smile. Surprised and stirred, she said that people had asked what would happen to the school when she was gone. Today she had the answer—"the boys will carry it on."

About to leave, the audience halted again as Gordon Keown, honor graduate of two years earlier, stepped forward. His voice breaking as it had on that other day, he offered her a purse of $53, in the name of the "old boys."

For the third time the crowd rose, then stopped. Professor Douglas lifted his hand and in the faculty's name produced a purse of $210. Each gift left Martha Berry more moved. "I know what these things mean, especially at a time such as this. They mean that you have given up much that you need. I think I'm richer than any millionaire." She looked down at her hands. "I hold the future of the school."

A call came from Atlanta. Governor Terrell had learned that

99

Andrew Carnegie, the steel magnate, would stop there briefly. The governor had arranged a reception at the executive mansion, and could Miss Berry attend? Martha had been ill, and Aunt Marth had been dosing her with not one, but two, tonics. In any case, it was almost time for the daily train to leave for Atlanta. For a moment she almost declined. Then she remembered Carnegie's many gifts to education, and so she accepted and hurriedly dressed. With her she took a reminder of more affluent days, a gown she had not worn in years, because she had little need for it—a rich blue satin, lace-trimmed, and a long full cape to match.

Although friends in Atlanta arranged for Martha to be in the receiving line with Carnegie and assured her that she would have opportunity for a conversation with the guest, Mr. Carnegie arrived late. The crowd was heavy, and she found herself, alas, separated from him by two others. These sympathetic individuals quietly moved down the line and edged her closer to Carnegie. Glancing over, he smiled, began to talk—and then a long file of newcomers halted them.

Once again he turned to her, and once again the throng intervened. Then Mr. Carnegie was gone, and she groaned at her luck. A man in the philanthropist's party, who understood her work, murmured to her: "The train's leaving soon, but if you can possibly come aboard, I'll try to make a chance for you to see him." After a brief hesitation, Martha rode to the station.

Aboard the train she met immediate disappointment; ushered on, Carnegie went promptly to bed. Her friend passed with a question: Could she stay on board for the night? He would make sure she sat beside the man at breakfast. Martha bit her lips. She had had no time even to change to her street clothes, and when and how would she return to Georgia? A moment later she dismissed these questions. Her school was more important than the way she looked or did not look in blue satin in the morning. Drawing the cape closer, she located the conductor, who provided a berth.

Up very early, Martha waited anxiously. Suppose, after all this effort, her co-conspirator could not manage it! Then his head appeared at the end of the coach and she hurried down the aisle, her evening cape shimmering around her. As she passed she ignored the whispers of fellow passengers. Mr. Carnegie had taken a table in the diner and, as promised, a chair was empty beside him. Smiling, he recalled their meeting and listened as she went into her story. While he seemed to pay close attention, she sensed that this man took no action without careful investigation. After a few minutes he nodded sagely and said he hoped to hear more "when you're East the next time."

With that he let her know that this part of the conversation had closed. Martha fought an angry impulse to leave. No, don't slam the door, she warned herself; keep the foot there. She laughed, told a mountain story and one about a peculiar highland tombstone. When Carnegie gave a deep laugh, she added another.

Washington was close, breakfast was over, and Martha needed no one to advise her to stop on a cheerful note. Shaking the capitalist's hand, she stepped down from the train to inquire about the next one back over the same route. Shivering in her flimsy dress, she searched for a store near the station and bought a woolen outfit for her return.

Her staff and family were much disturbed; just where had she been these past two days? Now that the need for action had ended she felt headachy again, and she resumed Aunt Marth's double tonics. Had she accomplished anything? She could not tell, but Mr. Carnegie was going to find her next visit to the East occurring far earlier than he anticipated!

For the moment, matters of school management intruded. After studying many catalogues, she addressed the president of the Mechanics' Institute at Rochester, New York:

> We need a man to take charge of the industrial work. I would like him to know how to work with his

hands as well as know the theory of the work. He must teach and supervise. He would live in the dormitory with the boys . . . He would eat at the table with them three times a day. He must be a man of fine character who will teach Sunday school on Sunday, in addition to teaching and working through the week. He must not smoke, drink nor swear, as I have very strict rules for my boys. I hope he will work for a small salary, as I feel I cannot pay more than $40 a month. If you know a young man who would meet these requirements please let me have his name.

Slightly bewildered, the institute official replied that to come upon someone with all those attributes and for that salary, "I believe you would have to get St. Peter to send one from above." However, he suggested a few possibilities, and she took a young man who, though not quite winged, pleased even Miss Brewster.

Soon after his arrival the new industrial supervisor asked Martha if she would mind looking at something. She followed him to a room shared by three boys, where a wren sat on her nest atop the bookcase. A big sign read: "The Man What Disturbs Her Ain't No Gentleman—Cause She Is A-Setting." Martha's campaign to preserve bird life was winning recruits!

The famous magazine editor, Dr. Albert Shaw, visited the school and drew it to the attention of President Theodore Roosevelt. Martha's hand shook as she read Dr. Shaw's letter: If she had occasion to be in Washington in the near future he thought the President would see her.

Roosevelt and also Carnegie . . . The prospect surely merited a trip North. New funds were imperative, and this might be the answer. Within a week a small figure in a shirtwaist and plain brown skirt and coat sat in the President's anteroom. It was a crowded day, with important-appearing people sharing the room. Only a few of the younger men noticed the good-looking woman who sat so quietly in the corner. Secretaries paid her little heed until a figure paused in a partly opened doorway, a big head cocked, and she heard: "Is that Miss Berry? Send her in."

The suddenness of the reception left her with moist hands and dry lips. But this time she had arrived somewhat prepared; she carried a thick black book of photographs and had outlined what she would say. "I won't waste your time, Mr. President," she began, and before the heavy man with the large teeth could do more than greet her she went to work.

She pointed to pictures of the school farm, the craft shops and dairy, shabby mountain cabins, bent men, and hollow-faced children. "This is Joe, Mr. President. He was twenty-three and couldn't write his name. In four years he finished courses that usually take eight, and now he's assistant manager of a store."

Martha told of Ernest, "who walked from so far away that his feet looked like two big blisters. He had to stay in bed for days to get better. He's one of the smartest boys we've ever had. Until he heard of us he was lost in a mountain cove, discontented but with no way to escape. And this one . . ."

Theodore Roosevelt rubbed his chin, flipped through the book, asked one question on top of another. A half hour had passed when his secretary re-entered. "Mr. President, the senator's still there, and the minister is getting ruffled."

"Let them wait!" The President of the United States pounded on his desk. "This is the real thing." As the secretary retreated Roosevelt faced her: "So the boys do everything, and when you need more rooms you just tack 'em on?"

Martha held her breath; the man seemed deeply stirred, and now he went on: "Young woman, you can guess that a lot of others have called on me like this. Most of them"—he made a gesture of impatience—"they're dreamers, with visions on paper. You're making it go." All at once he asked: "Please stay a day more in Washington. Mrs. Roosevelt and I are having a dinner tomorrow night, and I'd like you to tell those people the things you've told me."

In a happy confusion Martha left, and the next morning brought a messenger with a formal invitation to the White House. She had taken along a refurbished old evening dress, "weak in spots," for by this time formal costume had become a necessity in her work. When he received her again, President Roosevelt may have been astonished at the change from the drably attired caller of the previous day; tonight Martha carried herself with ease and elegance. As he led her forward he quietly informed her that the party included editors, publicists, and others who would be able to help her school if she drew their interest.

Martha had thought she might discuss the matter informally at dinner or later. To her surprise Roosevelt had made her his guest of honor; during the meal he talked of little else than her school. After the first course he rapped on the table: "Miss Berry will tell us all about the things she's doing." Without rising, Martha spoke for nearly forty-five minutes; each time she stopped, the others urged her to go on.

"I might as well have been eating corn shucks for all that I noticed of the food," she answered when friends pressed her later for details. After the dinner men went up to her, gave her their cards, and told her of their interest. At one point she heard Roosevelt's voice boom: "Miss Berry said yesterday that she hoped to admit the girls to her school." (She had merely indicated this ambition.) "You do that," he now advised her. "Give the same chance to those girls down in Georgia." And he announced: "When I finish my job here I'll make a trip for myself to see what this young woman is doing."

In later years Martha never ceased to praise Theodore Roosevelt for his impulsive interest and unstudied friendship. Not for some time did she realize the true value of his introductions to many men with power to shape American opinion. That evening in the White House opened countless doors to her.

There were no immediate contributions, however, and she had much work to do in New York, much money to try to raise. The next few days brought bad news from several sources. Many people whom she had hoped to see were out of town. Simultaneously the school sent word of a tornado that did heavy damage; the need in Georgia was mushrooming. Yet she received one refusal after another, and a friend explained: "You're here at a sad season. People have less money since the bad times started, and they're careful how they use it. There's so much want right here that few of us are inclined to send money far from home."

Worst of all was the matter of Andrew Carnegie. Though Martha had written in advance, she found it impossible to penetrate the web of secretaries at his office. What to do now? She asked it repeatedly, until Sunday came and, with it, an enforced pause in her calls. Much disturbed, she went out for an aimless walk, when a severe snowstorm began, the icy flakes cutting into her eyes and lips. (Whenever she arrived in New York, the weather turned against her, she said ironically.) As she shivered she caught a glimpse of a church spire against the gray skies, already half lost in the swirl. Moving toward it, she paused before the entrance of Grace Church and read two words on the door: "Strangers Welcome."

That was quite different from the spirit she had met so far on this trip, and she stepped inside. The services would not start for some time, and the minister saw her enter. Perhaps it was her dejected look, the slump of her body; in any event he went to her. With chattering teeth Martha responded to his smile; as Dr. Huntington took her hand he observed that it was very cold. "You see, I'm from the South," she said, and all at once she was speaking of her school and of the threat to its existence, until she halted. "I'm sorry. After all, I'm a beggar and it hurts me to beg, even for others. But if you could see those faces, you'd understand."

Dr. Huntington answered emphatically. "I do understand. And you must never again think of yourself as a beggar. Always remember—you're an ambassador of the King of Kings." Long afterward Martha Berry told of the effect of the minister's words, which came to her like a blessing.

Before she left, Dr. Huntington assured her that she could talk of her work before the women's guild of his church. A few days later, as the guild members listened, one after another put aside her needle and thread. When Martha left she had funds for several scholarships, promises of clothes that would fill several barrels, and, echoing in her ears, new encouragement which she had badly needed.

The events at Grace Church determined Martha's next step. In spite of misgivings she would make a last effort to see Andrew Carnegie. It might be unwise, but she had to try a new, direct approach. That night she rang at the door of the Carnegie mansion. The butler looked down (definitely down, she told friends) and said: "Mr. Carnegie cannot be disturbed."

As he started to close the door Martha appealed to him: "Wait, please." Drawing out her card, she scratched a message: Did Mr. Carnegie remember her stories on the train about those mountain tombstones? Within a few minutes the door reopened, and she was led to the library, where the steel man sat posing for a portrait by a European painter. Carnegie greeted her in friendly enough fashion, drew up a chair, and smiled. "I'm not supposed to speak while he works, but you go ahead."

He could hardly fail to hear her now, and Martha talked "as I suppose I've never talked before." Carnegie nodded, yet said nothing. Ten minutes passed, and the artist lowered his palette. "I'm sorry, Mr. Carnegie. These stories the lady tells . . . One moment I'm laughing so I cannot work, and the next I'm weeping so I cannot see."

Still without emotion, the capitalist escorted Martha to the next room. There he asked several pointed questions, and after getting apparently satisfactory answers he reached into a desk: "Miss Berry, this is how I do things. Fill out that form in full detail, and later, if I decide to help, I'll give a certain amount—provided you raise a similar amount from other sources."

"I understand." That sounded hopeful, or perhaps ominous. Martha could not analyze her feelings when she left; an hour later, as she sat in her room, she understood that she was scared. So many details, so many figures were called for in the form. . . . She telephoned her school helpers to speed the information to her. "Drop everything else, because nothing can be more important."

That night and for the next few days and nights Martha struggled over the blanks with ink, eraser, and sighs. After the data arrived from Georgia she left the bulky document at Carnegie's house. Should she wait in New York or go home? The millionaire's reply came sooner than she had anticipated. It was yes, for $25,000!

The amount took away her breath. Yet she could never touch it unless she found another $25,000. The prospect appalled her but propelled her into action. That same hour she wrote to a list of the first twenty friends of the school whose names occurred to her. After dropping the letters into the box, she resumed her telephone calls.

"Mayn't I come and explain?"

"It's a new development, and I'd be so grateful if you'd listen."

Martha went without sleep, she lost weight, she forgot meals. She was able to count a few quick results; Andrew Carnegie's interest was good for a $50 contribution in one place, $200 in another. Each day, however, saw her checking names off a dwindling list, and more and more often she heard the disconcerting words: "It's such a big total that you're trying to get. . . ."

107

When she had reached $7000 she groaned; for forty-eight hours she failed to accumulate an additional dollar. At that point Carnegie telephoned and listened to her apologies, then interrupted in amusement. "Why, it's not as bad as you think. Look, my wife and I are making a call tomorrow on Mrs. Russell Sage. You come along, and we'll see what happens."

Cora Neal, one of Martha's associates at the time, recalls that the head of the school had already met Mrs. Sage, who had made a small contribution but had not been immediately impressed. Like others, she wished Miss Berry would first "show a little more of what the school can do." The prospect of another meeting with the careful lady did not fill Martha with high enthusiasm. As always, however, she was ready to try.

The next day Martha enjoyed the ride along Fifth Avenue in the plush Carnegie carriage. If the boys could see her now, or Aunt Marth. In the Sage mansion their hostess led them to a richly hung drawing room, with an array of lace napkins, silver tea urn, and sandwiches on the table. Mrs. Sage served them with grace and style, and displayed a pleasant kindness toward the newcomer from Georgia. For a time the four talked casually, and then Mr. Carnegie aimed his weapon. He told graphically of Martha's work and added the amount he planned to give. "Mrs. Sage, wouldn't you like to help?" he inquired.

Eyebrows went up, and Martha scented gunpowder; Mrs. Sage had been startled, and not pleased, by this mixture of money-raising and the social arts. "Well . . . No. I'm afraid I'm already committed to too many things." The brief statement, in a tone of injury, made Martha's heart hurt. There went everything, perhaps the school itself.

She had reckoned without Andrew Carnegie. Smiling serenely, he returned to the attack. "Don't you remember, Mrs. Sage, you want me to do something with you in that project we last talked about?" His look became meaningful. "I think you really should give Miss Berry, say, $5000, so that I can know you're as interested in my work as I am in yours."

As Martha recounted the incident, she almost gasped aloud. Polite though it might be, this was blackmail. But it worked; after a short silence Mrs. Sage turned charming again. "Of course, my dear Miss Berry, I'm interested in work like yours, and perhaps, as our friend says, I should assist it." Before long, back in the carriage, Carnegie clapped his hands gleefully together. It was almost, Martha said, as if this were a million dollars and he had made Mrs. Sage promise it to him, not her.

A moment later she swallowed hard, as she realized that she still had $13,000 to raise. "Oh, you'll do it," the Scotsman murmured. "I have faith in you." But by now, she told herself glumly, she had exhausted every source she knew.

CHAPTER VII

ELEPHANTS, LIFTERS,

AND BIRTHDAYS

FOR THE NEXT week Martha trudged again from homes to offices to boardinghouse desk, listing new names, going over old ones. Several more $100 contributions arrived, and "one wonderful check for $350," then nothing except sympathy.
. . . Moving over the slippery streets, she caught a bad cold and returned at the end of a long, disheartening day with an inflamed throat and a thumping headache.

There was only one thing to do—go to bed. "My feet were swollen, and I had trouble getting them out of my shoes," she said. The alarmed maid knocked with hot milk and crackers. While Martha could eat nothing, the milk soothed her throat. Too tired to sleep, she reached for her Bible and opened it at random. "To minister, not to be ministered unto . . ." It had always been one of her favorite passages.

Apologetically the maid came in again, to say that someone wanted Martha on the telephone down the hall. She dragged herself out, her robe around her, and crept to the instrument on the wall. The man's voice, that of an elderly individual, had an odd, quizzical tone.

"I'm Mr. Miller, and my sister and I received your letter." The name meant nothing to Martha; she had been sending so many notes. . . . "Well, if you'll come up now we'll see you." Her first impulse was to refuse; it would be nine-thirty or ten before she could reach the address he gave. Why not tomorrow? Nevertheless she thought she detected a challenge, and she could not afford to reject any possibility at this point.

"I'll leave in a few minutes, sir." Back in her room, she recalled, she was tempted to fall on the bed and cry. Instead, she pulled on her dress and forced her feet back into her shoes. Her lips were pale with fatigue and cold when she finally climbed through a fresh sleet up the stairs of an imposing brownstone establishment.

Before the fire in an enormous library Martha wondered if she were dealing with an eccentric. A moment later she was certain of the fact. She almost jumped as she lifted her eyes to discover a small, ancient man, watching her closely from a few feet away. When he moved noiselessly over the thick carpet, white eyebrows stood up like birds' wings, and a wide mustache seemed to twitch. "Miss Berry? Would you like to look at my elephants?"

Elephants in a New York sleet storm! She remembered Judge Wright's warning about the strange life she would lead if she went on with her plans for a school. Had she not felt a dart of fear she might have laughed; for this, she had given up Oak Hill. A moment later a frail and kindly woman entered. "My dear, my brother is a collector of ivories, mostly elephants."

"I'd be delighted to see them." What could she do except go through with this? Ceremoniously Mr. Miller extended his arm and drew her across the hall into a parlor with an ornately carved fireplace. Martha realized that the ivories were extremely fine, but as she made the properly appreciative comments she cast about for excuses to leave. Before she could lead up to the subject, however, the sister, took her hand. "Now you must look at my Japanese dolls."

For another half hour the three of them went from floor to floor, sitting room to sun parlor, inspecting successive collections. Neither brother nor sister referred to her school, and Martha determined that she would not do so either. The house was greatly overheated, and she felt close to exhaustion. With an effort she finally told the Millers: "I've enjoyed this, but it's late for me." Despite herself, she had to add, much as she always did: "I hope you will come see my school in Georgia, and *my* collection—boys. Fine boys . . ."

The little man gave her an intent look. "Oh yes, we've inquired and learned it's a good school. We've wanted to talk to you about it. Why don't we sit down?" The astonished Martha followed the brother and sister back to the drawing room, where the maid brought coffee and well-buttered bread. Perhaps it was her relief, or the new excitement, but she was suddenly hungry. Between mouthfuls she talked at length of her work.

So these people had been interested all along. Yet why such curious behavior? Ultimately Mr. Miller explained: "This was a sort of test. We decided that if you loved your school as much as we'd heard, you'd come tonight and be patient with two lonely old individuals. Tomorrow we leave for France and may not come back." Mr. Miller caught his sister's glance and asked: "Shall we do it now?"

She nodded, and when he gave Martha a check her hand shook. As she hesitated Miss Miller smiled to encourage her to look, and she saw the figure: $10,000. Softly she told the Millers: "All my life I'll ask God to bless you." Her throat was better, and her headache had gone.

More hundreds remained to be raised, and all at once Martha

thought of an Atlantan, Mrs. Frank Inman. In that case, as in others, she said, something seemed to guide her at times—an instinct about people, a hunch as to the right step. From the moment she received the message, Mrs. Inman herself declares, "I knew I must accept, because we had to let those people up there see that the Southerners were also interested."

If Martha had erred about Mrs. Inman, it was only in underestimating her will and energy. The Atlantan went to one organization, to get only a vague response. Dropping it, she tried another and received mainly conversation. She went to a third, found that it had a small fund left over, which she took gladly. Then Mrs. Inman invited women to her home to "talk Berry," approached them at parties, organized Berry Circles in Atlanta and other cities.

With every hundred dollars she gathered, Mrs. Inman wired Martha. With such backing Martha pressed ahead in New York. But she had overtaxed herself again. Aunt Marth had given her a new tonic, and though she swallowed it steadily she could not shake off another heavy cold, which grew worse and worse. Christmas approached, and she longed to be home for the mountain children's tree. But she would not leave until she had the necessary funds or destroyed herself in getting them. Later she agreed with friends that she almost achieved the second goal.

After great effort by several of her partisans, a large women's group of New York agreed to have Martha speak. As she got up on the morning of the meeting she staggered and sank into a chair. It was some time before she could reach the washstand, bathe her cheeks, and begin the long effort of dressing. On her way downstairs the landlady saw her haggard face and protested. Martha refused to stay indoors but permitted her to call a horse-drawn cab. Expensive or not, she had to have one today.

Near the meeting place she closed her eyes, marshaling her strength. As she entered, the chairman stared at her in concern and whispered: They would understand if Miss Berry preferred to come back next month. They realized how hard she had been working, and they knew the amount she needed. . . .

Miss Berry rejected the suggestion. "I'm ready right now." After an introduction that seemed endless, she got to her unsteady feet. Resting her arm on the lectern, she forced herself to begin. "It was hardly the best talk I've made," she confessed eventually. "I'm afraid it was a bit—uncontrolled." Those who heard her said that her voice gave way several times with feeling. She pictured the days when the school went without heat, the boys who would lose their education if the doors closed. . . . She remembered no more.

Waking in a strange room, she saw a circle of women around her. "What happened?" she asked. Several of them murmured together, and the president bent down to her: "You fainted, but you'll be all right. Our officers have just met, and we're going to make up the rest of what you require. Yes, all of it." At that, Martha said later, "I almost fainted a second time."

It was weeks before she was well enough to walk around the campus again, and more weeks before she took stock and reached a new decision. This one had been taking shape for years. Repeatedly since her school's opening, young women had demanded or begged or cried for admittance. Scores had been turned away in spite of pathetic appeals: They had nowhere else to go for an education, and couldn't Miss Martha take them? Many, arriving and receiving a regretful refusal, would stay till dark in the hope that "ef we'd jes' set all day, we'd git in."

There was, for instance, Mary Manning from a cabin near Possum Trot. Martha could not forget the girl's great blue eyes as she appeared at intervals. "Miss Berry, don' yer have room fer me yit?" One day Mary materialized with clothes in a box. "I've thought what ter do. My brother's in school here, and I kin study from the same books and help with the plowin' and dairyin' the same as him. He'll tell yer how hard I kin work."

Sadly Martha had said no. "But when we get a school for girls, Mary, I promise you you'll be the first." Now, as 1908 advanced, she thought more and more of Mary and others like her, and dropped hints to her board. The trustees opposed her with groans over her "impracticality." Chairman Eagan spoke emphatically: "Martha, there isn't room for all the boys who want to come here. Why branch out and take girls?" He told her she would need new dormitories, classrooms, a double budget, double everything; she would "pile one big problem on top of another big one."

Other board members pointed out additional facts: Most mountain families would not wish their daughters to attend. She had persuaded many to send boys, but the highlanders saw no call for education of the girls. As one grizzled man asked Martha: "You says trainin'—trainin' fer what, I axe yer? A gel don' have ter go ter school ter fry meat an' make pone. Tell yer whut hit'd do—putt idees inter ther haids. Make 'em plumb dissatisfied."

To friends Martha admitted that the elderly fellow was precisely right in one respect; above all she expected to win the girls to ideas—ideas that would make them discontented with what they had. She hoped to turn them into better farm wives, better people. The average mountain girl was a drudge, who knew little of food preparation, of handicrafts, or the care that would change hovels into pleasant homes. Already the mountain boys at her school were moving ahead of their sisters.

While she speculated, board members brought up the subject in formal session, and all members voted against the project. Some years later, perhaps, provided things worked out and she had much more money . . . "Thank you, gentlemen," Martha told them. As they left the campus she walked to a hill a mile from the boys' school and let her eyes rove over the land. A lavender-gray dusk settled upon the rolling ground; a mist rose from the distance.

She thought of words she had learned as a child: "I will lift

115

up mine eyes unto the hills. From whence cometh my help? My help cometh from the Lord." She would go ahead, and use the 121st Psalm as a profession of faith for her girls' school.

The next morning she casually asked the boys if they thought there should be a school for the girls. She received a fervent yes; ultimately she said she decided that Theodore Roosevelt, the boys, and the girls themselves constituted a majority, and so she considered *her* motion carried. Later in the day she walked up to the school's foreman of construction.

"I wish you'd start tomorrow and cut down logs for several new buildings. Oh yes, the boys will do all the work." Before he could ask more questions Martha rode off to see old Captain Barnwell. Did he remember those rough drawings he had once made? Well, he could go right on with them. "You know," the captain smiled, "I had a feeling I'd be doing that."

Back at her desk, Martha sent out letters to college officials, friends, anyone who might have suggestions. She wanted a young woman with training in administration and skill in handling girls. From the replies, she winnowed through many candidates and settled on Alberta Patterson as prospective dean. After a few more weeks she assured Miss Patterson that she would be coming to Georgia to direct "the most wonderful girls' school in the South."

Miss Patterson replied that she had never worked for so low a salary, but, since Miss Berry herself was giving her services and the place offered so great an opportunity, she would accept. Martha met her at the train and "liked her at once." "She had a bright air, a real grace, none of the schoolma'am look." Driving out with the new dean, the older woman showed one building after another on the boys' campus, gesturing, pointing. Miss Patterson had no opportunity to speak until she finally interrupted: "But where is the girls' school?"

"Over the hill," came the blithe reply. They rode on for a time, and there, on a green rise, sat a pile of logs, a few frames

116

of a building, and a group of boys with hammers. Martha glanced from left to right. "Isn't it beautiful?"

"What? Where?" The young dean was wide-eyed.

Martha laughed lightly. "Why, right here, this lovely school. Can't you see the girls' happy faces as they walk up the paths—lined with violets, you know—and up the porches with their ivy and roses?"

As Miss Patterson told her story, all that *she* could see was confusion. "I thought . . ." she started, and Martha broke in: "The school will open this fall, and everything will be ready. You just go out and 'tag' the bright girls the way we tag our trees for transplanting." The dean "simply looked at Miss Berry and wondered." Then and for many months "I was a very doubting Thomas," she said. But she had agreed to come and she would stay.

Martha sent an immediate note to young Mary Manning, keeping her pledge that the girl would be the first student. Another message was one that she had hoped many times to write—to her old friend Emma, the city girl who had married the mountain boy. Would she and Jim like to send their daughter? The answer was that whenever Martha fixed the time the girl would be there.

The boys built wardrobes, bookcases, beds; if no other wood were available at the time, they turned to packing cases or supply boxes. Anything that would hasten the arrival of young femininity they would do. Martha continued to rob Oak Hill of whatever came to hand. She went to Georgia churches, and the Presbyterians gave kitchen utensils; the Episcopalians bedroom furnishings; Baptists dining-room supplies; and Methodists flatirons and laundry tubs.

As word trickled out of Martha's actions in defiance of their decision, board members were baffled. "What could we do except resign?" one asked. Nobody resigned, because they were all too much interested in the school's progress. When the trustees met in the fall, the first units of the new division were almost completed. Brightly Martha announced a "little surprise" and took them in buggies to the girls' campus. They accepted quietly.

With her instinct for the dramatic she set Thanksgiving Day of 1909 for the opening. Five girls arrived, and the number increased daily until it reached twenty-five. Last-minute problems delayed use of the first dormitory, and the girls were settled in several former tenant cottages, where conditions were even more primitive than on the boys' grounds. An ancient well provided water, and the students toted pails at all hours. Like the boys, the girls would have uniforms—long skirts, gathered waists, white collars and cuffs. The Singer Company donated a godsend, a new sewing machine, and during the next several years one mountain girl said she thought she heard it run night and day as the students worked in relays. "When it stopped I was sure something had gone wrong, and generally it had."

Also like the boys, the girls had work assignments for two hours of each day. An immediate responsibility was the care and feeding of school guests, as a demonstration of what the school could do. Quarters must be cheerful, food appetizing, of good quality, yet also kept within a strict budget. And all this had to be achieved with elementary equipment. "The old stove smoked," a teacher remembered. "It didn't even have a damper. Once when mighty important callers arrived, the stovepipe fell, and two girls had to hold it up with broom sticks while the others fixed dinner." She smiled in recollection. "But to most of the girls, who knew only the mountains, the whole place was paradise."

Paradise or not, it would be as antiseptic as Martha could make it. Repeatedly she lectured: "There's no perfume in the world like soap and water." Alice Wingo, one of the new staff, has told of the day Martha discovered that a screen door hung open at the log-cabin dining room, admitting dozens of flies.

With a blaze in her eyes Martha demanded that the student in charge come to her and "with considerable emphasis" let her know "this must not happen again." Asking for a swatter, she advanced to the attack. "Every one must be destroyed, every one!" After a moment she laughed: "Well, Leola, when you get married and your husband scolds you, you can have the comfort of feeling that nobody could have been as bad as Miss Berry."

One to whom the school seemed indeed paradise was young Lillian. One day at the barn Martha met a group who had returned from the pasture, and she noticed that Lillian's feet were wet. "You ought to wear your rubbers," she said. The girl lowered her head and milked on.

"Don't you have rubbers?"

"No'm." Lillian flushed.

"Then let's send to the store for them."

"No'm. Don't have no money and no credit there neither."

Asking more questions, Martha learned the story. There was nobody to whom Lillian could write; she lacked even stamp money. In their settlement her mother had died, leaving her, an older brother, and younger sister. For several years the father looked after the children. Then, when Lillian reached eleven, he married again and the new wife informed him they had "jis' too many young'uns around." The boy could stay to help on the farm; the others, no.

And so the father "opened the door and told the two little girls to go." They started off, frightened, crying. As Martha commented, the area had no policemen who might have found them, no children's organization or church society. After hours of wandering, Lillian thought of a place that lay miles away, her grandfather's, and they picked their way there over mountain trails.

The ailing man, a Civil War veteran in his late eighties, walked with difficulty, and his wife appeared only slightly less infirm. In their sagging two-room cabin the two children were only an additional care, and after a time they had to leave. No one else wanted them or could accept them, and they "worked here and there," doing house or field labor for bed and board or an occasional twenty-five or fifty cents. At last a farm family agreed to take in the younger girl, and Lillian, now twelve, went on alone.

In Atlanta a Salvation Army official came upon her and thought of Martha and her school. Arriving there, Lillian told Martha, she had her "first real home" since her mother's death. . . . The day they spoke, Lillian received credit for shoes at the school store, and the chance to do extra work for other expenses.

With the coming of the girls Martha remembered warnings given her by many mountain parents, who wanted "no mixin' with boys," no courting or even dancing. To some religious groups dancing was a thing of the devil, and in any case the way to keep the devil away was to prevent the girls from meeting the boys. As a faculty member explained: "That was how they wished it, and they weren't joking."

Of necessity Martha kept the girls' quarters well separated from the boys', with a line marking what the boys termed "no man's land." The girls were not allowed in town except with specific permission and under unusual circumstances. Eventually rules for both boys and girls would be made less stringent, but for the time they remained rigid. It would be years before dancing, for instance, was permitted.

As time went on Martha herself fostered weekly social gatherings and called occasionally for campus events to celebrate special happenings. Meanwhile at the edge of the boys' campus, many would take places and sing a refrain:

"On Jordan's stormy banks I stand and cast a wistful eye
To Canaan's fair and happy land where my possessions lie—
And Miss Patterson won't let me!"

The girls' dean did not favor the words or the music. Nevertheless Martha sometimes passed and laughed, and observers thought that when the crowd looked especially large she would announce a party for the students.

For years she had watched elderly highland women do old-fashioned weaving, and now the Berry girls were going to help keep alive the languishing art. From the Mechanics' Institute of Rochester, Martha hired a crafts teacher. The boys copied looms from old models in mountain houses; Martha and Miss Patterson located mountain women who demonstrated spinning and weaving. Then the girls went to work to reproduce patterns in coverlets, shawls, and bedspreads in the manner of their grandmothers.

"This be the 'Cat-Track and Snail-Trail.'" . . . "I allus had a likin' fer the 'Whig Rose.'" Other favorites developed, among them "Sun, Moon, and Stars," "The Chariot Wheel," and "Lee's Surrender." For wool the school obtained a herd of Angora goats, and as the girls washed, carded, and spun they sang Old English ballads and mountain songs. Invited to show their work, they hummed and spun at fairs and helped build new interest in the school—and, not least, sold products for Berry's benefit.

Suddenly the girls were working in a highly unexpected way, as a result of a blow that shook the institution. A railroad official announced that his line was going to cut a route through the girls' campus; if necessary it would expropriate land left and right. Hastily Martha saw Judge Wright and several attorneys, who told her with regret that the railroad could do exactly what it threatened.

This would hurt, perhaps wreck, her program, damaging the land, ending hope of later expansion. For a time her anger flared, and once she supposedly sent an ultimatum to the railroad men. Every time they put down a crosstie, her boys would take it up!

Martha Berry neither confirmed nor denied this tale. She developed a better strategy, using honey in place of vinegar.

Arranging a "grand barbecue," she invited leading railroaders of Rome, Atlanta, and Washington; her board members brought pressure of their own, and most of the officials accepted. The students labored over meats and sauces, and she rehearsed the girls in their part of the plan.

On the big day all students lined up to greet guests with smiles and bows. Miss Berry advanced with a bright look and compliments, showed the men about, and told true tales of her school, both funny and tragic. "The girls over there—they have an average spending money of ten cents a month." "That boy's supporting two brothers while he gets his own education."

The barbecue was aromatic, smoking and eminently satisfying. As the men sat back ("beaming and bemused," said an observer) Martha gave a signal, and the mountain girls slipped up in freshly pressed costumes, with gentle young smiles. In the front row, by arrangement, teachers had placed the prettier ones. Working at the spinning wheels, the girls sang a dozen old songs and finished with "one just composed by us."

> "Oh, we're the Little Sisters.
>   We cook and iron and sew,
> Just watch us in the next ten years
>   And see how we will grow."

The last lines were aimed directly at the iron hearts of the railroaders:

> "There's nothing now can stop us,
>   But you can help us grow."

By this time no man present wished to do anything to hurt the school or those girls. Not long afterward, as Martha expected, the head of the line made a brief announcement that the railroad would change its route. She sent her thanks—and received contributions in return.

Shortly before this crisis a thirteen-year-old boy, short,

scrawny, and timid, had stood wistfully watching the Berry boys march by and wondering how he could become one of them. Walter Johnson was originally from North Carolina, the oldest of three children whose father and mother had died in quick succession. Walter "learned early what trouble was," he said. Passed from one relative to another, he arrived in Georgia, where a cousin attended Martha Berry's school.

The day he first beheld the marchers, Walter began to hope. If only he could get in there, at least he would not be shunted from place to place. Directed to the principal of the boys' department, he made an appeal, only to have that official tell him: "No, you're too young and too little." Sadly the boy turned away. He had accustomed himself to disappointments, but when he saw Martha a few minutes later all his longing burst forth. "Miss Berry, I'm Walter Johnson"—his words ran together—"and I want to come here, and Mr. Adams says I'm too young and too little."

Martha's old instinct for a good one must have stirred. She looked down at the shy, determined boy. "Walter, you go back home and we'll find out about it." Within thirty days the principal himself wrote that Walter had been accepted. For a time the puny boy was a problem to the school. The farm foreman didn't want him; the dairy manager said no, and so did two or three others, until the dining hall dietitian thought she might try him at washing floors and cooking.

Here was a grudging welcome, and yet for the first time in his life Walter Johnson had found a place for himself. Spying Martha again, he forced back his timidity. "I'm Walter, the orphan, and I want to tell you I appreciate you havin' me here." She smiled and remembered the boy and after a time had him wait on her table and drive her buggy. After several years he came to know her better than did most students. Though he continued shy, Walter grew taller and wider; Berry milk and Berry friendships gave him another view of life.

He made another conquest. When he approached Oak Hill

on an errand, the scowling semi-tyrant called to him: "Walter Johnson, you git out. You cain't have a thing in this kitchen."

"Aunt Marth, you make the world's best cookies, and I'm weak from walkin' way over here. I'd sure enjoy having one or maybe two."

"Well, you don't git none. Now out!" Five minutes later the boy was still in, and five minutes after that he left with a handful of cakes. One conquest, however, Walter did not achieve. Mrs. Berry fixed a grim eye on his childlike form when Martha said he would drive them on a trip. "Show me how you can drive," she ordered. He complied, and she announced that she did not like the way he did it. "You just get another boy, Martha." Meekly the head of the school got another but still kept Walter as a friend.

Theodore Roosevelt had said casually that he would visit the place "when I finish my job up here." Soon after he left the White House he sent word that he would be there on October 8, 1910. It would be a chance to demonstrate to this good friend just what his help had meant. The surge of interest that followed his announcement made it clear that the nation would have its eye on her campus as never before.

For weeks the place roared with activity. Martha called one of the new men on the faculty, the young Dr. S. H. Cook, for detailed instructions. "Dr. Cook, you must be sure that the boys have clean overalls, nicely pressed. When the President talks, please have your pockets filled with cough drops and pass them around if any of the boys have to cough. And, oh, there'll be a lot of people from the outside, but our guests from the mountains must not be pushed aside. Will you see to that, Dr. Cook?"

Without waiting for Dr. Cook's reply Martha went on. "Now a lot of the ladies will have their babies, and I want them near the door in case the babies cry. If they do, Dr. Cook, you must take *every* crying baby *outside*, immediately." Before the bachelor Cook could raise a question she shook a finger. "We must have perfect order."

There was a pause, and Cook recognized his cue. "Everything will be ready, Miss Berry." She started off, only to turn back. "And don't let dogs fight and bark when President Roosevelt speaks. Control them, Dr. Cook." Dr. Cook nodded.

As "R-Day" came near, Martha had something else to fret her. The schools had not seen rain for six weeks, and roads lay deep in dust. That situation, too, demanded action. In Rome she borrowed a sprinkler wagon, and two boys worked through the preceding night. (Long ago Martha had decided that if a thing had to be ready at a certain time, the dark was as good as light.) Then at 4 A.M. rain started, and continued for hours. By 9 A.M. Martha gnawed anxiously at her lip. Surely God would be kind, and the showers would end before Mr. Roosevelt arrived?

The rain became even heavier, and parts of the campus flooded. Wherever she looked she saw widening ponds; students stood about dejectedly and the faculty was dripping wet. With a sad heart Martha borrowed all umbrellas on the campus, had Roanie and other horses hitched, and drove forth with several faculty members, Judge Wright, Mr. Eagan, and others to welcome the guest. Suppose he took one glance at the flood and turned back?

At the station hundreds of people milled about. As the train churned in and everyone ran forward, Martha made out a familiar big head, thick mustache, and goggle eyes. Roosevelt bounded off, pulled up his trouser legs, and beamed with all his teeth. When she apologized for the rain, he laughed. "Don't be discouraged. It's a bully rain."

Her spirits lifted, and so did those of her staff. Waiting for Roosevelt was the school's oxcart, driven by the two "tuition oxen" brought years ago by the young farm boy. When Martha described the incident, Roosevelt pounded his knee in appreciation. The 250 men students ran out and cried their greetings.

125

He waved his hands; music struck up, and a song started in defiance of the rain. Martha applauded, the faculty followed suit, and there began a day that was swift, happy, and at times teary.

"Welcome," declared a big sign on one side of the cart. "Seeing the Berry School" proclaimed one opposite it. Handed an umbrella, Roosevelt rejected it and called to the boy who held the reins, "Let me take your place." For the next few hours the burly former President drove, pointed his finger, cried out, and jumped down to study some point of interest. In the view of one observer, he was "just looking and looking as if he'd never seen anything before in his life."

Martha made certain that he saw everything: dormitories, kitchens, dining hall, bakery, cannery, laundry, barns, workshops, those chicken houses with the steeples. Roosevelt inspected farm lands and pasture, apple and peach orchards, a vineyard that had been created along the mountain, and always the boys in overalls. Questioning them, he heard about cover crops, soil building, special treatment of depleted soil. And then, like the impresario that she was, Martha led him to the girls' school, in whose history he had had his part.

As the cart drew up at Louise Hall (the dormitory named for the ever-active Louise Inman), fifty of them stood up in their long, full dresses to hail him with a song. If it had not been for his encouragement, they reminded him, they might not have been there.

When Martha told Roosevelt of her hope to find future Lincolns, he took it as a theme, and before long he assured her: "I've seen more potential Lincolns in this crowd than ever before in my life." Gifford Pinchot, who had been chief of the division of forestry in the Department of the Interior, had joined the party, and Roosevelt shouted: "Gifford, this is the only thing I know of that beats conservation!" The quick-witted Martha made a response that pleased both men: "Sir, it *is* conservation."

A towering youth who bore a certain resemblance to the Rail Splitter served among the welcomers as the party went into Recitation Hall for the chapel hour. He was scheduled to speak, but Roosevelt threw him off balance. "I've been listening to too many older people. Miss Berry, who's that Abraham Lincoln-looking young man?"

"His name is Percy Pentecost," she answered with some apprehension.

"Pentecost, tell us what you've learned at the Berry school."

Knees shaking, Percy changed part of his talk and spoke so earnestly that he moved many of his listeners. He finished in a thunder of oratory: "It is great for one to die for one's country, but we at Berry have learned it is greater to live for one's country!" Then, as the farmers, their wives, and the townspeople leaned forward to catch his words, Theodore Roosevelt declared that the school combined in an extraordinary degree "a very lofty ideal with the most practical common sense in realizing it."

The school was achieving, he said, "one of the greatest works for American citizenship that has been done within the decade." For his children as for others, including the Berry students before him, he wished the kind of success that would make each one "a lifter and not a leaner." The talk struck a happy note. More than ever the Berry people felt that they had a partisan in the generous-spirited, slightly bumbling man.

Lunch followed in another cabin, where little Walter Johnson had become head cook and waiter. As he listened to Martha's retelling of campus stories, Walter was anxious. Finally he touched her shoulder and whispered: "Don't forget to tell the President that all this food was raised on the place and cooked right here by the boys." Smiling at his pride and loyalty, she relayed the message. "Walter saw that I wasn't on the job." In a delighted confusion Walter retreated.

At the end of the afternoon Martha shook the President's hand and quoted some of his words. "Today, sir, *you* have been

the ideal citizen, as you always are—'lifting and not leaning.'"
The following morning the students adopted his words as a slogan: "Be a lifter and not a leaner." The building in which their guest had dined became "Roosevelt Cabin." Martha explained that it would "help us remember the day and the man." That was like her, the students said, "always wanting you to remember things."

And meanwhile she worked steadily to teach the Berry students about occasions and anniversaries, "hours that meant things." One of the girls from an especially remote spot had a birthday, and Martha insisted on a small party to commemorate it. All went well until the time for the cutting of the cake, and then the girl looked down.

"Please, cain't I have it around for a few days more, ter see and ter admire?" Her eyes lifted to Miss Berry. "You know, it's the first 'birthday' I ever had, and the first cake, too."

After a long pause Martha smiled. "Of course you want to keep your memory of tonight. Let's have a picture made of you and the cake and everybody else. That way you and the rest of us can eat it and have it, too." The plan worked well on that occasion and on many that followed. Hundreds of mountain girls kept photographs of their "first birthdays," their first Christmases, their first anniversaries at the school.

CHAPTER VIII

PRIME MINISTER
AND PUSHER

ON A VISIT to a small Eastern college Martha Berry stopped delightedly before a sign in one of the halls, which proclaimed: "Everybody Must Be Going Somewhere." That was precisely her philosophy; she had no taste for loitering. Thereafter she quoted the words on many an occasion.

Nineteen-eleven, 1912, 1913 . . . The Berry movement was definitely going somewhere. Despite detours, months of financial slowdown, almost of stoppage, she saw her work spread out in several directions, with more students, more buildings, and, though only after grinding effort, more funds. People were talking about the Berry plan, writing her from other states and countries. Schools on her model were being established in Tennessee, in North Carolina, and elsewhere. Royal Daniel of the *Atlanta Journal* informed his readers: "Martha Berry is the first woman to make me sorry I was born a man."

Learning of her work, teachers inquired if they might join

the faculty. This last development filled her with wonder. "Imagine somebody coming here without being urged into it!" But a few anxious people were saying the wrong things, to the school's temporary detriment. Certain mountain parents were reported planning to keep their sons and daughters away. Why? Because they knew for a fact that nobody could enter until some city doctors "cut 'em open" to see what was inside.

Martha was baffled by this rumor, until she realized its origin. Physical examinations occasionally indicated that an applicant had an inflamed appendix or other serious condition, and an operation seemed imperative. "We'll go on operating," Martha ruled, and they did.

Her nonsectarian program also caused a few complications. The school continued to have Bible study and services not connected with any particular denomination. Carefully she tried to make certain that no one would be offended; with equal care she answered all questions on the subject, including many from disturbed families who could not understand the situation.

At one time a number of the staff happened to be Presbyterian; they were said to be hunting converts. When a cross and lighted candles were placed on the altar, tales spread that Berry had "gone Catholic." Meanwhile, though an Episcopalian, Martha attended only the services on the campus and strongly encouraged the faculty to do the same thing. A former student declared: "Not till I left there did I find out *what* religion she was."

Because she liked "the look of it," Martha suggested at an early date that the choir be vested. Students gaped, parents wrote in about "Popery," and for years the choir went unvested. A number of visiting ministers wore robes, until Martha noticed that the mountain boys did not talk easily to them after the services. Then they, too, went unvested. Eventually, but only when she thought her students ready, vestments reappeared. When she had to, she could fight a wary fight.

As everything else expanded, so did Berry's business depart-

130

ment. Chairman John Eagan brought in a lean and taciturn individual to serve as comptroller. When Herman Hoge took over as watchdog of the treasury, Martha left most of the mechanics in his hands. Nearly always she respected Mr. Hoge and deferred to him, and yet they had their disputes. Once, he says, he sent in his notice when Martha complained that he had not gone out to find and bring back an important visitor. "That really wasn't my job," Mr. Hoge notes, "but in such cases not many of us told her that."

This time the comptroller stood his grounds, and the trouble smoothed over. For decades he continued to scrape the bottom of Berry's money chests to meet bills, and prodded debtors while he smoothed away creditors. "I hate to see you coming," Martha would joke to him. But Mr. Hoge extended Berry's reputation for "spending both sides of the dollar." If Berry had not achieved some such feat, it might have closed its gates at any time.

Other new faces were appearing on the campus. Men in their late twenties and thirties, older than the school had ever received, were applying as students. They had never been in a school and could not scratch out their names. Some had worked for years to help their families, to get their farms in running order. Now at last they wanted their own opportunity. "I always wished for this kind o' thing. . . ." "I hopes to know more and talk better."

A man of twenty-nine or thirty might arrive with a sixteen-year-old brother, and the younger would go to an upper grade, the older to a lower. Inevitably one element found this amusing, and strangers who walked around the grounds looked curiously at the elderly "boys." For a time Martha was uneasy. She realized also that the boys' school, in which both high school and lower grades were taught, had become badly overcrowded, and that they were turning away all too many students.

One incident settled her decision in the matter. A man stood

131

in the door of her office one day, a gaunt-cheeked, sharp-nosed fellow with a powerful frame. Martha smiled up at him. "Can I do something?" Shuffling his feet, he moved slowly forward. "I reckon so. Hit don' look jes' right fer a man ter be askin' a woman fer help. But I cain't read a line and thought yer might oblige by schoolin' me an' lettin' me do work as a swap."

Martha's interest rose at the prospect of superior new material. As he sat down the caller explained: "I'm John Henry Carson, and I'm twenty-four, and ma'am, I been mixed up in more things than you ever dreamed of." She quickly realized that John Henry was indeed an unusual type. "Miss Berry, I bin 'bout anything you kin name. Mostly a shell-game operator, a two-bit gambler, and a street barker with a circus. Broke lots o' laws in my time; it ain' a pretty life, gittin' as much money as yer kin out of folks and gittin' out ahead of the sheriff."

Martha listened in fascination while the enthusiastic John Henry Carson spoke of his boyhood days in a smoky cabin where his "prayin' maw" did the best she could with what she had. Restless, dissatisfied, he was "never one for religion," and he remembered her sadness as she talked to him of the subject. When still a boy, he felt impelled to leave the mountains, and his last sight was of his mother's thin form against the doorway as he rode away.

John Henry Carson spent months in one odd job after another and ended with a circus. The manager thought he had a gift for mimicry, and soon he was "barking" rural people into tents to see "bird women" and "half men, half fish." Then one day recently John Henry Carson had followed a crowd into a revival and undergone a conversion. Hearing of Berry, he decided to "do something with my life" and made his way there.

Martha gave him a long look. "Do you mean everything you've said?" After he nodded she thought again, for she liked this strange, voluble man, and she sensed an underlying determination. Though some of her staff might not approve, she would risk having him, and she shook his hand. "When the next term opens, you'll be with us."

Still considering the matter of John Henry Carson, she rode to another part of the campus. Several times this past month she had reflected upon a section nearly five miles away, a hilly wilderness which she had acquired at the foot of Lavendar Mountain. There she visualized a series of great changes. Within a few days she announced to the board that she was going to establish a separate grammar school in the area, and use the present boys' buildings for high school only. Thus they could take in more students of all ages, and the mature ones would not be on parade before gigglers.

The trustees frowned and appealed to statistics. Chairman Eagan spoke glumly: "You're duplicating costs again—separate heat, water, kitchens, barns. Martha, other people consolidate for economy, but you're spreading out." This was one of the complaints made at the time she started the girls' school. Martha listened and nodded, and assured the board that it marshaled its facts most convincingly. What she did might seem uneconomical, she conceded. "But economy isn't my main object," she explained. "It's education for as many as I can possibly get here. If you have a better way to provide that, tell me."

Getting no answer, Martha went ahead in her own way. To lose no time she chose an abandoned farmhouse as living quarters for the first group at the new grammar or "Mountain School." The superintendent was Grady Hamrick, who had recently been graduated at Berry, and with him came his wife Ethel, who had been a Berry girl. In this isolated spot classes began in early 1916. Martha and "the boys" had taken another step forward; more than ever, education at Berry had become a chain reaction.

For a long time the students of this division had only a bare bed in their rooms; the Mountain School had a minimum of decoration or even comfort. The boys' energies went to clear

133

the grounds and put up their quarters. Among the pines the buildings made their appearance, each on a small hill dominating its surroundings. Some structures used the log-cabin motif, while others had sections of stone. A great deal of rock was available nearby, and students used it for chimneys and walls.

In its setting of sloping earth the Mountain School had a rare beauty. Grounds followed the natural elevations, creeks, and valleys. No attempt would be made to give it too civilized a look, with clipped lawns and pruned bushes. This was a place of woodlands, winding roads, and tall trees silhouetted against the skies. In the autumn it had a carpeting of red and yellow leaves; spring came to the Mountain School in a swift blossoming of wild plants and flowering vine.

In this section of laurel, woodbine, and redbud, the boys found several good springs and created a pair of lakes, Moon and Mirror. A visitor from China designed a rustic bridge and lily pool, and Martha liked the effect so much that she added swans. But the Mountain students had only a limited time for landscaping; they seemed to be the hardest-working group at Berry. In class the older men had a great deal of learning to make up. Proudly Martha watched their swift progress, as they finished two years' work in one, skipping grades when they "got the hang of them big words."

John Henry Carson, onetime barker and gambler, had made his appearance as a student, and few would ever forget the lively, talkative individual. At the dairy he took an assignment to push a milk cart over the campus, making deliveries to the dining room and cottages. With the same energy that he had first shown Martha, he kept a book propped on the cart, a pencil in hand to dot passages he did not understand. When he met a teacher he would ask what the words meant, then shove the cart along, memorizing the explanations.

An instructor could hardly turn a corner without running into John Henry Carson, finger pointed to a confusing line. In the evening he put hundreds of questions to his teachers and classmates. Finishing grammar grades at Berry, he took high school work and decided to become a minister. Martha found an outsider who helped him attend a Bible school, and eventually John Henry Carson started a school near his old home, teaching through the week and preaching on Sunday. The Rockefellers became interested, and in time he conducted services as a visiting minister in the Riverside Church in New York. Martha said that in hours of discouragement the thought of John Henry Carson often helped her.

Another minister, who lived near the hamlet of Rising Fawn, provided the school with a half-dozen grown sons. It was not unusual to see them sitting long after hours at night with one or another of the teachers, trying to cram in additional lessons. In such cases few of the staff complained; pioneering spirit was high at the Mountain School.

Dr. S. H. Cook, the young faculty member, struggled especially hard with these overgrown charges. As he finished hours of study, one mountain boy cried out in admiration: "Doctor, if I knew half what you do I'd get out from here and *do* somethin' with myself!" Dr. Cook smiled.

For Martha herself the evenings brought a change. The last of her sisters had married and left home, and the aging Mrs. Berry asked if she could not spend more time with her at Oak Hill, especially in the evenings. Frances Berry, so long in command of affairs around her, was weakening slowly. One day she remarked that something had happened to the wisteria. "They're not nearly as bright as they used to be." Yet, in spite of her failing eyesight, she insisted on doing her own gardening. And Aunt Marth summed up the situation for Martha: "Time fer you ter git home fer a w'ile." Although drawn in two directions, Martha still spent ten or eleven hours a day on the campus.

For years she had hoped that someone would give the school a chapel of adequate size. Captain Barnwell had designed a log-cabin church of quiet beauty and appeal, but long ago it had been outgrown. Men students used the recitation hall, so overcrowded that they had to sit in twos and even threes at desks intended for one. The atmosphere hardly encouraged contemplation, Martha said.

During an Eastern trip she mentioned the need; following her talk an elderly woman spoke to her but did not reveal the extent of her interest. Not long afterward a man telephoned the office—a friend of the Eastern woman, he said, who was just passing through and wondered if he could attend church services. He sat with the staff in the tightly packed room and left almost on a run to make the train. The next night, as Martha discovered afterward, he telegraphed his employer that "Miss Berry has underestimated the need." He was the lady's business manager.

With a cry of delight Martha received the news. A chapel at last. . . . But someone else, who was still closer to the Easterner, intervened to say that Martha Berry could do without the building. The school was mainly a dream, he claimed. . . . The would-be benefactor changed her mind, and the new word sent Martha to bed, until one of *her* friends called on the lady, waited for hours, and pleaded. This time action was definite, an announcement that the school would receive a replica of Christ Church of Alexandria, where George Washington had worshiped. It would be a substantial brick building that would help transform the campus.

Even then the chapel appeared jinxed in advance. Its site was to be a point in the middle of a fine nearby grove, owned by a friend who had said he would sell the land to Martha when she raised the money. Rumors suddenly sprang up that the owner had received an offer from people who planned a country club. She was startled; to lose the property would be a setback.

Martha went to the friend, and he told her that if she paid $10,000 she could have the land. At once she took a three-month option, giving him a down payment to secure it. For several days, she said, she was afraid to let her associates know what she had done. She had scant prospects of getting any such amount. There was a single possible source—New York, and she went there without further delay.

In the East, Martha worked for weeks, only to be frustrated every time a hope arose. Disappointed, depressed, and over-worked, she suffered another of her periodic collapses, and lay sick for a long time in her boardinghouse. "The doctor strongly advised me to . . . go home or to a hospital, as I really needed rest, but I could not give up." Propped up in bed, she composed letters in pencil, copied them laboriously in ink, and in time raised a few thousand dollars. Even when Christmas approached she refused to return home. She had missed it before for the school, and she would have to miss it again. She wrote to friends that if they wanted to give her something, she hoped they would make it contributions for the land tract.

Slowly more funds accumulated, and then a frightening telegram came from her Georgia neighbor. He expected full payment on the day the option expired, which was less than a month off. The message provided a fresh spur. Again she went about, "making talks wherever anybody would let me," telephoning and writing. She had never recovered her strength, and she became so weak that she often asked permission to sit down for her speeches. Yet she did not collapse, "because I couldn't afford to do it." And thirty-six hours before her deadline she had the $10,000. She wired home to transfer the money and left New York.

At Oak Hill, Mrs. Berry said dourly that Martha looked like a death's-head, and Aunt Marth predicted: "You'll be gone 'fore any of us, you hear?" Martha heard, but happily. Work was starting on the chapel and at the site she had chosen.

In these years more and more Berry boys were marrying Berry

137

girls, and Martha turned fond eyes on such weddings, encouraging and helping plan them. As soon as the tall chapel rose, with its white Georgian entrance, she announced the first festive wedding. "Let's do it well," she said. She gave her full attention to arrangements, advising students on dress, the use of flowers, selection of attendants. Smilax, roses, and violets decorated the serene chapel; a reception followed on the lawn, with a big cake and photographs for the bride to keep. For some guests it was the first such ceremony they had ever seen. Then and later, no Berry bride could say she lacked a proper launching of her marriage.

Now and then Martha Berry had a moment of sadness on these occasions. Whenever possible, she gave the bride away. Once, she said, she had looked forward to a wedding of her own. "Every girl does, and some of us are lucky enough to have it." Then she smiled. "Instead I married my schools, and have thousands of children." But she never mentioned her one-time fiancé.

At Martha's side as she went about her duties was a youthful-looking man who had an ever larger role at Berry. Gordon Keown was the handsome boy who had shed tears during the early "tent commencement." Born in the mountains thirty-five miles from Rome, Gordon eventually saw something of the world, and many called him the keenest man in the county. At the same time he remained always the countryman, slow-moving, laconic. He drawled, he went about with seeming aimlessness as he talked to farmers, storekeepers, and sheriffs, and meanwhile he kept eyes and ears wide open.

A tall youth with well-cut features and an awkward walk, Gordon had known lean days. Until he reached twenty-one he had almost no education. Nearing twenty, after helping the family bring in its cotton, he tried his own crop and received less than $25 for a year's work. Earnestly he turned to sorghum cane, labored furiously, and netted $16 for the next year's struggle. "A little discouraged," Keown became a pioneer Berry student and began an identification with the school that lasted, except for a few interruptions, for nearly all his long life.

As a student Gordon impressed Martha with his shrewdness. One day she sent him to Oak Hill to borrow the family carriage for campus guests. Dropping into the kitchen, Gordon made a casual report to Aunt Marth and headed for the stables. "Wait a minute!" The dark dignitary strode after him, all her responsibility for Berry treasures gleaming in her eyes. "What fer? Dat 'casion don' soun' important enough for dem hawses an' de glass carriage, and dey ain' ter go. Go tell de boss dere ain' no 'casion."

Startled, Gordon left. Wait till Miss Martha erupted over this! He was startled a second time when Martha merely nodded. "Well, if Aunt Marth said that, we'll just have to make other arrangements." He did not forget the incident. On graduation young Keown found agriculture and land use an absorbing subject and took university courses in Georgia, Iowa, Kansas, and Arkansas. After three years Martha summoned him back to Berry for a series of positions. He married, sent his two children to the Berry schools, and his roots went steadily deeper into the soil.

Gordon's duties were a mystery to some people. At first he described himself as "the office boy" who did "whatever came up that didn't fit in elsewhere." One of his tasks became the management of guests who arrived to look over the school. As he directed them from one building to the next, pressing them on, the boys gave him a name, "the Pusher." Then Berry obtained its own post office and Martha made Keown postmaster. Seeing the initials P.M., the students dubbed him "the Prime Minister," and in some ways the title appeared accurate.

Over a period of years Martha listened closely to Gordon's opinions on matters affecting the country people. As a staff member noted: "She always wanted to know what he thought, even if she often didn't follow him. She respected his judgment, though she frequently assured him he was wrong."

Most important of all was what he termed "the trading end." A horse trader par excellence, Gordon Keown loved a deal of any kind. Recognizing his gift, Martha put it to work for the school. She had always wanted to expand her landholdings, for, as she once wrote, "Every acre of land added to the property of a school adds to its permanency . . . Buildings may be destroyed by storm or fire; land is safe from both." Keown recalled that she said to him: "After all the forms of endowment have vanished with changing times, the land, and also the trees, will be the best things we have left."

First, however, she had to get the land. Martha gave Keown authority to ride about the countryside to see what the farmers wished to do with their land. Most of the area about the schools was in small tracts, sections ranging from one acre to two hundred or so. To acquire them proved no simple operation; many owners showed suspicion or a plain unwillingness to sell. "It took a great deal of time and a great deal of thought, and, I sometimes fear," he said, "a great deal of just downright scheming—horse trading."

For a quarter century Gordon Keown served as Martha's purchasing agent. "We always bought; we never sold. We seldom pressed; we let people understand our interest, and waited." Years might pass before a deal solidified; months would go without a new purchase, and then five or six would develop in a row, until eventually the school had 30,000 acres. The closeness of the town of Rome was a complicating factor. To build so big a holding at the edge of a community which eventually reached 30,000 inhabitants called for true skill.

The "Prime Minister" had a set of simple rules. "When you want something, it's better to let someone sell it to you than to buy it." His poker face made him a rare bargainer. "You could never guess whether he had reached his limit or would go way higher," said one who observed him for years. "I don't suppose I ever saw him excited. He could size up a situation and settle in a minute, or hold on for five years—and finally get just what he wanted. After he'd won he'd sit down and give us cracker-barrel philosophy, but he never told everything."

The best deal, Gordon asserted, was "when everybody got what he liked, when all sides left satisfied." In one case the school hoped for a small tract of land, and already it owned plots on four sides of the strip. The owner delayed; she wanted at least $2000, "But I jes' don' know ef I wan' ter sell." She was accustomed to the spot, the water supply, the run of the land. Gordon did some research and returned with an offer. He had located a farm of the same size, with a good house, running water, and neighbors who were related to two of her friends. Would she trade? She would and she did. To obtain the new farm Gordon paid $4000, losing a possible $2000 in the deal. Yet each side had what it wished, and in time the woman's land would have a far greater value for Berry.

One old farmer made a face when Keown walked up. "Tell me," he asked the Berry agent, "why in hell does that school want more land? Must have clost to 20,000 acres now."

Gordon rubbed his long chin. "How many acres you got?"

"Two hundred."

"How many people you got?"

"Me an' the ol' lady."

"That's 100 acres apiece. At Berry we got about 500 students and 40 acres apiece. Why in hell do you and the old lady want so much land?"

"Never thought of it like that," the farmer snickered, and he sold.

Gordon enjoyed a light touch in his operations, and also a slight reputation for eccentricity. Once he disposed of several wagonloads of produce but had a large supply of cabbages left over. Nobody would buy, and so he went from house to house with a proposition:

"I'll let you have these cabbages for ten cents a head. If you

141

take two, you can have them both for a nickel. And if you take four, you can have 'em free with a piece of cookin' meat thrown in." As he told the story: "You know, I got rid of a lot of cabbages that way!" And he threw his head back and laughed his short, high-pitched laugh.

At one time the schools had too many mules, and Gordon pondered ways to free the campus of them. When a country boy walked in to buy farm equipment, Keown gave his prices. "For a wagon, $50. If you want a mule and wagon, you can have both for $25. If you take two mules and the wagon, it won't cost you anything at all." The youth retreated in confusion, and the next day his widowed mother came to investigate. "The boy didn't get you right," she began, and Gordon interrupted with a chuckle. "The boy got it just right," he said, and watched her unbelief as he repeated the offer.

At last she agreed and left, still shaking her head. Again, said Keown, it was the best kind of transaction. The widow got what she needed; Berry cut down its feed bill, and he had a good laugh.

Meanwhile Gordon went on buying land for Martha. They would hold long conferences during which she reminded him: "If that one over there is ever up for sale, get it. I'm like the rest of the country people; I want what 'jines me.'" Eventually Gordon would notify her that a public sale had been arranged. "Miss Berry, I think I can take it at a fair price if you'll only stay away. When you come with all that enthusiasm and bubbling up, like, these folks see how anxious you are, and the figures hit the sky." Eventually she learned to remain at home, but it took effort.

As Berry added bits of land, a map of its holdings resembled a crazy quilt; some of the farmers applied the adjective to Martha. Why would anybody want all *that?* Her board members also looked askance. "We're going to be land poor, flat broke." Listening carefully, Martha would reply: "You may well be right. But I'm going to take a chance anyway."

By general reputation, much of the new property was poor

soil, gullied and overused. For years the farmers had known of only one or two uses for it. They would burn over the small pines and clear the area for crops or for cattle. Crops meant one thing, the old single stand-by of cotton; year after year it ate at the soil, wearing it away. Now Martha and her staff set out to show new techniques to their neighborhood and to the South at large. Fields were built back to fertility, renewed for cultivation. Berry planted cotton but also many other things, and rotated, experimented, altered the pattern with the seasons.

At the same time the Berry staff went to work on other parts of their new properties, the piny "wild land." Martha told the Mountain School boys: "From now on we'll have a new crop over here—trees." With Gordon Keown and others, the students studied the land, picking good trees for special attention, thinning out one area after another.

"We're growing pine the way we grow roses and vegetables," Martha explained. "Later we'll harvest. For the time being we're planting and watching." There were some smiles at what seemed a silly preoccupation—men and big boys fooling around trees. Martha smiled in another fashion. "One day this land may run the school for us." It was years before the neighbors realized precisely what she or her program meant.

While they shared basic convictions about land, reforestation, and hard work, Martha and Gordon Keown also differed in several ways. Having learned rigid economy in his early life, Gordon never forgot his lessons. "When Martha did something impulsive he went behind her, trying to save a dollar here, a penny there," an observer declared. He hated "frills" or what he considered frills; he had little patience with planners whom he thought impractical—and that description sometimes included Martha herself. "If I were you I'd hold back a little," he would say. In certain cases, as another staff member noted, "he slowed her up, or at least tried to do it."

In many transactions they made a good team, one complementing the other. Yet frequently Martha would shrug off his restraint. Bridling, she told him in the hearing of others: "If it were left to you, Gordon, we'd have no schools here. A lot of black ink, yes, but no schools." He nodded. "Nothing wrong with black ink, Miss Berry." Meaningly he would murmur to her: "If we'd pray a bit more around here, instead of trying to *do* so much . . ." To that she once snapped: "We'll go right on as we have. We'll pray, and we'll do more, too."

In amusement she said once or twice: "Gordon is the perfect adviser. He waits till I've done something, then tells me how I did it wrong." Several times in their years of association her anger boiled over. Sent to meet an important delegation, he missed it, and Martha blamed him for a fiasco. Again, when she organized a group of Berry representatives to appear in New York, he drawled to her: "I'm plain not going, Miss Berry." Martha argued, demanded; stubbornly Gordon stayed home. He was one of the few on the campus who could have done that and survived.

At another time she conducted a months-long, one-sided feud with him, stalking past his office, head averted. Yet she would not dismiss him; she knew how valuable an aide he had made himself. Like the wise countryman he was, Keown sat things out. One morning, when she could no longer do without a specific kind of help, Martha went to his office as if nothing had happened between them. "Good morning, Gordon. You've heard about that new offer . . . ?" The team was at work again.

For years the school's water supply had been a problem. She asked one engineer after another for advice about the matter, and each shook his head. Then an imaginative expert pointed sadly. "If you only owned the mountain shed over there I could make you the finest supply in Georgia. There's a natural bottleneck right above us."

Martha gave him a slow smile. "As a matter of fact, we do own it. I bought it once after I 'lost my mind' over land." The students went to work under engineering direction to create a fifty-acre lake by throwing up a dirt dam across the gorge. That land purchase, like others, has paid itself back many times.

CHAPTER IX

HOME FIRES BURNING

IN THE EARLY spring of 1914 Martha Berry's endless, unsparing labor suddenly had the effect that Aunt Marth had predicted. She lost weight rapidly, she had trouble sleeping, and one morning as she tried to rise she fell helplessly back. The doctor ordered a complete rest—a prescription which made Mrs. Berry shake her head in anxiety. "She'll never take it while she's in range of those schools, or even in New York or those other places she's always going to."

Sister Laura, now Mrs. J. Bulow Campbell of Atlanta, had a solution. Why didn't Martha go to Europe, visit their other sister, Jennie, in Rome, and try one of the continental watering places that did people so much good? Laura would take care of the expenses, so that Martha couldn't claim she needed the funds for her work. Martha argued, smiled wanly, and gave in. She promised not to talk or think of the schools. She felt much too tired, she assured them.

As the steamer left the New York dock, according to friends, she waved a last good-by, then turned to look over the crowd on deck, and chose a pleasant woman who appeared to be enjoying the sparkle of the water. Finding a vacant chair, Martha eased into it. A few minutes later they were no longer strangers, and she was animatedly describing her enterprises. After a time she paused, and her new acquaintance touched her arm. "Please go on. I've always been interested in home missions." Though the last phrase made Martha start in surprise, she quickly continued. Long before the ship reached the English coast, the friend promised to visit Berry. Eventually she did, and as a result another building went up on the campus.

For years afterward the Berrys and the staff heard of other travelers who met Martha and learned of her work on the ship, in Europe, or on her return voyage. The vacation netted uncounted thousands of dollars. In Italy she visited briefly with Jennie, now the Princess Ruspoli, who summoned her own doctor and helped arrange transportation to Austria and the resort at Carlsbad. There Martha improved steadily and had settled down for a stay of several more weeks when the newspapers brought word of a shooting at a place named Sarajevo in not so distant Bosnia.

At her hotel apprehensive officials assured her that the trouble which followed would be over in a few days. Yet several titled Russian women, though seriously ill in their rooms, were carried to the railroad station on stretchers, and every few hours more French and English guests departed. A week later Martha found herself the only resident of the hotel. Men were being called up, cars requisitioned. On a frightening afternoon she watched a chauffeur with six children tell his family good-by, and realized that he expected never to return.

It was obviously time for her to go home. After standing in line for hours, day after day, she obtained a passport and military papers. The only ticket she could get took her a bare twenty miles; at the next station she waited six hours for a train which officials promptly sidetracked for troop movements. A trip that normally required fifteen hours stretched to six days.

As the train passed a bridge a passenger threw something from the window (innocently, it seemed), and a guard shot him to death. On the heavily overcrowded ship bound for New York, Martha slept on a tiny sofa, ate little, and "fairly wept" on arrival. A fellow passenger was the famous Madame Schumann-Heink; Martha had no way of knowing that their names would eventually be connected in a surprising fashion.

Back in Georgia again, she thought it a "blessed relief" to hear, not the endless tramp of armed men, but the pound of the Berry students crossing the campus. Gradually, however, the United States moved closer to hostilities, and then overnight it plunged into the conflict. The hour was a disturbing, challenging one. The government offered Martha "the opportunity to go to Europe on confidential business, to make a report on some conditions there." A Red Cross post also became available, with the prospect of stirring work.

After hesitating briefly, Martha declined the offers. Already Berry felt the war's effects, and even with her on hand it would suffer crippling changes. Funds for the school shrank as patrons explained that they must now buy war bonds. All over America a new phrase was heard—"the high cost of living." In time ten staff members had joined the Army or Navy. "Our best-trained boys, those who had been with us long enough to learn the use of tools and who could help train the younger boys," were going. New students were more youthful than before, less experienced, and double work had to be done with a reduced force.

A bad blow was the loss of Clifton Russell, a recent graduate who was building Berry's prize-winning herd. For Clifton the development of that herd had become a kind of crusade. On the day of his departure Martha passed the dairy and discovered him still with boots on, working intently. "Clifton," she cried to him, "I thought you were off to war!" Glancing at his watch, he replied: "So I am, but I still have an hour."

"Don't you know there's a party in Rome for the boys that go today?" she asked. Clifton frowned. "My only obligation is to make the train. I'll do it, and as soon as things are over I'll be right back here." He kept his promise. Becoming a lieutenant, Russell handled army stock with skill and eventually returned to continue at the school for more than a quarter century.

As always under war conditions, romance flourished. Martha encouraged a succession of soldier marriages, and smiled when Walter Johnson, the orphan boy of other years, later a young mathematics teacher at Berry and then in service, planned to marry Mabel Lloyd, another graduate. Because of a quarantine at nearby Camp Gordon, the wedding had to be postponed. Arriving unexpectedly at the campus, Walter explained to Martha that a new date must be set.

"Let's set it now, today." She beamed at him. "No time like the present.

"Oh, but the marriage license office has closed," Walter explained. "I don't have a ring, and we haven't arranged for a minister."

"Let's arrange it all right now," Martha nodded briskly. Walter called the court official at home, she rustled up a preacher, and Mrs. Dessie Bible loaned her wedding ring. A few hours later Berry's bells clanged for a special service. One of Walter's friends appeared with a coat and so was promptly made best man, and all of the students looked on as he and Mabel took their vows. As Martha repeated, there was no time like the present.

By the fall of 1917 several hundred Berry undergraduates and alumni had gone to training camps and on to dugouts in France. Women and younger boys took staff places, and Martha had to spend ten consecutive months without a rest or a break, to cope with troubles that developed almost daily. Chairman Eagan of the board became less available as war committees called him repeatedly to Washington. Watching her, her associate Alice Wingo decided that difficulties of one kind or another were "Miss Berry's daily stimulant. Nothing so stirred her to action as the sight of some monster of discouragement rising in her pathway."

All too many monsters rose before her. Boys whose classmates had gone overseas, who expected their own summons at any hour, found it hard to "sit still at a desk and look at a book." Restless, discontented, they slipped away from work or from the dormitories, and sulked at orders. Once more Martha asked her friend, Judge Wright, to give talks in assembly and to reason with difficult students. With his diplomacy added to hers, Berry held most of its waverers.

America began to realize how many young men remained isolated and without education in the Southern highlands. Hundreds resisted the draft, ignoring the summons which they could not read. Except for the training her school and staff had given her graduates, Martha said, some of them "might have been with the men . . . that our government has to hunt in the recesses of the mountains."

Letters arrived from England and France. The Berry boys were doing well, they said, though they thought often and sadly of the good days at school. One gratifying report came from an officer who told of the day he had inquired how many men in his company could cook. Seven hands went up. How many could do laundry work, carpentry, lay pipes? With every question the same seven hands rose. Where were they from? "The Berry schools." Martha's "training of hand and mind" had had its effect; the officer wrote to thank her.

Then a Philadelphian informed her that he had two Berry men in his company. When morale had begun to suffer, they kept spirits high and encouraged frightened, tormented soldiers around them. They had learned to "get along" with others and with conditions around them. The officer had made up his

149

mind to send a gift to keep such a school going, and he enclosed it.

After a time the staff received another kind of message, news of the deaths of Berry boys in trenches and village fighting. In each case Gordon Keown or one of the staff went to the distant home to comfort the mother and father. And still more students or graduates left for the fighting. These were the days when Americans talked of going "over the top," when place names like Chateau-Thierry and the river Marne were on Georgia lips. The French Government decorated a Berry boy with the Croix de Guerre, and Berry chins went higher. A French medal for a plain mountaineer . . . Who would have believed it?

There was applause, and there were tears, when a student who still served overseas sent his "representatives" to the 1918 commencement—his wife and baby. Martha made speeches about "fighting with our funds for our country." Students bought thrift stamps. At a war meeting, in spite of their own need, the seniors gave fifty cents each for a Liberty bond, and the others thirty cents; these were large amounts for the highland students. Teachers added their contributions, and the bond was oversubscribed.

Conditions grew harsher. The staff and students had a struggle to plant and harvest, look after cattle, raise pigs and other produce, teach neighbors about home production as the government asked—more sweet potatoes and lettuce and other crops in "war gardens." Funds still declined while prices rose. Several faculty members, seeing the school needs increase with every week, turned back to Berry a large portion of their monthly pay, "to do our bit."

One or two suggestions were made to Martha: With the situation so hard, might it be wise to close the school doors for a time and reopen when the war ended? Each time she stiffened and made a quick answer: She had been through worse times, and she intended to hold on as long as they had milk or water to drink and corn pone to eat. Sometimes they came close to that diet; for days at a time the menu consisted of vegetable soup, corn bread, and sorghum.

President Wilson, once a schoolteacher, appealed to Americans to keep the classes going, and Martha murmured a fervent "amen." Wilson continued a tradition of presidential interest in Berry. The first Mrs. Wilson had lived in Rome, and while in the White House sponsored an exhibition of her paintings for the school's benefit. . . . Meanwhile the students sang "There's a Long, Long Trail A-Winding," "Pack Up Your Troubles in Your Old Kit Bag" and, again and again, "Keep the Home Fires Burning." While the fires burned, five hundred Berry men went into the war, and eleven gave their lives, while many lost eyes, arms, and legs.

At last came the dark German losses of 1918, collapsing fronts, and at Berry a joyous shout: "The war's over!" Bells rang and rang at the chapel, and the school band led a parade over the road to Oak Hill. Martha and her mother hurried out, orators made speeches, and the boys sang school songs and a hymn of thanksgiving. The white-haired Mrs. Berry spoke of the time she and Martha's father returned here after the war with the Yankees. "It's been bad here lately, sure enough," she said. "But it was worse that other time."

Aunt Marth muttered fiercely to herself, cried a little, and smiled, and asked when Walter Johnson, Clifton Russell, and other favorites would return. Then Aunt Marth announced to everyone in hearing: "Time to tote ourself' back and git ter work." With her words the war had officially ended for Berry.

Within a few months the soldiers were toting themselves back to school, to take up old assignments or better ones. When Martha greeted a youth who had lost a leg she asked what he wanted to do next. Well, ma'am, he'd been thinking vaguely of studying dentistry, but with only one leg . . . "Of course you can be one," she told him. "You're going to be the best in your town." In time he became that.

The next year saw a fresh rush of applicants. The war had

brought thousands of boys out of secluded mountain homes, and Southerners were becoming aroused to the need for better schooling. Then the price of cotton slumped disastrously; farmers had to rotate crops to survive, and Berry could teach them better methods. Every student bed filled, and new ones went up in tiers, in halls, greenhouses, and in the narrow, stifling loft over the cannery, with a tin roof above.

A grandmother rode in with a young man and a crude tent. "Miss Martha, he won't take up your space because he can sleep under this, and he'll be proud to have other boys share it with him." Touched, Martha accepted the boy and the gift, and paused. Why not a great many more tents? She sent to the nearest army camp, and soon other tents were hauled there by army men who instructed the students in setting them up.

As the applicants increased, Martha tried to take most of them. "It may be their last chance to get an education," she told her aides. "Stretch a few points whenever you can." In the end, however, many were turned away. "We just don't have the money to support them." Each such rejection, she said, was like a tap upon her heart.

A delegation called. The boys wanted to give extra hours of labor to the schools, in appreciation of what had been done for them, and in memory of those who died in the war. They had heard Martha say she hoped to see a lake covering the low area beyond the girls' school, and the campus needed a road to the distant Mountain unit. They would provide both.

Soon afterward crews started before sunup, cutting brush, beginning a winding passage. At the same time others set out to construct a low dam. Eventually a small lake filled the place, with weeping willows and flowering shrubs. That day the girls volunteered to help in removing brush, and with dark, Martha topped off the occasion by arranging a party at the girls' school, with the boys invited to dine. After supper they talked over names and chose two: "Victory Lake" and "The Road of Remembrance." The campus was gaining in beauty with each year.

But one who had worked for a long time to help Berry emerge in richer colors would now leave them. At Mount Alto the saintly, white-bearded Captain Barnwell died in sight of the great sycamores under which he had designed the school's early buildings. With a student group Martha went to the white country house where two lay brothers of the Plymouth Brethren conducted services.

In his last days the captain had made his own pine coffin. Standing beside it, the Brethren offered no eulogy; they said only that he had "lived the Christian life among them," and, as he would have wished, they would read from the Word of God in which he trusted and sing some of his favorite hymns. Captain Barnwell had indicated he wanted no flowers, but Martha had yielded to an impulse to pick a handful beside the campus walks planned by this man of "large soul and white life." He had given of his arts to build Berry, and she wanted him to share something of it at the end.

Another old associate was leaving. The school paper reported that the ever dependable, matter-of-fact Elizabeth Brewster, by then principal of the girls' school, "has been compelled to go away for a month's rest." The month became several months, and Miss Brewster went to recuperate with relatives in California. She went back to Berry some years later, to continue for a short time. Through ebb and flow, good days and bad, she remained firmly herself. "When Elizabeth left," said Martha, "she took a whole and beloved part of our history with her."

Again new faces appeared, among them that of a Berry mainstay, G. Leland Green. Martha had never hesitated to reach far out for staff additions, and this time she set her eye upon a Yankee of Yankees, from Vermont. She got him, as she sometimes did, by refusing to take a refusal. She had made inquiries; a leading Harvard educator had recommended Leland

Green, principal of the Vermont State School of Agriculture.

Back from the war, the thirty-six-year-old Dr. Green received a note from Martha. Would he come help her develop her schools? Dr. Green had never heard of Berry and declined politely with the explanation that he expected to spend the rest of his life in his current assignment. Nine months later, during the winter's worst blizzard, his telephone rang. It was Martha Berry, who "happened to be passing" the village of Randolph Center, two miles from the Vermont school. She could not get out to him; would he mind going in to her?

Several hours later Dr. and Mrs. Green sat on a small hotel sofa beside her, and Martha told her story. "I had never heard anything like it," he recalls. "We were half crying, half laughing as she talked. When she finished, both of us were more stirred than we had been in our life."

She obtained a promise that the Greens would visit her school as soon as possible. In parting, Dr. Green, like any man with a family to support, inquired about salary. "Oh, that isn't important." She brushed off the inquiry. "We can always settle that." A month later, after spending several days on the campus, Leland Green got up at one of Martha's now famous joint chapels, and as he looked into the faces before him he knew what he was going to say. In the fall he arrived as principal of the school—at less than he had received in years.

"Ahead of us were months when we had to worry about finances, about even the continuation of the school," Dr. Green says. "It was the hardest work that I ever had. And still I don't think either of us ever felt we had made an unwise decision." A tolerant man, he proved rather less rigid than some of Martha's earlier associates. Quietly he worked to temper the ancient demerit system and helped strengthen scholastic standards through the years that followed.

In these days Martha counted increasingly on the warm support of another friend, Mrs. John Henry Hammond of New York. This great-granddaughter of old Commodore Vanderbilt gave to Berry of her means, her energy, and her eager imagination. She and Martha met when the school head visited friends before the war at Bar Harbor, Maine. "I fell under her influence that first evening," Mrs. Hammond says. "She had humanity, a rare style, a breadth of spirit that affected all of us." Almost at once Mrs. Hammond offered Martha the use of her Ninety-first Street mansion for gatherings to help the school, and Martha invited this new supporter to Berry.

From then on Mrs. Hammond went to the schools annually or more often for a quarter century. Once she took along two of her pretty daughters and, though they could not be regular students, Martha allowed them to spend about a month with the Berry girls. For both sides it was a new venture, but Mrs. Hammond's concern was only that her well-dressed, more sophisticated daughters "might have a bad effect on these fine mountain girls."

The young Hammonds put on plain uniforms and went from department to department, "doing everything." They lived in crowded quarters, learned to cook, spin and dye and weave, handle cows, and serve meals. In classes and on the campus they became friends of the highlanders, "and returned to New York better people," Mrs. Hammond believes.

By then Mrs. Hammond, a woman with a steady organizing hand, had decided that her own friends must know of Berry. To make sure that they saw the place she would bring them herself. She formed a band of "Berry Pilgrims" for a trip, confidently describing the original group as the "first annual party." Each spring thereafter she took thirty or forty people by train or plane for several days at the school. She telephoned and wrote to those she knew, cornered them at social gatherings, and called upon well-known ministers, editors, and men in public life. If necessary, she provided for the expenses of some who might otherwise not go.

Once, finding Mrs. Sara Delano Roosevelt sitting next to her at a luncheon, Mrs. Hammond spoke so enthusiastically of a forthcoming pilgrimage that Franklin D. Roosevelt's mother said: "I wish I were going." "Then why don't you come?" Mrs. Hammond demanded. Mrs. Roosevelt had several engagements that week and regretted that it would not be possible. Mrs. Hammond did not give up, but called her back until Mrs. Roosevelt cancelled the appointments and joined the band. Over a period of years hundreds of people went to the schools in this way.

Largely out of the "pilgrimages" Martha Berry evolved a dramatic pattern of programs for formal visitors. They always arrived after dark, and when the automobiles slowed up before the white gateway the newcomers saw a small flame of light, then another and another in an endless line. Every student— eventually 1200 of them—stood in a double file along the path, each holding a lighted candle at the level of his heart.

At a signal the automobile drivers switched off their headlights, and as the cars moved by, passengers made out the faces in the yellow glow. A boy, a girl . . . On it went for two miles or so against a background of pine forests. Each countenance, said a Texas visitor, seemed "a portrait against the canvas of the dark night." At the end waited the school band, pounding out a welcome, and then there were greetings, formal and informal, and the singing of songs.

Soon afterward the guests would retire to rustic log cabins built by the boys and furnished by the girls. Pine floors had hooked rugs in early American style, with four-poster beds and reproductions of colonial furniture in rooms whose fireplaces glowed with pine cones and cornhusks. In the morning the guests learned about Berry eggs and ham, grits and jelly and coffee, and at other meals about golden-browned chicken, heavily sliced ham, thick biscuits, heaps of vegetables and meats.

That day and during the one or two that followed, the pilgrims went to each school unit, passing lakes and woodlands and fields of ripening crops. They visited wells left from early days, and the original log cabins, including the one in which

Martha began her Sunday school, where the melodeon still stood ready. In the spring season azaleas, laurel, and flowering shrubs lined the highways and splashed the edges of the grounds, with Lavendar Mountain as a backdrop.

The callers saw workshops in which machines buzzed, canneries in which steaming vegetables piled up, packing plants near the orchards, buildings in which boys learned crafts, quarters in which spinning wheels whirled and girls mixed mountain dyes. The pilgrims walked to the chapel for the joint services, standing outside while the boys and girls marched toward them in long, curving files. The students approached from opposite directions, boys in blue shirts and overalls, girls in colored chambray. To the band's music the lines met in the center of the sweeping lawn and moved forward to the church. For some this procession of youth, heads lifted, arms swinging, provided the high point of their visit.

On the final night the guests sat talking together after dinner until someone, usually Martha Berry herself, caught a sound of soft steps outside. In the dark, scores of students had slipped up to the guest cabin, according to a plan as carefully prearranged as any of the others. Candles were lighted, one by one, and the young men and women stood there, faces outlined in the uncertain light under the shadowed trees and against the dogwood blossoms.

For an hour or so the pilgrims were serenaded with mountain ballads and plaintive songs, ending with "God Be With You Till We Meet Again." At the first stanza the student group began to break up, backing into the distance, still singing, their faces glowing in the dark. Slowly the candle flames dimmed and the voices died away until they were only far-off points and echoes, and at last there was only the night and the sound of wind in the pines.

But another sight which certain pilgrims remembered longest was one which developed from a revival of an ancient industry—the biggest water wheel in America. On land newly purchased by Berry, "Prime Minister" Gordon Keown had been fascinated by a section of an abandoned mill nearly 110 years old, which seemed to grow out of a mossy bank at the foot of the mountain. The school required a great deal of ground corn, and why not have their own mill?

They located the metal part of a massive wheel, and Berry technicians went at the problem. The largest overshot wheel in the country, they learned, was in Montana—42 feet high. They set this goal and passed it, with an object towering 44 feet in the air. Thousands of visitors have admired the sparkling display of water that pours down and moves the wheel by gravity's force.

Martha obtained Berry's first miller on a mountain trip during which she encountered an elderly individual with shaggy hair and patriarchal beard. He and his wife were looking after their grandchildren, eight, ten, and twelve years old. After their daughter died, the old couple had never been able to get the young ones to school. "You see, ma'am, it was sich a long ways off." Martha stared after these bright-eyed children of the American 1920s, who could not recognize their own names on a paper. But they were too young for dormitory life, and how could she fit them in at Berry?

"What work can you do?" she asked the bearded man. He had been a miller, a real fine one, he answered, and he could still match any young fellow she named. So Martha took the old and the young of the family to the campus and gave them quarters. The children started classes, and the mill got off to a good start.

The arrival of one new student in the early post-war days posed a dilemma that Martha first considered impossible to solve. Accepting Eugene Gunby with misgivings, she wondered for a time if she had made a mistake. Then she watched a triumph of the human will and spirit.

At the beginning everything was against young Gene Gunby. Born on a farm fifteen miles from the nearest railroad, one of nine children, he suffered an attack of infantile paralysis that destroyed all use of both legs. From the time he was five he could move only by crawling with his hands. Nevertheless he forced himself about, and if he could not crawl where he wanted to go, others lifted or carried him. The effort might be agonizing, but Gene chopped cotton, hoed corn, and milked like any of the other children.

Then and almost always, the handsome Gene Gunby was a smiling, cheerful individual. "And I prayed," he says, "prayed most of the time. Maybe I didn't know precisely what I prayed for. Still I did, and eventually I got it." Until he was eleven he stayed around the farm, wondering about the world beyond. Then Gene Gunby determined to learn something. The only school lay several miles away, a gray one reached by an uneven, up-and-down route. One of his brothers put him in a wheelbarrow and pushed him there every day. Depositing the boy on the front porch, he would call for him after classes.

Eventually one of the family broke a bull calf. Each morning his sister lifted Gene to the calf's back and led the animal to school, tied it to a sapling, and carried the boy inside. Though Gene started classes late, he went swiftly from grade to grade and finished before he reached fifteen. But how could he go on? Friends spoke of his case and mentioned it to Atlantans. In the city a new hospital had just opened, the Scottish Rite Hospital for Crippled Children, and after a great deal of arranging the forlorn yet determined boy made the trip there.

Long days of waiting were followed by word that he would be operated on. "I thought that it would be over in a few hours, and I'd go home well and strong," Eugene Gunby recalls. "It was just the beginning. Following the operation I stayed in a cast for eleven weeks, and then they told me there would be another operation and another, and after that I went back for more treatments." Finally doctors placed a heavy brace on one leg, gave him crutches, "and from now on it was up to me."

For the first time in more than ten years Eugene stood on his own legs. A moment later he crashed to the floor. "But I knew I could do it, and I told 'em to lift me up." He started again, moved a yard or so, and went smashing a second time to the floor. It did not matter; he would get the hang of the thing. With sweating effort he worked for many weeks at the agony of walking. Then an older friend, Mrs. William C. Wardlaw, mentioned Berry to him, and a new hope began inside him. "They'll have to take you, Gene," she assured the boy, and one day she drove him to the school.

For most of the day Berry officials shuttled the pair from department to department. "In their eyes I saw what they thought —they couldn't fit me in," he says. "And I could understand their viewpoint, in a way." To get him in and out of the buildings, other boys had to be called to lift him gently up and down the steps, and once or twice, because of his fright and embarrassment, his crutches slipped when he crossed the floors. At this place everybody had to work steadily, intensively, and how would that be possible for someone like Eugene Gunby? With each hour the youth's hopes dropped lower; he clung more tightly to his crutches, and the dull pain of the brace became worse.

But his friend Mrs. Wardlaw had a will of her own. She had first asked to see Martha, only to be told that the head of the school was busy with a dozen conferences. Realizing that Miss Berry had to pass down the front stairs when she left, Mrs. Wardlaw drove to that point, and they waited for a long time. At last Eugene heard tapping footsteps, "the steps of an alerted person, who knew just where she was going. I listened in fear and excitement, and I just don't recall breathing at the time."

Mrs. Wardlaw took Martha's arm. "Miss Berry, you may have heard about Gene Gunby, the crippled boy. I have him here."

Martha stiffened. "You should see the people you were told to see."

"We've seen them all."

Martha became still cooler. "If you did, that's the end of it."

Woman faced woman. "It isn't the end. Miss Berry, you're going to keep Gene here, or you'll have to keep him and me, too."

Suddenly Martha Berry threw back her head and laughed. "Bring him along." As she nodded to the boy, she gave him a quick look but said nothing. He hobbled after the two women, and onlookers carried him up to the office of Dr. Cook. After a few minutes of consultation with Dr. Cook, now the dean, Martha turned: "Eugene, you've had supper? Well, Doctor, see if you can find something for this boy to eat."

The crippled youth felt his heart beat faster than ever. Did that mean he could stay? It did. Mrs. Wardlaw gripped his hand, started to say something, and turned away. In his palm she left a good-by gift, a dollar bill, and Gene's new life was under way. Dr. Cook, a kind man, yet obviously uncertain about the whole matter, soon located a bed for Gene, and the boy took a pair of pajamas from the paper sack that held most of his possessions.

That night and through most of the next day Gene talked nervously at intervals to the students who clustered around him. Though they were friendly and interested in what would happen to him, his own spirits fell again. Staying on in the dormitory, he wondered if everybody had forgotten him. At 4 P.M. a car arrived, and a boy told him: "Miss Berry wants to see you." They picked him up and for an hour or so they rode around the campus.

Martha made no reference to Eugene's condition; instead she spoke of Berry, its work, the way assignments were handled. "You see that tree Eugene?" She went on to explain: "We plant and name them for people we're proud of." It was then that Eugene Gunby made up his mind: Someday he would have a tree with his name on it at Berry. A few minutes later Martha inquired: "Do you like the school? You do. Why?"

"Well, I've talked to the boys and I like their attitude."

"What's their attitude?" She was always asking such questions, the newcomer decided.

"Well, they're happy and good-humored, and they work hard to get things done."

Martha nodded, and the car rolled on in silence. "How are you going to get around here? It's a big campus, you know."

Gene faced her. "Where there's a will, there's a way, and I'll find it."

"I like *your* attitude, Eugene," she told him, and said nothing more on the subject. Her assistants discovered work that he could do, and he helped in the printing shop, in the library, and for a long time drove the horse and wagon for milk deliveries. Gene stayed at the reins while another boy jumped out to deposit the bottles. "I tried to make myself useful," he recalls, "and I think I did. I didn't play baseball or such things, and for that reason I sometimes might have worked a bit longer than some."

His fellow students fashioned a low cart with hand pedals; with his powerfully developed arm muscles he could move along at an easy clip. Sometimes the others pushed or pulled him from building to building. But when he walked too fast he frequently clattered to the ground, and, though Gene does not tell of it, his classmates remember that he had bad falls and other hard days. More and more, however, he moved about with the others, and they took him to their games, where he kept score or helped manage teams.

"It was wonderful to watch him sort of unfold," says one who worked close to Eugene Gunby. "He was a sharp boy, and we couldn't fool Gene about anything, even if any of us had wanted to. And nobody did. When he got sick at times, the whole boys' campus felt disturbed."

162

Eugene received frequent calls to ride with Martha Berry, "and apparently I found a way into her life." She gave him small assignments, extra duties, and talked with him for hours. She seldom spoke directly of his difficulties, "but I was surprised how much she seemed to know." One of the things she learned promptly was his class record; he finished five years of work in two years and a few months. When a mathematics expert gave tests to one of Gene's classes, the boy's instant mental calculations amazed the man.

At Oak Hill he made friends with Martha's mother, now growing feeble and not always in happy humor. With Aunt Marth he had a shattering first encounter. When he stood in the doorway on crutches, she scowled. "Boy, what you doin', hangin' aroun' here?" He started off, and was halted by her next words. "Where you goin'? Now don' you leave yit." She asked a few questions, received his answers, and nodded in satisfaction. A few minutes later the housekeeper handed him a paper bag with three ginger cakes, and Gene knew he was in. "She had a bad bark but she never once bit," he remembers. Years later, when Eugene made speeches or returned to address the students, Aunt Marth demanded that she be taken to hear him. "Gene Gunby got sense—more'n I kin say fer some 'round dere."

Eugene saw a happy Aunt Marth in the audience on the day Martha Berry presented him with his diploma. And another woman had a glowing pride in his achievement; she was Mrs. Wardlaw, who had faced Martha down to get the boy there. From Berry, Gene went to the University of Georgia and the Columbia Law School. In New York, however, the winters were too much for his health, and when his crutches slipped on ice and he broke one of his legs, he went back to Emory University in Georgia.

Eugene Gunby served with the Trust Company of Georgia and as a teacher in the Georgia Tech night school, then entered a law firm. About twelve years ago he was elected judge of the

Fulton County court, a position to which he has been re-elected several times since then. Repeatedly Judge Gunby has returned to the school to speak before students and guests. Martha had taken him against her better judgment, she said, only to discover how wrong she had been. And in time Gene Gunby achieved one of the things he wanted most in life—a tree with his name on the Berry campus.

CHAPTER X

SPINNING WHEEL
AT THE PLAZA

INEZ WOOTEN was one of eleven children of a farm family in southern Georgia. Six were younger than she, "and there never was time for me to play with dolls, because there was always a real baby to look after." Of necessity practically all of the family, including Grandma, worked the year round; the girls "made just about as good field hands as the boys."

Inez' earliest years were largely bound up in those younger children. By the time the girl reached six her mother felt it safe to leave her for a day to take care of the babies and to cook the family meal, which consisted usually of a pot of field peas, streak-ed meat, and corn pone. If she finished the churning in time Inez added a molasses cake. Often she dragged a chair to the old wood stove and stood on it to lift a potlid and stir the food.

In most cases Grandma prepared the churn and left it on the floor, so that Inez could stand beside it and lift the dasher up and down, pounding until the butter formed. Then the little girl had to wait until Grandma returned from the field to take up the creamy product. . . . The family of Eli Bryant Wooten, Inez' father, had owned land, only to lose it when Eli's father died before the boy reached thirteen; as the oldest child he had taken on a man's responsibilities.

Though Eli had spent only a few weeks in a country schoolhouse, he had struggled to teach himself to read and to handle figures. A good farmer, he had what some thought an overgenerous hand, with "messes of meat" as presents for all neighbors at hog-killing, long loans of plows and other equipment. Eventually, in his later years, he was to lose his own small acreage.

Inez remembered above all the kindnesses of her father, his lessons in behavior. As a child she muttered something uncomplimentary about an older acquaintance. The girl had her back to the door, and her father looked quickly toward it and called: "Come in, Miss Madge!" When Inez jumped as if lightning had hit Ty Ty Creek, he asked: "Now, do you know one nice thing to say about her?"

"Yes, plenty of 'em," the girl replied, and her father advised her: "Child, say only the things you'd say if she stood right here." Inez did not forget the lesson. Nor did she ever lose the wish for education that Eli planted in her. When she was five, hearing that a small school some miles away had opened for a few months, she decided to attend. As one of the family declared, if Inez made up her mind to a thing she generally did it. In this case the pert-faced, intent girl rose before daylight and walked to the school for the seven-thirty bell, crossing Rocky Creek by a foot-log.

Often the creek ran high, and parents and children feared the risky passage. Many used the danger as an excuse for missing class. A stick in her hand, tongue between her teeth, Inez always got across. Though she slipped occasionally and arrived with wet skirts, she never failed to reach school.

In her spare minutes the bright little girl took care of any sick or injured animals on the farm—a habit that was to alter her life. An early favorite was a small crippled chicken, wrapped in flour sacking during the winter and kept in a cardboard box behind the cookstove. In time "Crip" hopped everywhere after Inez, until one day when he heard her approach and jumped out to meet her. She did not see him in time to avoid stepping on him, and he died a few moments later.

Her next patient was a young black and white goat, which dogs had wounded in a night raid. The following morning the girl discovered it nearly dead, her throat ripped open. A new and larger box was placed behind the stove and, by virtue of much nursing, Sarah, the goat, survived, though she would always hold her head to one side.

Inez was growing up and watching steadily over the junior children. Toward her brother Clint she felt a particular affection. She helped him with his schoolwork, supervised his house chores, and advised him when, at ten, he began to tend his own small crop of corn and beans. And meanwhile she gave part of her attention to her third pet—Star, a red calf with a broken leg. Inez bound the leg with an old meal sack and brought grass and water to the injured animal. Eventually he hopped around on three legs, following her from yard to fence and back.

The girl had completed work in her country school, and one day she talked to a Berry graduate who told her of the school where she might work her way. Inez thought about the matter for a long time and wrote to the Berry school. Miss Lily, her first teacher, who conducted seven grades in one room, had spoken often of her hope that Inez might get further training, and her father and mother said they would be glad if she could find some way to manage it. Before long Berry officials replied to her letter, accepting her.

But how was she to get there? Had transportation required as little as a dollar, she would have lacked it. For weeks she tried to think of methods of raising the money, and not one occurred to her. Then unexpectedly a party of bank agents drove by and asked Inez about the farm. "I don't own it," she told them. "I don't own anything except this little old calf." With that she had her inspiration. Foolish as it might sound, she would ask, "Would you like to buy Star? I'll sell him for $9.60. That's what I need for my one-way ticket to the Berry schools at Rome, Georgia."

One of the men began to laugh, then stopped and stared. "You want to go real bad, don't you?"

When Inez said she sure did, he reached down and handed her a ten-dollar bill. As he rode away with Star in his wagon she called out: "You'll watch good after him, won't you?" The agent turned back. "I sure will." The extra forty cents, Inez told herself, would help her get started in school. A few days later she said good-by to her father and mother, young Clint, and the rest, and went off on her first train ride—her first trip of any kind out of her immediate neighborhood.

On an August afternoon of 1919 Inez Wooten paused as she entered the campus to watch sunburned girls in uniform going briskly past her, and boys in blue shirts and overalls. Ahead stood a white-pillared, red brick hall, set among tall trees and sweeping lawns. It was so peaceful, like nothing she had ever known, and Inez, a Bible student, thought of Scripture: "Put off thy shoes from off thy feet, for the place whereon thou standest is holy ground."

Next day the thin girl gazed—"my eyes popped out on stems" —as she stopped before Martha Berry's home at Oak Hill, with its wide porch and tall columns. Like others before and after her, Inez had been assigned to work there. The new arrival heard a quick, springing step, saw a face with a calm smile, and heard a light voice. "You've come to help, child?" A moment later Martha Berry directed her to the kitchen. "Aunt Marth will let you know what to do."

Inez expected to meet a favorite relative; instead she found the slightly stooped Negro in a long, old-fashioned dress with gingham apron and red kerchief over her head. Swinging around, Aunt Marth dropped her dishcloth: "Dey gits less sense at dat school ever' day dey lives! I sen' fer a girl to help wid de wuk—not somethin' scared ter deat' ter raise!" Aunt Marth's throaty voice conveyed complete disgust. "I bet you couldn' even fin' de broom."

Inez trembled. "No, but if you will please show me where, I'll try to remember."

Softening slightly, Aunt Marth led her away. "Well, seein' you's willin' ter learn . . ." With each step, however, she mumbled. "Dey don' know straight up. Don' know sooey!"

Thus began Inez Wooten's decades of connection with the Berry schools and her friendship with the two Marthas. A day later she went to her first chapel and saw Miss Berry in action. Not yet in uniform, Inez marched close to the end of the long lines of students. She rose with the rest when Martha and the faculty walked up the center aisle. Stretching to make out the small figure in gray suit with white blouse in the boxlike fashion of the day, Inez saw another smile but also thought she detected a certain anxiety. Within a few minutes Martha Berry confirmed her impression.

Moving to the front of the platform, Martha extended a greeting to them all, and then said she had to tell them of a serious disappointment. A few minutes earlier she had noticed that six small trees on the chapel hill had been broken down; the boy who tended the cows had neglected to close the gates. She was grieved because of the loss, but also "because the boy was careless and others of you may have been careless too. Though some must have seen the cows out there, you didn't investigate since it wasn't your responsibility."

The silence deepening, Martha continued: "Years ago I picked those trees and had them planted so that you and thousands like you could benefit by looking at them. I dreamed that one day I'd be put to rest beside them, where the boys and girls would march and sing and pray."

169

Her listeners sat with lowered eyes, but still Martha spoke of the six trees. "I want this opening day to teach us something. Everything we have here has been given us because friends believed in us. Berry is ours in trust. Won't you help to make and keep it beautiful and pass it on in the same way to those that come after us?"

The light eyes moved over her audience from older students to Inez, the newest recruit. "I wouldn't want to find that any of you had marked a hymnbook. I'd feel sad if any boy cut even a small gash in a pew. No matter what your department is, take an interest in all departments; if you see something that needs attention, investigate. Protect our property and protect our name." Inez Wooten promised herself that she would do that, and as she glanced around she sensed that the others were promising the same thing.

For Inez the next few years were hard, crowded, often exciting, and wherever she looked she met something new. "After all, most anything would have been new to someone like me." She discovered teachers and fellow students who had been to towns and cities, who knew words and had had experiences as foreign to her as those of the Orient. She did algebra and hand weaving; she learned English and gardening, advanced composition, science, and proper bedmaking.

Inez wrote home to tell the family of the world that was widening around her. Her father's health declined, and the Wootens could still provide little or no money. The extra forty cents she had brought with her went more quickly than she anticipated, and she did extra work to accumulate nickels and dimes for expenses. Someday, she told herself, she would be able to send something to the family. With Mr. Wooten's illness, young Clint had taken over part of the farm work; in particular she hoped to help Clint.

Martha Berry complimented Inez on her improvement in manner and speech; the students all learned that Martha considered such matters vital ones. She did not often correct a girl,

170

but a quick look told how she felt, "and she didn't like to look very often." Approving of Inez' assistance at Oak Hill, Martha thought of other assignments for her.

"You work hard, child, and you have what's just as important, an imagination and a touch of humor," she told her. "None of that hurt anybody yet. Let's use it all." One day she informed Inez: "You're going to learn to type right away." The girl had no time to ask what this meant; Miss Berry had already planned the details. An experienced typist at the office stood ready to instruct her, and Martha propelled Inez toward the next room.

Daily thereafter Inez concentrated upon the typewriter. Martha had a machine sent to the girl's room, and there Inez worked red-eyed beyond the usual retiring time. A bit later Martha gave her a "three-week vacation"—to study shorthand. After that Inez attended two chapel sessions a week, took down everything and transcribed it, "for practice." Practice for what? Martha did not say, and Inez did not inquire.

Some months later Martha had gone to New York on a fund-raising expedition, and Inez knew her plans only in a general way. Miss Berry was staying at the Plaza Hotel, a name which even the Berry girls realized meant a high point in splendor.

One Sunday evening Inez was sitting in the chapel balcony when Gordon Keown tiptoed in, a yellow sheet in his hand. "She's telegraphed for you to go to New York on the next train, with the spinning wheel."

Inez' mouth fell open. "What can I do up there with a spinning wheel?"

Keown answered laconically. "Fill up space if you can't do anything else. She's got an exhibit of our weaving at some art center, and she must have more room than she has exhibit." Keown and two teachers consulted as Inez packed, contributed coats and other extra garments, gave her a ticket and a few dollars and also assorted advice. In the morning, panic-stricken, with the spinning wheel at her side, she set out on the great adventure. She had to change trains in Atlanta and again in Washington, and she was still asking how to do it when her coach pulled out of Rome.

After several near catastrophes Inez reached Pennsylvania Station in New York. All the people in the city must be in that station; surely she would find Mrs. Hammond or one or the other of the five or six New Yorkers she had met at the school. Then a hand gripped her arm: "Little girl, do you know where you're going?"

The eyes of the Travelers' Aid representative had taken in the spinning wheel, Inez' "country" air, and other pertinent details. The "little girl" of sixteen tried to appear poised and efficient. "Oh yes, I'm to join Miss Martha Berry at the Plaza Hotel." The stranger was unimpressed: "She expects you? I'll telephone her and see."

"Please, she's busy and you mustn't disturb . . ." Already the agent had given the number to the operator. A few minutes later she reported, with a doubtful frown, that Miss Berry thought Inez fully capable of getting to the hotel. With a look of vindication the girl left. In the lobby of the Plaza—where she became possibly the first guest to arrive with a spinning wheel—she walked anxiously to the clerk's desk and followed the bellboy for her first ride in an elevator.

Round-eyed, still breathless from this last experience, she knocked on a door and heard the longed-for, familiar voice. "Is that you, Inez?" The girl drawled: "I'm not sure, but if you'll open the door we can see." Martha threw her arms around Inez and explained the schedule ahead of them. The girl was to be part of the exhibit and also help Martha with her correspondence.

That day Inez, in mountain costume with bonnet and apron, sat on a platform and spent the first of many hours in being a highlander before thousands of New Yorkers. People pointed, put questions she considered foolish and sometimes laughed heartily for reasons she could not understand. Inez kept her eyes open and enjoyed everything, or nearly everything.

Martha herself was seldom away. To all who came up she explained the spinning, told about mountain weaving and also about the Berry schools in general. (By this time the schools were generally referred to in the plural.) "Nobody got away without learning something of our work," said Inez. Martha handed out pamphlets, descriptive data, blanks for contributions. This was a new life, and a new Miss Berry.

As Inez sat there she received a flood of whispered directions: Tell them this. Remember that. Let them know about the girl who . . . the boy that . . . "And smile, child, smile. You have a nice smile, so use it." One day a dark, Latin gentleman looked musingly at Inez' garb and told her: "You remind me so much of my grandmother!" Before the girl could decide how to respond to this doubtful compliment, Martha recognized the speaker as Martinelli, the opera singer.

In the spirited exchange that followed the pungently accented Martinelli announced gaily that Inez spoke a more peculiar English than he did. She flushed, but she had already discovered that most New Yorkers could comprehend only half of the things she said, and she had equal difficulty with their speech. "When they said something, I asked what," Inez explained. "When I opened my mouth they just grinned." One hotel attendant inquired: "What land you come from, honey?"

The girl had had scant experience in telephoning, and to Northerners on the line her Georgia voice proved unintelligible. Once, when Martha asked her to get someone by phone, she stood for several minutes trying to make herself understood. "I got so embarrassed I wanted to throw the thing out of the window."

With that Martha led her by the hand to friends the older woman had made in the hotel telephone exchange. While Inez writhed, Martha conferred over the problem. "Miss Wright, you have such a charming voice. Would you allow Inez to sit

173

and listen for a while? I must have someone to give my numbers clearly, you know." Patting Inez, she walked away.

The girl sensed the operators' amusement as they pronounced the words: "*But-ter-field*, not *Buddahfeel*, sweetie . . . Four, ni-un, fif-teen . . . And speak up, don't swallow it." With thanks and a red face, Inez left after her lesson. From then on she had less difficulty, and she received a reward when, passing through the lobby with her, Miss Berry stopped to tell Miss Wright: "My dear, you've been so good that she can say them all. Say them for Miss Wright, Inez."

Most of the staff appeared to know who Martha was and what she did; she talked to everybody, and sooner or later they heard all about the Berry schools. But the girl was not prepared for the way Martha took over the Plaza dining room. Aunt Marth had sent a tin of brown biscuits, and the students had added several jars of jelly. One morning Martha gathered the gifts and ordered a light breakfast of coffee and toast. Then she opened Aunt Marth's box.

"Could I have my little biscuits warmed in the kitchen?" she asked. Country girl though she was, Inez suspected that few Plaza guests did that. But the waiter, well charmed, agreed at once, and other attendants moved closer to watch. Cheerfully Martha continued: "You see, the people at my schools prepare these especially, and they're the best in the country."

Men and women at three or four other tables were listening, and Martha included them in her conversation. Her voice rose clearly: "The Berry schools, you know, down in Georgia, where we give work and education to the mountain boys and girls. We make this jelly—oh, very fine jelly. Ah, here are the biscuits, and beautifully warmed, too, thank you."

Lifting the napkin, Martha called for extra plates, put biscuits on them, added helpings of jelly, and instructed the waiters: "Do pass them around." She addressed the next table: "Wouldn't you like to try them? And here are some for you, too, sir." Then she went on gaily about Berry and its program.

174

Inez sampled biscuits and jelly. While they were good, she had had better at the school. By now, however, Martha had built up her products so well that the other guests were nodding and complimenting her. "Best I ever had. . . ." "What's the name of that school?" That gave Martha the cue for which she had been waiting. "Inez, take some of our pamphlets around. And you might get that kind gentleman's card if he has it. We sometimes have a large supply of jelly and send it to our friends."

By the time the two women left the room Berry dominated the tables, guests smiled, and waiters beamed. For once the Plaza had a real folksy air. On their way out Martha dropped off a gift for the manager, a gentleman who, Inez surmised, seldom received jelly from those he accommodated. Inez took several cards, and months later the jelly was making more friends for Berry.

Yet there were moments when Inez wondered why Miss Berry did not send her home on the next train. To the little Georgian, New York was a mad, rushing place. She stared when she first saw people come "boiling up" from the ground. Informed that they were taking subway trains to save time, she replied that it was foolish to be in that much of a hurry. Martha, however, loved subways, and pushed Inez down the steps before her. "What do you really think of New York?" she once demanded, and chuckled at the girl's response: "It has too many people and not enough folks."

When Mrs. Hammond asked Martha to Sunday dinner, Inez was included. The novice kept a wary eye on the forks, followed the lead of Mrs. Hammond, and survived. On the way back to the hotel Martha complimented her. "I was very proud. But why did you go all around the room to put down your coffee cup?" Inez explained that she had been overwhelmed by Mr. Hammond's hunting trophies. "I didn't want to step on those beautiful white animal pieces and their fine eyes and teeth, and the only way was to walk along the wall."

175

When the Berry exhibit closed, Inez' work seemed only to increase. Every few hours she received new assignments to hunt addresses, locate correspondence, carry messages. For the first time she perceived the full range of Martha's friendships and connections. Each day meant new contacts, meetings, renewals of previous acquaintances. The size of Martha's correspondence was astonishing; no less astonishing was the way she thought about each person and his interest before she wrote him.

When she sent letters without a secretary, Martha tended to the telegraphic style. Messages to the staff consisted of choppy sentences, phrases, and isolated words, separated by commas and hyphens. "Until you got used to them, they made very little sense," a faculty member declared. "When you did, she sometimes dashed off cards in such a rush that you still needed help in translation." Her personal notes are generally disappointing to those who seek distinguished writing or personal revelations, for Martha's gift for eloquence did not extend to her pen.

Now, however, Inez Wooten was learning to put Martha Berry's messages on paper. The girl bent over a pad, and Martha walked up and down the room, tossing off directions, pausing in the middle of a letter as she recalled something else, getting back to the letter, and going on to another subject. At first everything appeared disorganized, hopelessly confused, so that Inez closed her eyes and thought of dying. Then she learned to take a deep breath and go ahead, and finally it all made sense.

Though Martha's mind jumped from topic to topic, it seldom lost track of main themes or basic lines of work. When Inez reminded her of a suspended thought, she would wave her hand. "Child, I'm still working on that. We'll get to it sometime." She dictated in a sort of shorthand: "Oh, you'll know to finish." Or: "Say something about how bad things are going." Inez would cogitate, improvise, use words she thought her superior would use. While she generally succeeded, she received an occasional stinging comment. "Child, this letter isn't fit to send to a cat." That brought improvement!

Inez found that Martha Berry had a sharp eye and ear for names, identifications, connections. If she did not catch a name she asked it again and committed it to paper. Inez discovered that she must acquire this same facility. Martha's whispered directions were specific: "My dear, make sure you know where she lives." "Get both their addresses—any way you can." For the country girl these attempts were agonizing. How could she speak to these glossy people in the effortless way that Martha managed when they had to ask three times what she was trying to say?

Still worse were the times when Martha drew her aside. "Inez, I have to take these people away. But Mrs. Burr over there—she can help us a great deal, and you must get her interested in the school." Such a command tended to turn the tiny Georgian into "a bowl of clabber." Nevertheless Inez did it, haltingly, fumblingly, and yet she managed, "because I had to manage." That, she concluded, was one of Martha Berry's arts: "You rose to the occasion because she wanted you, willed you, to it."

Meanwhile the secretarial work, usually at night, grew even heavier. After they had worked for hours Martha would retire to her adjoining room, with the door open between them. For more hours Inez typed as Martha sat up in bed, scratching out rough notes—a name, a phrase—and throwing them to the floor. Eventually Martha would turn out her light, but Inez would type on until 2 A.M., then go to bed.

At times Martha would toss restlessly, still wrestling with her uncertainties. Then she might suddenly develop a new idea, a different approach to a dilemma and jump out of bed: "Child, child, let's go to work." Wearily Inez would crawl forth, to see that it was almost 3:30 A.M. She would make no protest, no complaint, for Martha could shame her with a soft reproof.

177

After all, wasn't it for the schools . . . ? It might be 4 A.M. before they finished, and Martha would turn to her with a happy sigh: "Now, Inez, we will go to bed and get a good night's sleep." At eight they would be up again for a hard day's work.

One day a friend urged Martha to seek out a certain philanthropist. What to say to him? That night, while Inez pored over other letters, she stood at the window or moved restlessly about her room. The going was hard. . . . At last her face calmed. "Inez, the thing to do is pray the Lord will guide us."

After some experience Inez understood just what that meant. Shifting her typewriter close to her bed, she put pad and pencil on the table beside her. At 3 A.M., just as Inez dozed, she heard the familiar voice: "My dear, we can get up and write the letter. The Lord has answered."

The girl jumped to her feet in an instant, and twenty minutes later the letter lay ready for Martha's signature. "Now, child, we must lose no more time." Throwing on her coat, Inez peeped into the hall and carried the message to the mail chute. On her return Martha greeted her with a look of satisfaction and the inevitable comment: "And now, Inez, we will get a fine night's sleep." In this case the Lord's answer had been a good one. Before they left New York the philanthropist sent for Martha, and she emerged with a contribution that made her happy for weeks.

On their way home Inez had a few shocking lessons in living costs outside of Berry. At Hot Springs, Virginia, the girl protested when an attendant told her the room rate. "For one night? It's robbery." Embarrassed, Martha laughed off the subject. But Inez, knowing that Miss Berry herself paid all the traveling expenses, declined to go to the dining room for the evening meal. Instead she walked two miles to the dark village, bought bread and two slabs of cheese, and returned with them. Martha joined her for the supper.

The next day they took a long mountain drive, and Martha

heard her name called. It was William G. McAdoo, Woodrow Wilson's son-in-law, the guiding spirit of the Hudson tunnel. (McAdoo once declared that he would rather have built the Berry schools than the tunnel itself.) The McAdoos took Martha and Inez to lunch at an excellent restaurant, and Martha advised her protégée: "Inez, eat as much as you can. Our friends are giving us this treat." With a smile she told the story of their bread and cheese of the previous evening.

When she and Inez left the resort the McAdoos caught the same train, a sparsely equipped local. To the surprise of all passengers, it halted for a long stop and a waiter walked through, crying: "First call for lunch." McAdoo got up. "Miss Berry, I wanted to see that you and Miss Wooten didn't leave hungry this time." He had arranged for a special dining car, and later Inez watched him hand the attendant a bill, the first $100 one she had ever beheld.

From such luxury they returned to the simplicity of Berry, and Inez settled into her new role, that of part-time secretary, general helper, and student. It meant an effort such as she had never known. Though Martha continued to use her regular office secretary, Inez worked with her in her home and also on her many trips. Daily, as she rode around the campus with her superior, she would jot down notes, take instructions as they occurred to Martha, and carry them out when she left the car.

At times she gasped with the load of duties, and Martha patted her. "Child, when I'm interested in someone I make a special effort to put him in a hard place. Struggles strengthen character, you know. Maybe you think I'm a little demanding, but remember, I'm interested in your future." A moment later she smiled. "And also in what you can do for our schools."

Most of Inez' extra money went home and, as pennies for postage became more plentiful, she wrote the Wootens of her exciting life, with notes and postal cards from all the places she visited. Whenever she made long trips with Martha she picked

179

up colored cards, and her brother Clint received dozens of these pictures of the outer world.

While she said nothing to anyone, Inez had begun to plan to bring Clint to the schools. He would make a name for himself and for the family, she was sure. The bright youth had shown a marked liking for books; regularly she passed hers on to him. Replying to her notes, the boy continually asked what things were like at Berry. What were the students doing at this season, and how was the dairy? By now she had made up her mind that Clint had to come here without delay.

As vacation approached, Inez told herself it would be a different and happier summer for the Wootens. She wrapped small gifts for each member. Clint would get a new picture book "for himself," the first he had ever owned. Then, just before midnight one evening, Inez felt a tap on her shoulder. There was a long-distance call for her. Her older brother spoke in a muffled voice: Clint had died a few hours earlier.

Back in her room Inez stared at the brightly colored picture book, and pulled out her belongings to pack. No train left for southern Georgia until morning; it arrived in Rome four hours late, and then down the line was sidetracked for hours longer. When Inez got home she met the family on their return from the country graveyard. They had given up hope that she would be there in time. On a table beside the boy's bed Inez picked up a shoe box, which held every card and letter that she had sent Clint. Toward the end, her mother told her, the boy had taken them out and talked about her and those great places he had never seen. . . . The next few weeks were indeed different for Inez and the Wootens.

Twice during the following year Inez went home to be with her sick father. Once he asked her to think hard; could she remember a time when he had treated her badly? She could not. Again she recalled the early lesson by which he taught her never to speak harshly of others. More than anyone she knew, her father had lived up to his own rule.

As death came near, Eli Wooten talked to Inez of his hope that some of the younger Wootens might have the same chance for an education that she had received. Would she ask Miss Berry? At Berry, Inez went to her older friend, who assured her she would help. For the next twelve years there would always be a Wooten brother or sister at Berry. Inez stayed on, and her own life centered there. For a long time she kept near her a memento of the great transition—the spinning wheel that she took to the Plaza.

CHAPTER XI

ALL ROADS LED TO ROME,
GEORGIA

FOR THE NEXT eight or ten years, as Inez Wooten remembers, she "always seemed to be studying something extra, taking a course of one kind or another." Her work as Martha Berry's secretary brought her much closer to her superior, and every few weeks Martha found something that Inez should learn for her own good and for Berry's.

At times it appeared to the onetime farm girl that she was enrolled in practically every subject in the schools' curriculums. After she received her diploma she continued post-graduate studies at Berry, and then Martha sent her off to summer schools, to Chautauqua in New York, to New York University, to conferences and institutes. "Whenever she spied a spare minute or a spare part of me, she enrolled me in something to fill it," Inez recalls.

Anyone who worked near Martha Berry, Inez concluded, needed to keep at hand a good pair of walking shoes (track shoes would be even better, she sometimes thought), paper, pencil, and, not least, his wits. Passing a line of campus trees, Martha evolved a project and dictated a letter on the spot. Meeting Inez in the hall, she would have a burst of creative energy and fire out a memorandum and two letters. On the porch outside, a chance word or a name would spur her to more messages. After she had filled pages of notes, the girl would race upstairs and translate them into action.

When they entertained a guest who might help the schools, Inez stood nearby, pencil inconspicuously available for instant use. "You mentioned a Mr. Gordon, who has an interest in contracting," Martha would say. "Where does he live in New York State?" Or: "Are there others in your city with the same connections?" Once Inez neglected to take down some such fact, and that night Martha told her graphically what her error might mean. "My dear, that could have been the man who would keep us some day from bankruptcy. You do understand?"

Her secretary understood. Martha, she had decided, was alert during every waking minute "and expected you to be that way too." For Martha Berry, all roads led to Rome, Georgia, and on to her schools. For her associates the rule must be the same. Very early Inez had discovered her device for drawing from almost anyone she met some fact, some viewpoint, some information to help the schools. "Practically everybody's an expert in something." An architect would be taken over the grounds, shown each building, asked for suggestions. An authority on foods would see menus, stoves, storage places, bookkeeping methods.

When an important visitor planned a call, Martha prepared for him. If his field were dairies, she talked to her dairy officials, read up on the subject, organized a supper circle with that in mind. For all of his stay the order would be: Push dairies. The staff members were to speak frankly, answer all questions; they were also to ask him for information—trends in the field, new construction methods, improved care for animals.

183

"Thinking back, I realize she was always asking somebody's advice about something," a staff member observes. "As she said, if she got ten suggestions, at least two or three of them would be good or better." Ultimately Martha would make up her mind; meanwhile she heard everything she could on the subject. "Learn to listen. Listening can be far better than talking," she maintained. Sometimes she received recommendations she already had, or had even put into effect; nevertheless she responded with enthusiasm. "Thank you, that sounds wonderful." "Thank you for telling us; you're so kind to help." To her faculty she explained: "If you ask a question and then say you already know what the other person tells you, he's naturally let down. Keep your ears open, and he'll nearly always give you something new."

Out of years of reading, travel, and a great range of interests, Martha accumulated knowledge on many subjects. She loved conversation, and she enjoyed meeting strangers. It was not long before she found a common denominator with almost anyone she encountered. She smiled and charmed strangers, yet her wise eyes missed nothing, and she seldom failed to use whatever she saw to advance her program.

A businessman said that as he first shook Martha's hand he felt certain she was "simply a delightful woman, very feminine, and very much in need of help." Ten minutes later he decided that he had come into contact with one of the keenest minds he had ever known. "A half hour afterward I had committed myself as I never intended, and I was enjoying the whole thing." He could never discover how she worked her magic, except that she was a master of the right word, the perfect phrase. "She made me feel this was the most important thing in the world, that I had happened along at just the moment to accomplish the great deed. After that the spell never quite went away."

A Southerner whom Martha brought to membership on her board about this time remembers the experience. "When I first met her at a hospital, where both of us were under checkup, I'd barely heard of her school. That morning we got into conversation, and at once I saw how intelligent she was. But only gradually did I find quite *how* intelligent she could be, and how persistent in getting what she went after."

On his return to his home the manufacturer learned that Martha Berry wanted him as one of her trustees. "Had I been foresighted I would have reconciled myself to joining it then and there." For two years, however, he resisted, and with a great many arguments: He had no time for extra duties; his home was too far from the schools; he planned to be away for months. None of these reasons mattered, as she had counterarguments for each. Martha sent Inez Wooten six times as an emissary, and she wrote a series of letters, casual or earnest or in-between in mood. She forwarded clippings on subjects of interest to his business; his wife was drawn in, his advice sought. "I understood what it was like to be wooed, and by a master of the art," he says with a grin.

Then one night the manufacturer went to a dinner at Berry, and was surrounded by staff members whose conversation fascinated him. How intelligent they were, how well informed. . . . All at once he sensed that they had been selected and selected well for the occasion. Martha Berry sat in command, and everyone spoke as she wanted him to speak. "She was like an organist at the keyboard; when she touched the key she got exactly what she wanted. She got me, and I never regretted it." He remained on the board long after her death.

Might this have been considered too calculated? Few people thought so, it would appear. As William McChesney Martin, Jr., chairman of the Federal Reserve Board in Washington and in time head of her trustees, put the matter: "She carried it off practically every time, and she did so because her motives were good. Had that not been so, had she worked for anything except the complete interests of her schools, she might have failed. Her conviction came through. If she used art in her

185

preparation, it was good art. You might shake your head eventually in amusement or astonishment; you never ceased to respect what she had done."

As still another board member declared: "Martha Berry was the most—well, the most concentrated person I've ever met, but, as odd as it may seem, in a relaxed way. She found what meant something to you, and she related it to the schools. She understood the appeals to pride, to a sense of work well done, to idealism and sentiment. She could enter a conversation on any topic—medical science, the prospects of war, the Dionne quintuplets, the raising of hound dogs. And eventually she got the talk around to her schools, adroitly, firmly. Then if she saw that the man or woman wasn't really intrigued, that was it. She wasted no more time!"

Meanwhile Inez was learning more about Martha's methods of producing good performances. Miss Berry warmly praised the staff members to each other: "That girl can get the quickest results with a little talk." "Nobody handles a meal better than Alice." Wryly Inez had recalled some of Martha's pointed remarks about the skill of the office secretary in handling telephone messages. The wryness vanished the day Inez heard Martha tell a newcomer: "You must learn to handle the telephone; just listen to Inez and see how well she does it." Inez had arrived!

When Martha wanted something done, she assumed it could be done. One day she telephoned Harvey Roberts of the school staff about a letter that had to be written in an emergency. "Harvey," she asked, "can you take dictation?"

"No, Miss Berry, I sure can't."

"Well, take this letter." Finishing the long telephone message, she ordered: "Get it off in the next mail," and hung up before Harvey could protest. He got it off.

In her office Martha spoke with cheerful frankness, as in the case when she asked a staff member: "That visitor today—did he give us a scholarship?"

"I'm afraid not," answered the assistant who had shown the stranger around.

Martha smiled. "Don't you know I want to get a scholarship out of everybody who comes?"

"Miss Berry, you can't always do that."

Calmly she proceeded with her inquiries. "Then did you find some good names of other people?"

"I'm afraid I didn't."

"Anybody can do anything he tries." That was always one of her favorite beliefs, and she sighed. "Ah, John. You're so Southern you'll never make a good beggar."

Willie Sue Sullivan, supervisor of handicrafts in the girls' school, was another staff member who found that Martha indeed believed that anybody could do anything. At Oak Hill was a small, subtly colored Aubusson rug, treasured by Mrs. Berry. It would be wonderful, Martha announced, to copy it in the weaving room. In great detail Willie Sue explained differences of technique, the impossibility of copying an Aubusson on their looms, but Martha ignored all objections. Of course Willie Sue could do it, and think what a showpiece it would be for their exhibits. Willie Sue did it; it took a great deal of experiment, and 900 hours of work, but there it was at last, almost indistinguishable from the original, the time-faded colors perfectly matched.

At times Martha announced that the school would take anything presented to it, "from a set of false teeth to a four-legged white elephant," and make use of it. While she never received these precise items, she did get almost everything else.

Once she had an offer of free manure from a government camp. Much of the campus grounds needed enrichment, and she accepted—fifty full carloads. "We could hardly live here," one of the staff said in recollection of the pungent weeks that followed. "She laughed and told us that good could come out of anything, especially manure. We lived to see the fine result."

Not long afterward a well-meaning friend presented Martha with a shiny black limousine, too big for her purposes and also a heavy consumer of gasoline. She made a series of calls and sold the thing to someone who required it "only for short trips" —a local undertaker.

For years she had received donations from R. Fulton Cutting, the Wall Street broker who had given her that first check of $500. One day unexpected word arrived that the elderly man had decided to visit the school. Uneasily Martha reflected that Mr. Cutting lived in an environment very different from Berry's. She arranged books, informed staff members of Mr. Cutting's interests, and made certain that noises were kept to a minimum.

The visit went well enough. Mr. Cutting saw everything, nodded approval—and then stunned her with an announcement. "Miss Berry, for fifty years I've dressed for dinner, and I'll feel more comfortable if I can do it tonight." She reassured him and looked up Alice Barnes, supervisor of the "practice cottage" meals. "String out the supper to make it look like a dinner. Add soup and serve things in courses if you can. And, oh yes, light candles and brighten the place any way you can manage."

Then Martha went out to her early-model automobile. "Charlie, drive fast." In a moment she was speaking hurriedly to the school nurse, an Englishwoman who had received several war decorations. "Miss Beverly, you must be at dinner tonight in your black velvet gown with all your medals." Miss Beverly stared. "I haven't unpacked it this year—haven't needed it here, you know. And the medals are at the bottom of a trunk. Well, I'll do my best."

On her way again Martha thought of Dean Cook. He came from Richmond, and of course he'd have a dinner jacket. Dr. Cook disappointed her by telling her he had left it at his sister's house in Virginia. "But somebody's got to keep Mr. Cutting company," she groaned. A moment later she remembered that last week a Philadelphia church guild had sent a box of used clothes, and she had seen a dress suit among other items. "It will come nearer fitting you than any man we have," she said happily.

Whatever Dr. Cook thought about wearing such hand-me-downs, she took him to the school store, where the clothes were on sale at very low rates to the students. Luckily no Berry boy had discovered a need for a formal suit, and they arranged for a hasty pressing of the costume. Meanwhile Inez received a message: "Wear that blue floor-length dress you take on your trips." Martha herself got out her black lace dinner dress; though "weak in spots" like some of her others, it retained semblances of elegance.

When all of them gathered in the softly lighted dining room, Dr. Cook took care to sit down slowly in order to protect the seat of his tight trousers, but no one noticed that or other problems. Miss Beverly brought along phonograph records of proper dinner music, and everything went as smoothly as if dressing for dinner were a nightly custom in rural Georgia.

The years saw the departure of old friends, the coming of new ones. Martha wrote a careful note to Adolph Ochs, the generous-spirited publisher of the New York *Times*. Receiving her, he listened intently, invited her and Inez to a luncheon, and ended by saying he hoped to inspect her schools someday. Like Andrew Carnegie, he was a man who would want to know a great deal before he acted. As they left they could only wonder if anything would come of their encounter.

Months passed, and then one day Dr. Leland Green darted upstairs to whisper: "Mr. Ochs of the *Times* is signing the visitors' register." Martha fired out instructions: "Bring him right up." "Inez, take the wrappers off those *Times*', and spread them all over the big table." "Phone the guest cottage and say

189

we'll be there in a half hour, and we want a real dinner." When Mr. Ochs entered, his eyes caught sight of the papers and he murmured with a wise smile: "A smart woman." As if she had expected him for weeks, Martha started out with him.

Her efforts were a success to the extent of a $100,000 endowment. The more he learned, the more impressed Adolph Ochs became. Some Georgians, he concluded, knew less about Martha Berry's work than did people of other sections. He started a drive which tapped thousands of new sources in this area. For a time he also planned an endowment campaign outside the state, until he and Martha decided reluctantly that such an effort would conflict with her annual campaigns for regular operating funds; and meanwhile the schools must continue to run. . . . Nevertheless the New York publisher remained an alert and active friend of the Berry movement.

About the same time the friendship of a wealthy woman and a comparatively poor one produced one of the schools' best buildings. An invalid, the wealthy Mrs. Walter Ladd of New Jersey, had heard of Martha's work and, wondering about it, decided to see for herself. Though she spent most of her time in a wheel chair, she set out with her nurse-companion, the young Miss Alice Lemley.

While waiting in Atlanta for the connecting train, Mrs. Ladd was taken past a well-known candy store. Stopping, she put in a telephone call to the schools: How many students did Miss Berry have? Soon afterward Mrs. Ladd asked for the store manager and explained: She would leave in a few hours for Rome and wondered if she could have a box of candy for each student—about 800 of them?

After a few minutes of puzzled consultation the manager closed his shop and put all his force to work to fill the boxes. Late that evening Mrs. Ladd and Miss Lemley, the nurse, arrived at the schools. In the morning the delicate woman visited a few buildings but soon had to retire to her room, while Miss

Lemley went around the rest of the campus with Inez and others. After a time, when Mrs. Ladd gave the boxes, the students thanked her so courteously, she said she made up her mind to send them all candy thereafter for Christmas.

Meanwhile the nurse returned from her tour in a glow. "I saw so much, so many things I'd never imagined," she told Mrs. Ladd. Alone with her patient in the quiet guest room, Miss Lemley asked Mrs. Ladd a question, and went to Martha Berry herself. "I haven't much money," she said, "but I'm a good hand with a needle. Some of Mrs. Ladd's friends have told me they like my work. From now on I'll try to sell it and send the money to you down here."

Martha was much pleased, though she wondered if it would be possible for the young woman to earn a great deal in that way. From then on, however, the nurse regularly contributed her earnings, and they reached, in all, more than $2500— enough to give full schooling to a large number of highlanders.

One day news came from New Jersey that the strong young woman had caught pneumonia and died, leaving behind her invalid patient. When executors opened Miss Lemley's will they discovered she had left much of her small estate to the schools. Mrs. Ladd had been saddened by the death of the girl who had given her such loving care; now she was touched by the generous act. In the name of her nurse, the older woman gave the schools Alice Lemley Hall.

A chapel was needed at the remote Mountain School for boys and overage men. The schools were like a growing child, Martha said. When she provided a pair of shoes to fit, it had outgrown its coat; by the time she had that, it needed larger trousers. As the Mountain School students hunched awkwardly over chairs in their church room, she decided they could scarcely worship well under such conditions. One day she set out on the lawn a small white wooden cross with black lettering:

191

CHAPEL WANTED

For months the cross remained there unnoticed. Martha was feeling discouraged when a letter arrived from Los Angeles, from a man who had been reading of her schools and wanted more information. The signature, Howard Frost, was new to her; in her reply she invited him, as she often did in such cases, to visit whenever he found himself nearby.

A month or so afterward, on a sullen spring morning, the telephone rang. It was floodtime, and Rome's three rivers lapped at their banks. The speaker gave the name of Howard Frost; he had hoped to get to Berry, but the people in Chattanooga insisted he could not reach the schools. "They say you're cut off from the world."

"Not quite," Martha told him. "Give me the name of your hotel and stay there just two hours." In a dubious voice Mr. Frost promised to wait with his wife. Martha sped across the campus to challenge Tracy Byers, an adventurous new staff member. He enjoyed traveling through the back country, and she assured him it was just possible to make his way to the Tennessee city if he took side roads and out-of-the-way trails. A few consultations with boys from the area, an extra supply of gas, and Tracy chugged off.

The two-hour limit had barely passed when Berry's emissary entered the Chattanooga hotel lobby. The astonished Frosts jumped into the machine; by midafternoon Martha received a signal that the car had returned, and she went out to meet her guests. For hours the middle-aged couple explored the campus, absorbing everything.

Toward evening, when they made motions to leave, Martha asked: "Why don't you stay and see the rest?" From the school store they obtained a razor, toothbrushes, and other supplies; faculty members loaned a nightgown and a pair of pajamas. Martha listened carefully to the Frosts. There was something, a certain pensiveness in their manner, the way they looked at the boys, that touched her and made her speculate to herself.

The next day the two callers appeared particularly interested in the older students, and Martha concentrated on the Mountain School area. It was Sunday, and the guests stood silently beside her as the boys marched, sang, and prayed. After services the couple told Martha that they had lost their only son when he was about the age of these youths. "Hadn't you guessed it was something like that?" Mr. Frost asked.

"I had," she answered.

The Californian continued: For a long time he and his wife had considered a memorial to the boy, and perhaps a chapel would be a good thought. At this point Martha realized that she must press for nothing; instead she smiled. "Let's look at a few more things you've missed." She pointed out the way many of the buildings were placed in the Mountain School section, each on a separate hill, dominating its surroundings.

As she perhaps intended, the couple discovered a certain spot that intrigued them. The elevation had a great deal to offer, except that there was one serious drawback. It was much too flat on one side and too steep on the other. "Don't mind a thing like that." Martha gestured. "We can take the part that's too high and put it over where it's too low." Howard Frost shook his head in admiration. "The Bible tells us if we have faith we can move mountains, and I think *you* could do it."

So the Mountain School was going to get its chapel. A little later the Frosts wrote to ask if the building could be finished by the next spring, when they would like to attend the dedication. Martha sent a prompt promise to that effect, and the boys started energetically to put up the structure. By midsummer work was up to schedule, so that the following April would find everything in order. Suddenly a telegram declared that Mr. and Mrs. Frost expected to pass through Rome in early fall and would like to dedicate the building then; they would bring their minister and arrive in mid-October.

In her office, as her associates remember that burning day, Martha sat briefly fingering the message. Then she rang one electric bell after another, for Inez Wooten, for the departmental heads of the school, for all who had any connection with the project. "We've got to complete the chapel six months early," she stated flatly. The industrial manager was aghast; the business manager explained how very difficult it would be to get doors, windows, and other sections. Everybody argued, but with each argument Martha became more determined.

"Please, no excuses." Turning to Inez, she dictated a reply: She would be delighted to have the Frosts here in October, when everything would be ready. As Martha walked out of the office, one of the staff sidled over to Inez to whisper: The day's mail had left the campus, and by tomorrow Miss Berry might have thought the matter over. If Inez could only delay a little . . . Before he had the words out, Miss Berry hurried back in. "Finish the letter, Inez, and put on a special-delivery stamp. I'll drive in to Rome and mail it from there."

Impatiently Martha waited, and when they dropped the note at the Rome post office she swung around. "Now let's go to the spot and change *can't* into *can*." Why had she made up her mind to try the impossible? No one could be certain, but perhaps this was another challenge, and Martha enjoyed challenges. Then, too, she probably felt she owed it to the Frosts. In any event, she went every afternoon to the site, and if any part of the work began to fall behind the new, stepped-up schedule, she ordered more help. If one material proved unavailable, she called a conference and located a substitute.

Soon the industrial manager reported that, as he had predicted, the doors could not be shipped in time. "Very well"—Martha nodded—"we'll make our own, and it will mean more to the boys and us, too." Plans changed again, and more work shifts were added, more boys assigned to the project.

For Martha Berry the chapel had to approach perfection. Walking over a downhill gravel path from the building, she stopped at a turn. "This should have a little more curve," she said, and directed the boys to move it about eight or nine inches. In the rush the young workers were being directed by a succession of new foremen. As she turned away she heard a newly arrived student ask his companions: "You suppose she could be another foreman?" Martha walked off with a chuckle.

Work raced along, and still the job seemed hopeless. On top of everything the donors sent a letter saying that they would arrive three days earlier than expected! Once again Martha rang bells, again helpers groaned, again the schedule quickened.

On the day of the Frosts' arrival Martha left to meet them with the beat of hammers and the yelling of directions still in her ears. A little later she waited beside the donors as they looked at their memorial to their son. "It's beautiful," said Mrs. Frost in a soft voice; her husband was unable to speak. They went inside, inspecting windows and altar and floors. "Oh, but you don't have any pews," Mr. Frost noted. "Can we dedicate a chapel without pews?"

"Wait," Martha murmured. At ten-thirty that night she asked if he would go to see something, and a staff member took him to the boys' shop. There fifty youths sawed, brushed, and polished at a furious rate, and Mr. Frost stepped up to a seventeen-year-old worker. "Son, it looks as though you're running a night shift here."

"Yes, sir." The boy continued to rub as he spoke. "Some friends was good enough to give a chapel, and we ain't goin' to let Miss Berry and them folks down." Outside Mr. Frost discovered another night crew—planting shrubbery by flashlight! And on the dedication day itself, as the couple and Martha Berry watched the long line of students marching over the hill, the staff understood the value of the sharpened curve that she had ordered for the walk.

"So often," Martha once said, "matters worked out in a way that we had not intended. One thing led to another, and then

195

we couldn't go back." She was speaking of the addition at Berry of a group of much younger children than had ever been accepted before.

One day she heard of a sickly seven-year-old who had to take care of the house for her father and an older brother. The mother and two sisters had died of a fever. Madge did all cooking, washing, and other work, and the child was having "a real bad time."

Martha drove out in the morning and after hours of search located the place. The friend who made the report had underestimated the situation. Madge was a sad, emaciated creature with milk-white skin, bright red locks, and hollow eyes; she appeared broken in health as she faced Martha over the blazing coals. With one hand Madge tried to hold her long hair from the fire, as she fried greasy meat with the other.

To Martha Berry the filth was indescribable; it was "no wonder that the mother and sisters had died." The man and his son stayed away most of the day, presumably working the bare farm. With each half-frightened answer Martha learned more of Madge's helplessness. Several hours later the bearded father arrived with his dogs, and Martha reasoned with him: Madge needed rest and care that she could never get at home. Would he let them take her and assist her?

Madge's father shook his head. No child of his'n was a-goin' to be taken off. Anyway, he was sick hisself and needed her to look after the place. Martha left and stopped at another cabin in the same area, where she offered money to the highland wife if she would only help clean Madge's quarters. Sharply the woman refused. That was a "mean, contrary" man, and she would not risk going near him.

As Martha tried to sleep that night she saw Madge's lusterless eyes, and "the face haunted me." Unless she did something the child might soon be dead. The next day was Sunday, and she drove all the way back, to argue more strongly: If anything happened to the girl, she told the father, it would be on his soul. Did he realize that? The man's soul evidently did not concern him greatly. For an hour she appealed, all but threatened, and finally offered a compromise. Why wouldn't he allow her to keep Madge for a month, if only to bring her back to strength?

With a sigh the father agreed, and Martha bundled the child up and rode off. At the school she and the trained nurse took Madge to a warm room, where they found her body "so encrusted with dirt that it took a long time to get her clean." During the rubbing and scraping Madge nearly fainted. "We had to wrap her in a soft blanket and give her some milk . . . let her rest awhile before continuing the cleansing."

Under medical care Madge ate better than ever before in her life. Her eyes lost their dull look, her face its deep lines, and after two weeks she smiled. Martha had to make a decision. She realized she would have to make another division of the school for the children who were too young for the dormitory. For that she needed a separate cottage, another step on "her plank of faith."

The boys sawed more logs and built another cabin, which she called Faith Cottage, "because I had no idea how I'd raise the money for it." On a recent trip Martha had met a young couple without children and liked them at sight. They should make an ideal father and mother for this new brood, and she asked them to join the staff.

The Nesbitts stayed for years in charge of a shifting population at Faith Cottage. In occasional emergencies other small girls came for temporary care before going on to relatives, but a dozen between two and fourteen years old were usually in residence. When they reached the later age they joined the regular students. To fit the children to the "Berry way" most of them had duties after classwork—the keeping of the garden, care of walks, the handling of rabbits and other yard animals. Each cottager tended her own small plot of vegetables. The smallest of the band had a miniature broom of her own. Martha, who remembered her own joy with a childhood pony, provided one and a cart in which they rode over the campus, and in time a young cottager became a prize-winning pony rider at county fairs.

Martha helped plant roses over the doorway, directed the placing of a flagstoned walk, and set her favorite violets along the path, "because if I had my own daughters I'd want them to have surroundings like that." Among those who helped educate the Cottagers was a surprise arrival—an old friend, the now white-haired Miss Ida McCullough, Martha's haloed governess of the far-gone days. After years as a missionary in India, Miss Ida had returned to South Carolina. Soon after she learned this news, Martha had begun inquiries to bring her to Berry.

"She has exactly what these young ones need. She can make a written page live and sparkle," Martha recalled. At the school Miss McCullough looked around in disbelief at the transformation of the grounds, and at times when neither woman was weighted down with duties they talked of earlier times, Martha's younger sisters, and her dead father. So much had happened to Martha and to this place since they had last seen each other. . . .

Remembering costumes she had admired in France, Martha ordered uniforms for the Faith Cottagers—red capes with a hood over white cotton dresses, with white sunbonnets for summer. Like other Berry students, they marched to assemblies and special events as part of the general procession. Most visitors to Berry eventually found themselves at Faith Cottage, where the children sang, played the violin, and curtsied as the governess taught them.

Mrs. Nesbitt, the foster mother, worked to teach the Cottagers politeness and good behavior, with emphasis on table manners. For some at Berry the children became pets, for others occasional problems. There was danger that they might not get the full care they needed; there was also danger that they might be spoiled. Martha admitted that she looked on them with particular affection, taking them on walks and outings and automobile trips. "But we have a lot to make up to them," she said.

After the children grew up, most of them completed schoolwork at Berry and went out to establish their own families. Several married other Berry graduates, and Martha arranged marriage ceremonies in the chapel. All of her life she kept up her interest in the Faith Cottagers, writing, sending gifts, getting reports on their progress.

When she suggested a reunion of the former cottage children, they arrived from several states. Mary, one of the smallest of the group, brought three of her own. As the youngest, less than four years old, sat carefully serving herself with her left hand in her lap, onlookers said they could see the influence of the foster mother, Mrs. Nesbitt. It was another of Martha's "special events," and a joyful one.

When Ann, a cottager who had married a Berry boy, died, funeral ceremonies were held on the campus, the place that had shaped her life. The scene was the chapel in which she had received her certificate a few years earlier and, only a day afterward, gone down the aisle with her husband-to-be. Last services were conducted by another Berry man, a classmate of Ann's and her husband's. The young widower, a baby in the crook of his arm while he held another child by the hand, followed the casket from the building.

CHAPTER XII

SWING YOUR PARTNER!

EARLY ON a cool day in 1923 Martha answered the telephone, and her breath caught when the speaker on the other end informed her that Mr. and Mrs. Henry Ford were accepting her invitation to luncheon and had already started for Berry. That the visit might be important she knew well; not for some time did she realize that this was probably the most vital message that ever reached her schools.

Minutes later Martha's small feet were flying over the campus. Conferring with "Prime Minister" Keown, she received his opinion on matters to be stressed with the Fords and set him into action. For the next two hours half the people at Berry stirred themselves in one way or another. As she moved, Martha perhaps reflected on the long effort she had made to get the Fords to the schools, and also the warnings she had been given about the difficulties that lay ahead of her.

To have issued a direct invitation to the automobile manufacturer might have been fatal. The man, brilliant in many ways, kept the world at a distance. He distrusted most institutions of learning and the things they taught. He had little sympathy with the efforts of the large majority of agencies and philanthropists to help the poor or handicapped. And in much of his thinking this man, whose mass-production methods had done so much to broaden life for Americans of his generation, looked not to a future which he helped create but to the past of his forefathers.

So much for one side of Henry Ford, the nation's most famous personage of his day, and the richest. In another aspect he was a man of generosity toward individuals, one with a fantastic capacity for labor and concentration, and a respect for others with the same abilities. And, though he had few if any close friends, Ford showed occasionally an almost wistful longing to be liked by others. For all his unprecedented power, he was a lonely individual. For a long time Martha had thought about this strange, contradictory titan of the twentieth century. With some of his beliefs, as it developed, she did not have a complete sympathy; with others she felt an emphatic agreement.

She had reached the Fords through their friends, the Thomas Edisons, and only by a roundabout process. The Daughters of the American Revolution asked her to speak to them, and the inventor's wife came up from the audience. Would Martha like to address a meeting of Mrs. Edison's D.A.R. chapter at the Edison home, in the interest of her schools? Delighted with the opportunity, the school director met the deaf inventor, who, though he missed half her words, expressed his own interest.

Later Martha read in a newspaper that Edison was passing through Georgia. (She and her staff watched constantly for such items.) She sent him a wire, and from his train Edison replied that he hoped he might accept her invitation to visit Berry. After several optimistic days she was disappointed to learn that he would not have the time. Tracking down the train, she found that it would stop briefly some miles from Rome.

With only an hour to spare, she went in search of Inez Wooten.

"Get our best angel cake, and pick a big bunch of violets," she instructed the girl. Martha believed that Berry students made rare angel food; caught cakeless once or twice, she thereafter had several kept ready for an emergency. When Inez brought the offerings she took her arm. "You're coming with me, my dear, but first go in and compose a poem to go with the cake."

Inez stood flabbergasted, since she had never written poetry in her life. Sensing her protégée's dismay, Martha called out: "Oh yes, you can do it," and motioned her on. Inez spent twenty agonized minutes, trying lines, scratching them out, and starting again. When at last she finished the words at least rhymed, and she and Martha rode away. They pushed their way onto the train, handed the amused Edison the cake and violets, and Inez read her "poem." As the conductor cried a warning to them, they hurried off.

Though Edison himself never saw the schools, the effort had its effect. The Edisons' interest increased, and Mrs. Edison visited Berry over a period of several years. Through her, Martha met Mrs. Henry Ford, a kind and unpretentious woman, and for some time she and Mrs. Ford exchanged notes. Once or twice she had an opportunity to shake hands with Henry, but all too casually. And then, again from the papers, Martha discovered that the Fords were due in the Muscle Shoals area of Alabama. Dropping everything else, she rode there.

The automobile man and his wife were staying in their private car, she learned when she arrived at her hotel, and she sent a friendly note to Mrs. Ford. What a fine surprise to find them here! She hoped she might see them in the next few days. Patiently she waited for a response, and later said she would have been willing to spend a week to get it. At last Mrs. Ford replied that Henry was heavily engaged, but she had persuaded him to set aside some of his work. Could Miss Berry call at eight that evening?

This might be the hardest interview of her life, Martha thought, and she prepared for it. Mrs. Ford greeted her pleasantly; the tycoon appeared preoccupied, with a hint of the defensive in his manner. While Martha addressed both of them she aimed her remarks at Ford. "Our school is different," she observed. "We think the head and the hand should be acquainted with one another, and that boys and girls learn by doing things as well as by reading about them." She spoke of her father's advice on land and timber, on "hard work yet intelligent work," and his cautions against too-easy giving. "There's no charity in anything we do at Berry," she advised this man who also did not believe in charity.

As he listened, Henry Ford turned directly to her. The hawklike face softened and he nodded, threw in a few words, and before long he was telling her how much he agreed and adding observations of his own childhood. Martha had reached fifty-seven, Ford sixty, and they had a number of recollections in common. When they laughed together Martha decided that she liked the man, and clearly he returned her feeling. The events that followed would otherwise never have been possible.

Henry Ford asked questions: Could anybody go to Berry without working, and did the girls have work assignments too? As she answered Martha smiled. "Couldn't you and Mrs. Ford see for yourselves?" Cautiously Ford said that he would try, and at last the Fords were riding toward the schools.

On duty in the girls' kitchen, Inez Wooten had been taken in hand by her supervisor and planted with a clock at the ancient wood-burning stove. A turkey was roasting in the oven, and Inez had orders to baste it on the dot. "Not a second too soon, not a second too late, and don't move till I get back." The turkey had work to do for Berry. Inez sat and basted, basted and perspired. In time the supervisor returned to ask: "Is the bird well cooked?"

"I'm not sure about the old bird," Inez answered, "but I

203

know I'm well cooked myself." A few seconds later came word that the Fords were arriving with Martha (in the school's Ford, of course). Under several tall oaks the uniformed girls gathered to sing a song written by one of their teachers for them and for this spot: " 'Tis with pleasure we meet, Our good friends to greet, 'Neath the shade of our old oak trees . . ." Brightly Martha led the visitors into a dining room as crowded as any the Fords had ever seen. Students at one table had to stand until those at the next could be seated. All chairs could not be pulled out at the same time, and those who served had to corkscrew their way along the narrow spaces.

During the meal Martha talked energetically: "This is a home-grown meal, a home-cooked dinner, and a homespun school." Mrs. Ford was obviously enjoying herself, and so was her husband; he seemed more relaxed, more interested than ever.

When dinner ended, Mrs. Ford inquired: "May I look at the kitchen?" Although used to large staffs, she still liked cooking and housekeeping, and Martha had heard she was a meticulous housewife. "Certainly." Martha smiled as she answered. (Later she said she asked God that the place be very, very clean.)

Entering the kitchen, she sighed in relief, for the girls moved quickly, almost silently, drying dishes and piling them in an atmosphere of almost antiseptic neatness. Mrs. Ford faced her husband with a look of satisfaction: "They've done it all in such a small space and with such old equipment. They really need a much larger stove. This one's practically worn-out."

Her glance dropped, and she made out long seams in three places along the pine flooring. "Henry, they've pieced the floor here, and there, and over there."

Martha shrugged. "Oh, when you have a child that's growing and you can't afford a new dress you let the old one out and add a ruffle. We push our walls out and add a ruffle to the floors."

204

As they left Mrs. Ford glanced back. "Well, I'd like to see what these girls could do with something to work with."

Henry Ford tapped his wife's shoulder. "Callie, maybe you'd like to give them a bigger stove."

"They certainly deserve one."

Martha remained carefully silent, and the visitors let the subject drop. After a trip around the campus the couple rode off on their way to Florida. A week passed and another, and Martha wondered if they would get a stove or even a frying pan. Then from a pile of mail she snatched an envelope. Mrs. Ford had written to ask if a Ford business representative might study the schools. Posthaste Martha replied that she would be delighted. A business representative . . . Wouldn't that mean more than a stove or even a kitchen?

Yet she must not be overoptimistic. The representative proved an easy-mannered but noncommunicative man who looked and asked and prodded while Martha alternated between hope and fear. Was he finding the wrong things? After he left, another two weeks went by, and Mrs. Ford wrote again to say how impressed she and her husband were with the schools. Martha's heart quickened at the next words. The Fords particularly liked the girls' department and wished to have a little share in it. Which kind of building did it need most?

She had achieved the thing that people had said she could never do! In the words of an associate, "She had touched the Fords, struck the note that others had missed." She sent her warm thanks and assured the couple that they would never know how much this meant to her and her schools. As for the building, Berry had hundreds of girls on its application lists, well qualified and anxious for an education. Probably it would be best to add a dormitory to care for a hundred more.

Of course, Martha went on, she might be putting the cart before the horse, because the school had already outgrown its dining hall-kitchen. But she would "feed them in shifts" if she received the new living quarters. The letter was a master stroke, an innocently shrewd appeal. While *she* wanted the dormitory, the Fords had indicated a special interest in the dining room. Now she would see what happened.

The note accomplished all she might have hoped for. Mrs. Ford wrote that she would give both dormitory and dining hall-kitchen, and asked if Miss Berry would get her architect to draw plans. Already Martha had chosen her man, a well-recognized Bostonian, and she knew what she wanted—not a log cabin, but a permanent stone structure, the first unit in a separate girls' campus, to be built from the bottom up in Gothic.

Addressing the architect, she explained that they must not ask too much, "just nice buildings that we and the Fords won't be ashamed of." His designs looked magnificent to her, and she dispatched them to Detroit. A reply arrived—a rejection. The plans were fine, but couldn't Miss Berry arrange for better buildings? Beyond doubt the Fords wished something much grander. Martha called the architect again: "I want you to make a full study and arrange the most beautiful kitchen and dining room any mortal ever imagined, and a finer dormitory too."

New plans, more extensive and more sweeping, went off, and Martha worried once more. Perhaps she had made them too lavish? For a second time the answer was a rejection. Mrs. Ford still hoped for something more, and would Martha mind if the Fords' architect made a few changes? In time there evolved drawings for a dining room of arched ceilings and long expanses. Because the units were so large the Berry boys could not build them, outside contractors bid for and received the jobs; and thereby developed a furore within Berry's board of directors.

Thus far Henry Ford had signed no contracts. In his dealings with Martha, neither mentioned amounts of money. He would approve a project, his experts would pass on it, and she or the schools would send him the bill. The first work involved more than a half million dollars, and Martha's trustees became fidgety. Board Chairman Robert C. Alston remonstrated with Martha. Surely they couldn't go ahead without a written promise of some sort? Martha shook her head. "We have to do it this way, Mr. Ford's way." She signed the papers, making the schools responsible, and the board members grew more nervous than ever. Eventually the money came in, though Mr. Alston said he could not sleep easily for months.

Berry hummed with the work of hundreds of new men, including a colony of Italian stonecutters. At times Martha might well have been dazzled by Gothic towers, Mediterranean stoneworkers, buildings that cost millions. Not many years before, she had feared to spend a thousand dollars on one of their structures! Even after construction began, Ford representatives expanded the projects. A kitchen expert frowned at the drawings. "Good equipment, but not the best." He substituted a metal kitchen interior which added $60,000 to the cost and made the room last almost perfectly for decades.

From then on, for more than twenty years, Henry and Clara Ford went to Berry about once a year. They brought Ford aides and members of the family; they walked or rode over all the campus and made suggestions. What they saw never failed to stir them. They enjoyed gatherings of the students, talks with Martha, and inspections of the operations. Ford delighted in telling of a particular incident. Near their guest cottage the schools had a field, and about ten-thirty one night he heard a noise. A half dozen Ford tractors were running with lights on.

Throwing on his coat, the industrialist strolled over to the edge of the field, and one of the boys stopped his machine. "Son," said Ford, "you seem to be saving a day, working like this."

The serious student shook his head. "No, sir, we're savin' a year. If we don't get this crop planted at the right time, we'll have to wait till next year." The thought that his tractors could "save a year" pleased the multimillionaire. He wanted to see still more tractors at Berry, and he advised Gordon Keown to dispose of Berry's last mules, then provided more of his own tractors as substitutes.

Mrs. Ford attended all chapel services, whereas Henry enjoyed puttering around machinery on the campus and might or might not arrive in time for the meetings. Martha had been warned that he disliked to speak, but on one of his early visits she took a chance. As he entered the chapel, she dispatched Inez, now her regular secretary, to bring him forward. "He won't come," Mrs. Ford whispered.

Inez bent over him, and slowly Ford rose from his seat. "Well, if Miss Berry sent for me, I have to go." On the platform he began wryly: "If I were going to make a talk, I think it would be easier here than anywhere else." He went on to expand upon one of his themes, the unity of mind and hands.

After a while Ford noticed that, instead of throwing away cornhusks, the students made them into neat rugs and table mats. "That's certainly using what you find," he said approvingly. About the same time he saw the schools' large flour bill and told Martha: "Let me send what you need of that." For a long time thereafter Berry received much of its flour from the Ford enterprises. The flour sacks bore letters in color, and he learned that the girls were bleaching out the marks and coloring the cloth with peach leaves, red clay, and other natural dyes. "Those fine dresses were once flour sacks?" he asked. Then he instructed his secretary: "Let's save them the trouble of taking out the letters. From now on put the Berry flour in plain bags."

The multimillionaire became a friend of the slow-talking Gordon Keown, and they spent hours together, inspecting fields or buildings or exploring the countryside. Ford was evermore interested in mills, ancient machinery, and other possible acquisitions for his museum collections. "Whenever he came I'd try to have something lined up that appealed to him," Keown explained. They would stop to speak to a farmer, who would "pretty near fall dead" when he recognized the automobile king.

The countryman Keown warned Ford: Let *him* do the bargaining, or the industrialist would be "held up by these folks." Quietly Ford agreed. When he wanted an old gin, Gordon ferreted out a hand-fed type and dickered to get it for only fifty dollars. Another time they met a driver on a covered apple wagon with a high stick at the front and prongs from which the fruit dangled for display. At first sight Ford itched for the antique, until Keown whispered: "I know where he'll go in town and I'll slip up on his blind side." Back in Rome, Keown talked first of buying a mere bushel of fruit, then the wagonload, and eventually got mules, apples, wagon, and all, to be shipped to Detroit.

As he heard Martha and Gordon talk of their belief in land and their successive purchases, Henry Ford was in enthusiastic agreement. They must let him know how they got along, he said, and also if they had any trouble in acquiring new property. On the Fords' next visit the canny Keown hesitated and explained that he *had* a problem. A fine tract had become available, but Berry just didn't have the kind of funds it required. A few days later it had.

On his trips around the neighborhood, Ford discovered a brick plant and indirectly put Martha Berry into the brick business. "Why don't you buy it?" he asked her and Gordon. "It would save you money and give the boys training." When he investigated, the "Prime Minister" learned that only a week or so earlier the owners had sold to absentee purchasers who would put in tens of thousands of dollars' worth of new equipment. "Just wait," Keown counseled, and Henry and Martha agreed to do so.

Months later the absentees failed, and when the plant went up for sale Keown ambled to the scene and bid it in for only $10,000. He valued it at $150,000, including all of that almost unused equipment. "We made money by keeping still," he said in a transport of delight. Ford paid the bill, and from then on hundreds of Berry boys mastered one more phase of building under the direction of expert brick makers.

Arriving on another visit, Henry and Clara Ford smiled when the Berry girls lined up to meet them. As always, the girls sang their old song:

> "Oh, we're the little sisters,
> We cook and iron and sew . . ."

And as usual the chorus declared:

> "There's nothing that can stop us,
> But you can help us grow."

In the middle of the song Henry Ford caught a phrase:

> "We need a recitation hall,
> With rooms about a score . . ."

A moment later, beaming, the manufacturer turned toward his wife. "Callie, let's give them the recreation hall."

"Henry, they didn't say 'recreation,' but 'recitation.'"

Ford grinned and rubbed his hands as a happy thought occurred to him. "Well, we'll give them that too." Without delay he set the machinery in motion to provide both halls, and in time put up even more buildings for the schools. What he did was always under Martha's careful lead. She had prepared an elaborate design for an expansion of the girls' campus—an expansion that few of her associates even knew she had in mind. It was to be a magnificent quadrangle, with an oblong blue pool in the center, other reflecting pools, a series of tall stone structures, and a richly landscaped area of trees and shrubs.

At some point—no one understood quite when or how—Martha let the Fords see the architects' visualization of her plan. They might not have realized that she hoped to have *them* build all of those units, but by the end of the 1920s they had

210

done precisely that. One of Ford's agents arrived in Atlanta to make a deposit of more than one million dollars for part of the construction, and the incident stirred the city's financial circles. What magic had Martha Berry worked with the tycoon?

The schools "grew deeper and deeper inside the man's heart," one of her associates remarked. Ford would stride through half-cleared woods, breathing the fresh Georgia air. He went zestfully to Possum Trot, the old church school in which Martha had pioneered, and there he inspected the words from Scriptures that she had painted on the walls. He would walk alone up the slope of Lavendar Mountain, to stand for long minutes watching the view. At one time, surveying the campus, he looked slowly from one group of structures to the other. "All the money on earth couldn't have built this school," he said.

At the Berry schools Henry Ford shed much of his suspicion, his protective covering against the world. As Ralph McGill declared, at Berry he "somehow found ways to express best, and with most enjoyment, his gentle and humane qualities and instincts." Here, the Georgia editor thought, he was happier than at any other place to which his travels took him. Here the Fords "basked in their affection for the school."

The automobile maker's confidence in Martha Berry's work meant a great deal to her. In Gordon Keown's words, Ford "believed in everything Miss Berry was doing and everything she proposed to do." This phenomenal man who, in spite of his capacities, also inspired hate and ridicule, responded to Martha as he did to few human beings. People who were too obvious in their self-interest could not reach him; more sophisticated persons found it equally impossible to do so. She had made her contact, discovered that common denominator.

In the late 1920s the Fords sent word that galvanized the campus. They were on their way with a seven-piece orchestra, to do what they had talked of doing for some time: teach Berry boys and girls all about dancing—folk, square dancing, the waltz. Curiously the art was one of Henry's favorite subjects, and he loved it and proselyted for it. For years dancing had been a somewhat delicate subject at Berry. While attitudes were changing, some of the mountain people still considered it a carnal exercise, to be shunned like Satan himself.

But now Martha's good friends the Fords were coming to Berry again, and if they wanted dancing, they were going to have it. Nevertheless, like the skillful general that she was, she went to work to protect the rear of her forces. As public relations director of the dance project she picked a conservative church deacon, Dr. Cook of the faculty. Years ago the youthful Cook had been assigned to quiet barking dogs and crying babies; this time he would cope with the prospect of disturbed parents.

Mr. and Mrs. Ford arrived in a swirl of dust with grinning fiddlers, dance-callers, and folk singers. A grand opening evening was arranged, and everybody on the campus was invited to the gala shenanigans. A smiling, slightly flushed Martha stepped forward with Henry Ford, bowed, and struck a waltz pose. As Henry took his own position, the students applauded.

Mrs. Ford moved up with a partner of her own. Shyly awkward youths faced their partners, and groups formed for mass instruction. "Slow now . . . and easy. Glide, just glide." For many students it was not only the first waltz, but the first dance of any kind, and they loved it from start to finish. Then came folk dances with the specialists to call directions. They did "Chase the Squirrel," "Grand Right and Left," and "Step a Little Bit, Turn Around and Stand Still," and the Virginia reel, schottisches, and more waltzes. Henry Ford danced with Inez; he was determined, he said, that she learn folk dancing. He'd stay at Berry until she did learn. Awkwardly, she trod on his feet and said, "At this rate I reckon you'll just have to move in and stay for good." She danced, too, as often as she could without attracting attention, with Will Henry, a Berry graduate who worked in the schools' store. It was all very grand to have Henry

212

Ford as dance instructor, but Inez thought a lot more of those dances with Will. Berry had "never seen the like."

In spite of the churchly sanction of Dr. Cook, a small number of students would have none of such sinful carryings-on. They looked as if they smelled something bad, and went swiftly to campus prayer meetings, at which they sent up petitions for the dancers' souls. The Fords stayed for days, and Martha gave them and their musicians a free run. Though classes were not interrupted, all vacant periods went for dance instruction and practice, and in the evenings nearly everybody was on the floor. Henry also provided a victrola, and for a full week Berry continued on, happily dance-crazy. The Fords danced with students, with faculty members; Martha danced with Henry, the staff, and the boys.

For a long time Berry would remember the most remarkable sight of all, Mr. and Mrs. Ford circling and circling, whirling easily in one of the old, old waltzes. From that week on, square dancing became a pleasing tradition at the schools.

The Ford structures were nearly completed, and Gordon Keown took Henry Ford to inspect them. They cost more than $3,500,000, and today the figures would be much higher, of course. The man who had put up the funds and given his time and personal interest to the program stood before the buildings, and his glance was almost casual, until his eyes lighted and he pointed to the high tower. "The clock isn't running," he exclaimed.

Ford had always been intrigued with clocks, kitchen ones, parlor types, all kinds of clocks like all kinds of machinery. Now he had to fix this one. With Keown puffing behind him, he climbed the long stairway to the tower and after that the shaky ladder to the works behind the timepiece. Adjusting the mechanism, the manufacturer let himself down, slapped his hands together, and gave another cursory look around the great quad-

213

rangle. "He seemed to feel that he had seen the whole thing," said Keown, and he left.

The Ford buildings had beauty and a fine symmetry. An American adaptation of English collegiate Gothic, they have been called one of the nation's best examples of the style. The buildings had vaulted roofs, leaded-glass windows, arched doorways, and wood carvings. The group's medieval air gave the unit a strong contrast to other parts of the "homespun" campus, but, as Alice Wingo pointed out, it had a number of "Martha Berry adaptations." Mural designs contained her favorite Twenty-third Psalm and texts from Scripture, and, like everything else at the school, including those chicken coops, the buildings had slender spires rising at many points.

Henry Ford introduced Berry to some of his theories of diet. At times he distrusted fruit juices; again it was milk, though once he had a notion that "manufactured milk" would be better than the "cow kind." For a year or two he worked to enlist Berry in his soybean crusade, and the obliging Martha and Inez attended a meal which he arranged with soybean soup for the first course, soy loaf for the main dish, soy bread, soy coffee, and soy cake. To several of the guests that was a lot of soy. In any case, when the Fords returned again he had switched affections to whole-wheat products, and eventually he went back to milk.

In at least one respect Martha, as Gordon Keown said, "put the brakes" on Ford. For some time he had a plan to erect a plant in the vicinity to manufacture Ford parts and perhaps other machinery. The boys would do the work on a mass-production basis and learn about industry at the same time, he believed. (He used similar plans at home.) Tactfully yet clearly Martha let her friend know that while she admired such efforts, she saw flaws for Berry in the project. She explained that she tried always to offer her boys a rounded training in agriculture, dairying, and a variety of other subjects—a phase of building, a phase of industry, office operations, and so on. She did not like

214

the thought of the students doing one thing over and over again. Her primary goal was the development of well-rounded abilities in every Berry graduate, so that he could fit into a variety of occupations.

Quietly Henry Ford agreed and gave way.

Martha never ceased to thank and praise the automobile maker; he did as much for her schools as any person in their history. And yet his generosity resulted in problems for her and her work. Erroneous rumors spread: "Berry's rich now, and it doesn't need my help any more." "Whatever they want, Ford gives."

But each big building involved big expenses for upkeep and repair, and Henry Ford did not provide for such maintenance. His gifts meant a large increase in the amounts which Martha must raise annually to keep the schools going. The new students whom he made it possible for her to bring to Berry also meant additional mouths to be fed, additional teachers and supervisors. She must still go out annually to gather funds, or Berry might shut down within a month or two.

PART THREE

"Something Wonderful

Around the Corner"

CHAPTER XIII

AND STILL THE HIGHLANDS

SHE HAD a waiting list of thousands, daily recommendations of boys and girls, and special requests for acceptance. But Martha Berry could not forget that many of their best graduates were those she had hunted out and fought hardest to draw to the schools. And, despite the progress that she saw all about her, there remained remote highland pockets still to be explored.

It was with these in mind that Martha, in her sixties, would jump to her feet and call to her secretary: "Inez, let's get out and start hand-picking again!" Her eyes brightening, she shoved aside a pile of papers, buzzed for a student driver, and went so quickly down the stairs that Inez Wooten could not keep pace. After leaving a message or two, they would drive off, to be gone as long as she thought necessary.

The staff might wonder if, with so much to do, it was good management to leave the main office. Whether they understood or not, Martha was refreshing her spirit, renewing herself.

Those families in the mountains were the ones for whom her schools existed, the roots from which Berry had grown.

She never wanted to lose time in reaching her destination. When automobiles arrived she welcomed them, in her words, "with a glad cry." "They're just what I've been waiting for," she said, as the early cars whizzed her along at dizzying speeds of twenty, twenty-five, thirty miles an hour. While familiar landmarks darted past she would sigh: "Inez, now we're getting somewhere."

When engines improved, Martha was delighted. With the speedometer hitting fifty, then sixty miles an hour, she prodded the chauffeur: "We're crawling, and I ought to be in Chattanooga." If another machine roared by, she would bend forward to question the student driver: "Why'd you let him get ahead of us?"

Once or twice the boy at the wheel would defend his caution. "Because I want you to live, Miss Berry, and me too." At that she might subside with a little laugh, but a few minutes later she would be urging him on again. "Can't we get around that fellow?"

Here, as in other situations, she used her old technique of praising Peter to spur on Paul. As the car rocked around a curve on the way toward Atlanta she asked: "How long has it been since we left school?"

"Just an hour and ten minutes." By then the driver would be muttering to himself.

"Hm. Harvey's made the whole distance in an hour and forty minutes." When the current chauffeur muttered and set foot to the accelerator, the cowering Inez sent up petitions to the sky. Once Inez gathered up courage to protest vigorously. "Now, Miss Berry, this *isn't* wonderful—it's plain terrible. If we had a blowout we'd all be dead."

"Is that so?" Martha glanced serenely at her tense assistant. "Well, think of it. We must never do that, child. Go a bit slower, Ged—just a bit." But if Ged complied she would soon be pressing him again for speed.

On her trips to the mountains Martha met other challenges and accepted them. Any road which she had not already covered stirred her to speculation, and from speculation to action. "Where do you think that leads, Inez?" Hoping to discourage her, Inez would shake her head. "Just a little old path, and I'm sure it goes nowhere, Miss Berry."

"Ah, let's find out. Ged, turn right here and keep on going till something happens." In a moment they would be jolting along, missing tree stumps by inches, fighting mud, water, or dust. Inez clutched the seat and prayed as Martha chortled. "Marvelous, marvelous! I'm sure this is the first car that ever came here." Generally, Inez groaned, it was.

Along the route they stopped whenever Martha's eye caught a sight that appealed to her. One day a young woman who worked with a plow at the edge of a field made her cry halt. "Notice that determination, and the way she hasn't looked up once. The girl has a powerful will, hasn't she?" A moment later Martha was out of the car and on her way to the fence for a talk. A boy who struggled doggedly to fix a harness might intrigue her, or a group of older people in a yard, a circle of children around a well. As a matter of fact, Inez Wooten said, almost anything that Martha saw became grist to the schools' mill.

Soon she had even the most suspicious highlanders interested. "I'm Martha Berry and I have a school where we do spinning and weaving," she began an interview. "That fine quilt—why, it's a pattern I've never seen. Did you do it? You know, we like to get the real old patterns to teach the girls." The mountain woman might sell the quilt and the school would make use of it, but sometimes Martha was merely preparing the way for a friendlier relationship.

She lost little time in drawing the children into their conversation. "What's your name, and where do you go to school? I'm

221

sure you have brothers and sisters." To gain good will she brought candy for them, the "streak-ed" kind, and in a few minutes they clustered around her. "Those flowers over there—what do you call them?" Then she would address the grand-mother. "Did I tell you we collect mountain songs at my school? Mrs. Burch, you must remember a few, and won't you favor us with one?"

Eventually Martha and Inez joined the family in a refrain that it had not sung for a decade. In that way they made a number of musical finds, and Inez would be hard put to jot down words and try to fill out the melody. Meanwhile Martha had learned more about the family than many of its closest neighbors knew; as she had spread word of her school and planted seeds for future cultivation.

"Wouldn't you like to learn to read, May Anne?" she would ask. Softly she would insinuate: "That fine boy should know his ciphers, Mrs. Burch." Or: "Did you hear of our Berry graduate, from right near here, who's turned into a doctor for the whole valley?" On departure she would say: "I'd like to leave a little sweater for Mary, this one that I just happened to bring with me." Or: "Now you must let me pay for the pattern. It's worth a nice amount to the school, and they'll be seeing your coverlet all over the North."

Long ago Martha had discovered that in the mountains, as anywhere else, it was wise not to visit too long. As she said good-by she was surrounded by all of the family who could walk, laden with flowers that she had admired and cuttings for the school gardens. "You 'uns must come back," the mother would call, and Inez told herself that the highland woman need have no worry on that point. Martha had her eye on three of that family, and her assistant would have hazarded a bet that at least two eventually appeared at Berry.

Frequently the mountain trips were planned with an objec-tive—a certain youth of whom Martha had heard favorable re-ports, or a family whose fine prospects, or difficulties, had been described to her. She had informal "agents" at crossroads, people who wrote her when they had information, good or bad, to pass on. After her death Harvey Roberts of the Berry staff came upon a boy who advised him that his father was "one of Miss Martha's main helpers." The old fellow had been a rural letter carrier, who kept his eyes open for potential students. Who could have known his area better than such a man?

On one trip Martha and Inez set out to locate a particularly obscure cabin. They drove for hours, until they met an ancient individual with stooped figure and long white beard. Could he help them find the Price place? The mountaineer lifted his broad-brimmed straw hat, bowed low, and assured them: "Wall, yer headed in the right direction. Keep a-goin' on and on till the road gits dimmer and dimmer. When yer git ter whar they ain' no road, yer purty nigh thar. An' ef'n you got an ax you mought make hit."

The highlander was right, for the road did grow steadily more faint, and the driver made good use of his hand ax, part of his mountain-riding equipment, to clear their path of fallen trees. Yet the search proved to be worth all the effort. When they finally reached the almost inaccessible hut, the girl Elizabeth, about whom they had received word, was working at the long vegetable rows beside her house.

Despite the heavy freckling of her face and her sun-bleached hair, Elizabeth was a beauty. She had an excellent carriage, clear hazel eyes, a look of dignity. Martha had heard hints of difficulties that might confront her here, and she began at once: "They tell me you'd like to come to my school, Elizabeth."

"That's sure right, ma'am. But my paw, he wouldn't never let me go nowhere."

But Martha had also been told of the grandfather, a patriarch who owned the land and had ideas of his own, if he were approached properly. With Elizabeth she went to him in the cabin, where he saluted her with reserve and explained the prob-

223

lem: "She's our oldest, and her paw says he don't know how he'd make out 'thout 'er."

Martha talked persuasively. "Doesn't she sit up every night before the fire, trying to read all the papers she gets her hands on? And weren't there people in your family that could read a generation back?"

As the grandfather nodded, Martha described what three or four years of education could do for the fifteen-year-old, recalling cases of other girls of the area who had become teachers and storekeepers and members of happy families. "Your wife's dead, and so is Elizabeth's mother. I don't think you want her to kill herself with grinding labor the way they did."

After an hour Martha had persuaded the grandfather. "Still," he murmured, "ef her paw come in now, he'd stop her right off."

Martha thought she caught the hint in his words and in his manner. "How long before he'll be home again?"

"Couple o' hours, I reckon."

She had already jumped to her feet. "By the time he gets back, Elizabeth will be on the way with us. And then you can let him know just what you think of all this, can't you?" Grandpa reckoned that he could; Inez helped the girl in her hasty packing, and they rode off as if the furies were behind them. Elizabeth became a star pupil, and, while her father never attended any of the Berry ceremonies in which she had a part, her grandfather went to every one. When she graduated a few years later with highest honors, he and her brothers and sisters made the long trip to watch and applaud.

On another occasion Martha and Inez started in search of a boy called Albert, who had written from a vague address. He could not be certain, Albert said, yet he hoped his parents would allow him to go to Berry. Something in the letter—a poignant note, the boy's humble manner of expression—impressed Martha. After considerable effort and several false leads, her car stopped before a shabby gate and a middle-aged woman walked out to her. She had lost all of her teeth and talked with difficulty.

She had seven boys, she said, and one answered to the name of Albert, all right. "He's out a-plowin' his patch o' cotton, a-hopin' ter save a bit from the boll weevil ter he'p git his eddication. A smart boy, Miss Berry. Ciphers at night an' all thet."

Then the mother hesitated. "We'd like 'im to go ter school, yes. His pap and me, though, we don' hol' with charity or suchlike. We don' wan' Albert to tek somethin' fer nothin'." Martha assured her, the youth, and his father that if Albert provided his own transportation, he could work at Berry to earn his tuition. Details settled, she prepared to leave, when the mother began to talk of the older son.

"Now Bob, *he* was our peartest boy, and he got kilt in that scrap our country had with them Germans. Bob went to help out our side, and 'fore long the mail brung a yaller piece of paper to tell us 'at Bob was kilt. The Germans never sent 'im home after shootin' 'im down, not even fer decent buryin'." The mother's voice thickened. "After that they fotched us another paper a-tellin' that money was bein' offered fer Bob's life, an' we said we didn't wan' it."

"You mean you didn't take the insurance money?"

"No'm." The reply had an emphatic ring. "We ain' sol' our son, an' we ain' takin' no money fer his life." Sitting down again, Martha argued that the insurance funds were their right and that they were not being fair to themselves and their other children in refusing to accept them. An hour later she convinced the family and helped set machinery in motion to recover payments due to it. When Albert finished at Berry, he took over management of the refurbished farm and the bank account as well.

Repeatedly Martha demonstrated a virtuoso artistry in achieving the impossible. A Southern judge who accompanied

225

her on a trip remembers the way she halted as they passed a bleak farm. "I didn't notice anything particular; she did—a kid at the end of a plowline. To me it was just a little old Georgia boy, but after she had spoken to him five minutes I realized she had made up her mind to get him. The things that happened next were like nothing I've ever seen."

The boy's mother became curious and joined the party in the field. With two or three sentences Martha won her to her side. The father emerged, "and I've never known any lawyer to handle a witness as she did, so smoothly, so skillfully. He told her flatly that he would not let the boy go to Berry; he couldn't spare him and that was that. Well, Miss Berry led the father from question to question and got him to say just what he was supposed to say. Didn't he feel some kind of obligation to his family? Didn't he agree he owed something to the son? Surely he realized that the boy would be a better man, that the younger children would have a better life?"

With each answer the father was caught more tightly in Martha's trap. Finally she asked: Why couldn't the boy try out Berry, and if he didn't like it he could leave in an hour? The man himself could call at any time, and if *he* was not pleased he could take Mike home. "I listened and marveled," continued the judge, who saw it all happen. At last, though with extreme reluctance, the father was hooked. He guessed it might be all right. . . . Two or three seconds later Martha cinched the deal: "Very well, we'll take Mike with us right now."

The boy stared in surprise, and so did his father. "Right now, Miss Martha?" Mike appeared almost frightened. "Now, he don' have no clothes fit to wear"—the father protested—"not even no valise."

"He won't need them," Martha snapped. "We'll get him a toothbrush and a few things at the store down the road. Mike, you say good-by to your family, and don't forget your sister over there." Before the family quite realized it, Mike was off, and as they rolled away, "that little old country boy just beamed and beamed and beamed." Hardly a half hour earlier he had before him a stunted existence in the mountains; now life had opened before him.

In the weeks that followed, the father went several times to the Berry schools, almost hopefully, to ask if Mike wanted to leave. "Oh no, Pap, I'm having me a wonderful time. Real wonderful." Sometimes, Martha said with a twinkle, "you have to work real fast."

In these days Martha and Inez drove at times to Mentone, Alabama, a Lookout Mountain resort at which the Berrys maintained a small camp. In a rustic setting the head of the school rested, but also worked over correspondence and school problems and went regularly to scour the vicinity for potential students. The Alabama section yielded a large number of Berry boys and girls.

In the Mentone camp as at home, Martha liked extra places at her table for the "drop company." About lunch time one day a mountain woman arrived with her children—fifteen of them. Inez stripped pantry shelves, made lemonade to supplement the milk, and stretched out meat, eggs, and corn bread, and Martha listened as the highlander described her troubles.

Her husband had died only a few weeks earlier, leaving her with "my drove." She had "tuck 'em to a singin' t'other day at Valley Head, an' a man thar drawed a pitcher of 'em." From her checked apron the mother took a post-card photograph of fourteen in a row and herself with the baby in her arms. Pointing a large brown finger, she identified them "down the doorstep line." "Thet's Donald, and Dick, Dewitt, Dora, Donna, Della, Dolly, David, Dan, Dock, D-Noka, D-Roma, D-Velmie, D-Rose, and Daisy."

Martha was fascinated. "How did you find all those D's?"

The matriarch shrugged. "It warn't too bad. I named the first six 'fore I thought 'bout 'em all a-startin' with the same letter, an' then I figgered I had to stick to D. I liked the name Rose so much I got to have one like thet, so I put a D in front. D-Noka? I ain' rightly sure 'bout thet one. I guess my poor husban' jes' felt like it sounded nice."

As her guest talked and ate and the children sat silent and ate, Martha did not probe for the purpose of the visit. At last it came out when the mother pushed back her plate. "Miss Berry, I heerd about you 'uns' school, and I'm here 'bout my drove."

"Which of the boys and girls would you like to get in?"

The mother responded without a moment's pause. "Wall, I'd like fer you 'uns ter take the top twelve o' 'em."

That might not be easy, and yet Inez realized that Martha looked with an approving eye on the husky children around her. The highland woman feared that she could not keep up her farm much longer, and she had to find a new home. Most of the brood were much too young for the regular Berry work. Inez took the children outside to sit in the sun, and the other two women conferred for a long time and made arrangements. The mother moved to the vicinity of Possum Trot, Martha helped her locate work, and most of the "top twelve" attended day classes at the school, from kindergarten up.

A sequel followed. The mountain wife remarried, produced several additions to "the drove," and all of them went to Berry's classes as well.

The latter-day mountain excursions did not always meet with success. For many months Martha referred unhappily to the case of Lorette, which haunted her sleep. In the middle of winter she had received word that the girl, who had just passed fourteen, "hankered after learning," and had told several people that she would "give anything if she could get to Berry." The next weekend and the next, Martha planned to go to the Briar Creek area, but each time urgent matters delayed the trip to Lorette's farm. When Martha and Inez ultimately arrived they were invited in by a lean woman who rubbed her hands nervously on her apron.

"Lorette ain' here, Miss Marthy," the mother told her. "If you'd only came a week back! She got plumb tired o' plowin', washin', scrubbin' floors, and cookin', and run off with Judson Crabtree, the eighteen-year-old feller up at Wild Cat Holler."

Lorette's mother dropped her head and went on between sobs. "Miss Marthy, that's what I done in my day too. Run away when I was fo'teen, 'cause I got sick o' a-pickin' berries and a-doin' washin' day and night. Now it's Lorette, and her chil'ren will be a-doin' it after a while." It appeared that the new marriage had begun badly, and the girl regretted it already.

Gently Martha inquired the way to Judson Crabtree's house, where Lorette and her young husband had moved in with his family, and she and Inez went there, partly by car, partly on foot. They discovered Lorette doing the washing; earlier she had finished the dishes, after cooking and serving dinner for the family. Now she spent most of her time at "the very things she had run away from," Martha noted—with a difference: She worked for more people.

With a sad stare Lorette talked to them of the situation and then of her main ambition of the moment—somehow to save enough money to buy a pair of shoes. She had never owned shoes, and thought she should have them to "go to meetin', like a married woman should." There seemed little more to be said. As Martha walked toward her car, Lorette whispered to her: "I wish't you'd of come sooner. I wish't it so!"

Martha remembered her girlhood friend Emma, who had sent her mountain daughter to be one of the first children in the girls' school. Trying to console Lorette, she said: "I'll have a place for your children. Be sure to let me know and get them to me, will you?" With a nod Lorette agreed. When Martha looked back she saw the girl outlined against the cabin, her hand against the sun, as her eyes followed them down the road. Long afterward, she said, she could hear the words echoing in her mind: "I wish't you'd of come sooner."

This failure was balanced when Martha accidently found a

student on another kind of errand. "Prime Minister" Gordon Keown had located a piece of property for purchase, and they started off with a third passenger to inspect the area. Reaching the road's end, they continued on foot and passed a house before which a white-faced woman sat propped at the edge of the porch. The plaintive pose drew Martha's attention, and she made a detour to approach the cabin.

"You be Miss Martha Berry?" The question had a suggestion of desperation.

As Martha went nearer, the tired woman extended her hand. "Miss Berry, I been hopin' somehow ter see yer. Would of came ef'n I could walk a-tall. I know I ain' got much time ter live, and I been thinkin' a long time 'bout my Agnes here." From the doorway a girl stepped forward to stand beside her mother. "She's a good, bright 'un, and there'll be nobody to look after 'er. I'd go happier ef'n you'd take 'er to yer school."

Martha promised, and went on to speak of the mother's ailment. "It hurts me to move a-tall, but I'm managin'." On the path outside Martha drew Keown aside. "If she had a wheel chair at least she could get around without such pain. Gordon, there must be a dozen wheel chairs stuck away in attics around the country, and let's find one." For the time they put aside the land purchase, and Gordon hunted until he got what they wanted. After a few months the woman died, and the girl joined the younger students at Berry.

That same month another trip produced a roaring dispute, of the kind that Martha tried always to avoid. Riding out of Georgia, she and Inez saw a tent near a crossroads store, and a farmer's wife smiled at them as she explained: "New preacher's arrived, and ever'body's headin' there fer a big testimonial service." Martha turned to her assistant, a fresh light in her eye. "Inez, it's been years since I attended one!"

For her secretary the prospect also had its appeal. A few hours later, sitting in places of honor near the front of the lamplighted tent, they watched as one mountaineer after another told of his sins. Though young, the evangelist preached a burning sermon and made many a convert. A young woman "turned herself inside out" to confess a habit of talebearing, and a man wept as he described how he had beaten his wife.

All went well until a bedraggled, unshaven individual struggled forward and gasped out his announcement. He was a moonshiner, no good and ornery, he said, but tonight he realized his mistakes. "I sells to ever'body hereabouts," he shouted, flinging his arms about him, and he proceeded to name names and places and times.

A mountain wife on the bench near him glared and jumped to her feet, pointing a quivering finger. "So now I know whar my man's a-gettin' the dirty stuff. Hit's you. I'm a-goin' to have the law on yer termorrer if hit's the last thing I do!"

Two other women rushed up, screaming denunciations of the sinner. At the same time, however, his sister and two male relatives went to his defense. "Hit's a shame to use a poor feller's own words agin' 'im." "Sich behavior's a turrible thing in the sight o' God!"

The minister showed his lack of experience; the fight had gone beyond his control, and he stood back in panic. Inez Wooten, who had seen mountain fighting in her day, sat icily apart. Shootings and knifings could start at any minute.

At that point Martha Berry acted. When she got up and raised her hands, the unaccustomed sight made the shouters fall back in a temporary silence. She spoke in a voice softer, lower than usual, so that they had to lean forward to catch her words. "I'm sure it's helpful to express our feelings in meetings like this." Her smile was disarming. "Sometimes, though, I think it may be even better for us to let God speak in His words. Now everybody has his favorite Bible verse, and I've always found John 3:16 helpful. 'For God so loved the world that he gave his only begotten Son that whosoever believeth in Him should not perish, but have everlasting life.'"

The crowd stared in surprise. Trouble might boil up again in a moment, however, and Martha continued the diversion. Turning toward the first indignant wife, she smiled pleasantly again. "Mrs. White, I'm sure you have a favorite verse."

The highlander blinked and answered with difficulty. "Well, I guess . . . I allus liked 'Be ye kind ter one another.' " Martha accepted that with thanks and looked toward the student who accompanied her and Inez. "This young man from the school is a good song leader, and I wonder if he could lead us now?" When she faced the minister, that much relieved dignitary made his contribution to peace by suggesting that they all join in "I'm Bound for the Promised Land." On that high note the dove of harmony floated back into the revival tent.

For all these mountain trips Inez Wooten had to prepare to function as a traveling amanuensis. Neither dust nor rocky roads nor flood nor storm could interrupt Martha's flow of plans for Berry. As they drove along, the older woman would close her eyes for a moment, then open them. "My dear girl, now I know exactly what we must say to the governor."

Inez would brace herself against the seat, pull out her dictation pad, and take it all down. While they walked a bit later through a wood, inspiration might strike again, and without warning Martha would fire off a new letter. When they had a flat tire Martha seized the chance to work and explore the surrounding terrain at the same time. In chipper mood she would start, pointing out sights to Inez as the girl struggled behind her.

After a moment a bright new project might suggest itself. "Dear child, will you take this?" She would compose a letter of congratulations, an adroit appeal, a long memorandum to the staff. Still racing to keep up with her, physically as well as mentally, Inez would lower her head to put down a sentence, lift it to avoid the branch of a tree, lower it again. And so they would go on for an hour, until the car caught up with them.

On one ride they came to a road with water flowing over it

from a nearby creek. The machine stalled, Martha nodded as the student went off to get help, and motioned to Inez to resume the taking of dictation. When the boy returned an hour later he saw them still intently at work. The muddy water had crept a foot higher and would soon be inside the car, but neither woman had permitted it to distract her.

At this time Inez was constantly taking on new duties and accompanying Martha on every trip. Then all at once her superior said quietly that Inez might soon make a formal speech in her place, and the south Georgia girl turned a greenish white. "Miss Berry, they wouldn't make out a word I said. Anyway, I couldn't think of doing it."

"Yes, Inez, you can." The smile was kind, the words unwavering. "You can talk nicely when you try. Just open your mouth wide, and you won't sound like corn pone at all." Then she took up another subject, and Inez decided that the speech-making idea was a forgotten fancy. The next week she realized that Martha had meant exactly what she said.

"My dear," Miss Berry told her, "you're going to talk to that crowd, and I know it will turn out well." Inez thought of fainting, but even as she did she knew it would be hopeless. Unless she died, she would have to get up before that audience.

She did, and she survived, "though I ended wringing wet, and only one person came up and asked what I had meant by 'grain-to-the-gallon' coffee," Inez recalls. "When I got home I told Miss Berry I never wanted to be put through that again. Even as she nodded, I suspected that I would." Thereafter Inez spoke repeatedly and with growing effectiveness at small meetings and large ones, formal dinners, teas, and great rallies.

As the burden of correspondence became steadily heavier, Martha hired public stenographers from Atlanta for stretches of special duty. The first such importation had an experience that blasted her composure. Miss Berry was accustomed to Inez' comprehension of her meanings, a comprehension which must occasionally have approached the psychic. With the new-

233

comer Martha plunged ahead much as usual. Working the first day in the outer office, Inez glanced up as the new stenographer emerged from a session of dictation with glazed eyes and felt her way unsteadily to her desk.

There the middle-aged woman stared at one page of short-hand notes after another, and her face reddened; in another moment she wept. Inez tiptoed over to her and asked: "Can't I help?" The stenographer cried harder than ever. "I've done this now for twenty-five years, and for the first time I can't read my own notes! She doesn't give you half the names, and she walks around the room so that you can hardly hear her. She talks so fast; she jumps from one thing to the other. In the middle of the sentence she looks out of the window and calls to a boy not to hurt the tree, because he's digging too close to the roots, and to somebody else to cut the grass on the other side. . . ." The stenographer's lips trembled. "I never know whether she's dictating or just talking with whoever's going by!"

Inez managed to soothe her. "Don't let her see you crying, and don't ever tell her you didn't understand." Years ago Inez had learned that Martha's aides must get it right the first time. "She'll go home presently, and we'll work things out."

Later the stenographer read a few words and Inez filled in a sentence. They struggled successfully with names, appointment dates, messages to staff members—everything except a note which appeared incomprehensible even to Inez. When they made a hash of that letter, Martha reacted vigorously. "My girl, this isn't fit to send to a goat!" During Inez' apprenticeship an offending message had been unworthy of a cat. This was perhaps an improvement.

Meanwhile there continued, year in, year out, a stream of youths from the mountains to the campus, and Inez and those around her saw another kind of miracle. The first day that Martha met a girl whose eyes had been crossed from birth, who had suffered agonies of embarrassment, she realized what she would do about it. On the morning of the young woman's arrival Martha took her to a doctor, and before long the patient emerged from the hospital with a happy pride that she had never known before. A boy whose hand had been badly twisted in an accident and neglected for years agreed reluctantly to a series of operations and long exercises, and then he used it again for the first time in a dozen years.

Girls with harelips, boys with club feet, others with hearing troubles . . . In each case Martha talked a long time with the student, the doctors, the parents. To gain a family's consent she might drive long distances to the home, draw in the neighborhood minister, a country practitioner, or an older friend. During all of her career she maintained close relations with medical men within a wide radius—men on whom she could call for quick action or for long, slow treatment.

"I'm not quite sure how she managed it," one woman said. "But those doctors would do things for Martha that they'd do for nobody else on earth. They'd drop other cases and ride miles because she asked it. One of them spent seven hours in an operation I thought would never end. Of course, he might have treated any other case in the same way, and still I couldn't help feeling that the long talk she had with him—the way she described that boy's family, the good things that would happen if the doctor succeeded—had something to do with the fine result he had."

Now and then the chance of a favorable result was a long one, and the medical man had a dubious air. "Perhaps we shouldn't try. . . ." Martha Berry halted such reservations. "We'll try." For hours she would leave other work to comfort a frightened girl or stand beside a troubled mother in the hospital anteroom. And at the end, in case after case, Martha opened those long-closed doors to the world outside and gave the mountaineers their chance "to grow a mind and a soul."

CHAPTER XIV

SORGHUM AND
INSURANCE POLICIES

ALL AT ONCE it seemed that the world was Martha Berry's. The 1920s saw a surge of national attention, a recognition that neither she nor her associates had anticipated. The years that followed brought hundreds of tributes, both planned and spontaneous. And for the first time many Georgians, who had stared at her in puzzlement, began to realize that this woman had made a distinctive place for herself and her work in the American imagination.

Martha was called to the Georgia governor's office, to the White House, to the headquarters of national organizations. In the pulpits of New York churches ministers used her work as subjects for sermons. Educators studied her experiences, asked her advice in planning their own programs. Citations, medals, awards naming her the leading feminine figure of the year . . . The flow of honors was to continue for the rest of her life. She took it with humor, sometimes a wry look, and with thanks on behalf of "the boys and girls."

More vital to her, she indicated, was the fact that her principles were spreading to other schools, reaching other young people. And students were coming to Berry from an ever-widening area, from the Blue Ridge Mountains of Georgia, the Cumberlands of Tennessee and Kentucky, and the Smokies of Carolina. Beyond those regions the schools now drew students from the Ozark ridges of Arkansas, the West Virginia and Virginia highlands, the Florida cotton and corn patches, marshes of the Sea Islands and the Atlantic coast, hills of north Louisiana, and the Mississippi barrens.

When she was asked about the flood of new recognition, Martha chuckled. "I might begin to believe some of it if I didn't know how much we still had to do down here." Then, more seriously: "And also if I didn't know what we had to do simply to keep things on an even keel—even to keep going." And repeatedly she mentioned the fact that the school had a waiting list of 4000 to 5000. "How can we say we're doing what we should when so many can't get a simple education?"

In 1925 Ida Tarbell picked Martha Berry as one of the country's fifty greatest women. When *Good Housekeeping* magazine had a national ballot, its voters chose her among the dozen most important women of the nation, along with Jane Addams, Willa Cather, Minnie Maddern Fiske, and Ernestine Schumann-Heink, her fellow passenger on the trans-Atlantic trip. Officials of the competition praised "the magnificent unselfishness of this woman, whose life has been one amazing, burning, passionate rescue of highland youth." Before his death Theodore Roosevelt declared her "the greatest of them all."

The 1924 legislature of her state bestowed on Martha a title never before awarded to one of its people, "Distinguished Citizen of Georgia." United States Senator William J. Harris said that while the state had had a hundred senators and innumerable governors, Martha Berry stood forth as the first resident of "Georgia and, in fact, of the South."

Two years later Martha received a request to go to the White House where, with two men, she accepted the Theodore Roosevelt Memorial Medal for Distinguished Service. Granted the privilege of taking five guests, she selected a group of recent Berry students, "because they deserve this a lot more than I do." While General John J. Pershing, Herbert Hoover, and James R. Garfield looked on, she met the two other honorees, George Bird Grinnell and a man she had seen fifteen years earlier, Gifford Pinchot, Theodore Roosevelt's authority on conservation.

President Coolidge told Martha that, greatly pleased though the late President would have been to know the distinction given to his other two friends, "he would yet be most stirred to see this Roosevelt medal bestowed upon you." Coolidge continued:

> "In building out of nothing a great educational institution for the children of the mountains, you have contributed to our time one of its most creative achievements. Because of you, thousands have been released from the bondage of ignorance, and countless thousands of the generations to come will walk . . . in light . . . Few are privileged to receive so clear an answer to their petitions."

In reply Martha accepted the presentation "humbly for myself, but proudly for my boys and girls." As she looked about her on this return to the White House, she may have felt that her petitions had indeed been answered. "Except that," in the words of one of the Berry graduates beside her, "we knew she wanted to get out of there and back to Rome, because something new was stirring—the chance for another dormitory. And in the automobile on the way to the station she spoke a few

238

minutes about the medal, then dropped the subject. For the rest of the trip she planned ways to cinch the building!"

For the year 1927 *Pictorial Review* gave Martha Berry its Achievement Award of $5000. A committee of men and women selected her as the woman who "made the most distinctive contribution to American life during that year." In this connection Genevieve Parkhurst wrote: "In a legion of cabins tucked away in the fastnesses of mountain, swamp, and hidden valley, she has fed the flickering candle of human vitality . . . Out of a land of decay she has fashioned a land of promise."

A dozen universities North and South had begun to honor Martha with degrees. She was soon to win the American Town Hall Medal, the Colonial Dames biennial National Service Award, the award of the American Institute of Social Sciences, the Daughters of the American Revolution medal. She was to be made the first woman regent of Georgia's university system, the first woman member of Georgia's planning board. In the meantime, more important in many ways, was the event to which she and her schools had looked forward for years—Berry's twenty-fifth anniversary, starting on January 13, 1927. On that day and others which followed, the movement celebrated its silver jubilee.

The institution that many had believed could not survive had thus far weathered every threat. For the alumni observance hundreds gathered—students, graduates, faculty, trustees, friends. It was a time for stocktaking, for applause and laughter and tears. Through the gates, along the Road of Remembrance, Victory Lake, and past the units of the now far-spread campus, men and women passed, to look and to think back to other days.

They saw a pageant with figures impersonating famous friends or visitors to Berry: Theodore Roosevelt, Henry Ford, Gifford Pinchot, William Jennings Bryan. Other scenes showed the first barrel-pattern butter churn, and then the barrels sawed in two for tubs in that historic showdown between Martha and

239

the first students, and the twenty-five-year change from old equipment to new.

Each graduating class from the school's beginning had representatives. The student body marched, the faculty marched, and the children of Faith Cottage sped along in their uniforms with flying capes. Within a few feet of one another went a man, one of the early graduates, and his son, whom he had sent to Berry; a woman graduate and her son and daughter who had studied here; a husband and wife, both former students, with three of their children who had also gone to the schools. These were "Berry families," and, as many predicted on this day, there would eventually be grandchildren of graduates who would enroll.

The procession stopped, a silence fell, and toward them rumbled an ancient, repolished buggy drawn by a somewhat unsteady steed. It was the buggy of Martha's first mountainstorming days, pulled along by old Roanie, her "Sunday horse." And in the driver's seat, as in those earlier years, sat Martha Berry herself.

The long legs of the once gangling colt looked more than a bit shaky, but as a band struck up, Roanie's ears lifted, he shook his mane, and, for all his years, he began to prance. Some thought he might collapse, and yet Roanie made it. The spectators murmured and pushed forward, and now Martha smiled as the buggy approached.

In a moment the crowd was shouting, boys whistling, girls cheering. Alumni ran forward and board members followed; men and women from New York and Philadelphia, Texas and Louisiana, North Carolina and Illinois surrounded the buggy to reach Miss Berry's hand or touch her arm. It was a public demonstration of love and admiration such as she had seldom known in her life.

All of them filed into the red brick chapel for a meeting that lasted two hours or more, with speakers who gave stirring addresses and learned tributes. As the program ended, men and women, boys and young girls rose from every part of the room. In spontaneous outbursts they "testified," with words that would not be denied.

"I want to say . . ." "I just got to tell you today . . ." Some spoke in broken sentences, their excitement betraying them; others talked more eloquently. They held gifts for Berry—checks, small objects which they thought the school could use. Many of the presents were small, but clearly they represented sacrifices. Through it all Martha sat silent, her lips moving at times.

A student in blue shirt and overalls pushed his way to the platform and called out: "Miss Berry, I wanted to take up something so you'd know I appreciate what the school has done for me. I didn't have any money, so I went home this weekend to help Pa make his sorghum and brought you this here surrup." With that he held up a tin can.

Martha smiled: "This is a gift from the heart, and I value it beyond price." Awkwardly the boy moved toward his seat, and as he did so a young man with crutches struggled up—Eugene Gunby, the judge-to-be.

Eugene raised his hand. "Miss Berry, may I suggest we sell the can of syrup and present the money to the schools? I claim the privilege of opening the bidding. Twenty-five dollars, I say, for that half gallon of sorghum!"

Behind him another alumnus jumped to his feet. "Thirty-five!" "Forty!" "Forty-five!" . . . The can went for $200, and the last bidder cried: "Now, Miss Berry, let the schools have the money each of us has bid, and the can of syrup, too, your 'priceless gift.'" Accepting the dollars and the syrup, Martha lowered her head a moment, then lifted it in happiness.

Yet, for some, the high moment of the silver year came when a recent graduate approached Martha on the platform with an envelope. "This isn't a great deal," he said, "but it's the best I've got, and I'm presenting it, ma'am, in hopes it may encourage richer people to do more."

241

Martha opened the envelope and faced the audience. "It is a thousand dollar paid-up life insurance policy." The former student had a wife and two children, and he had intended the policy as a protection for them. "But what we want most," he explained, "is for Berry to have it. The schools are just beginning."

Martha Berry looked at him and covered her eyes.

Shortly afterward the schools' long-time friend, Mrs. Hammond of New York, held a silver birthday party for Berry in the ballroom of the Roosevelt Hotel. Its purpose was to increase the small endowment, with the interest going to provide scholarships. Thirteen hundred men and women joined in a tribute of friendship and solid support. As illuminated birthday cakes were wheeled in, electric lights went out, and all 1300 stood in the candlelight for a "silent wish."

Members of the Berry Pilgrims told of their visits, of the things that the schools meant to them. R. Fulton Cutting, the early benefactor, announced that he would "endow a day," Martha's birthday of October 7, for $2500. Turning, he also endowed Mrs. Hammond's birthday in September. To continuing applause he asked Martha: "May I have the day of the Berry graduate at your side?"

Thus called upon, Inez Wooten stood in confusion. With eleven children, her mother had never recorded the birth dates and could not be definite regarding the earlier ones. But she said she knew Inez' was near mid-December. Eager to have Berry lose no possible dollar, Inez called out December 17, and on her return told her mother that the question had been settled once and for all.

On a great calendar other dates were marked with red letters as other men and women endowed other occasions—mothers' birthdays, a child's birthday, a wedding anniversary. Some endowed a half day, an hour, a minute, until the amounts reached $100,000.

242

Meanwhile Martha prepared for her next step in extending the scope of the schools, and perhaps her next fight. For years she had quietly helped leading graduates who finished Berry's high-school work and wished to go on to college. She had persuaded people to provide scholarships or assist them in earning their way, and many Berry youths had made records in higher education.

Conditions were changing in the mountain areas. After World War I many families started slow migrations from distant coves to crossroad settlements. From such settlements others moved toward the towns. The mountains and mountaineers would remain, but a certain proportion of the students now went on to live in regions different from their earlier homes, and more and more often they asked: "Can't we keep on at school here and learn more things at Berry?"

At the same time Martha found it harder to get them into colleges, which had very limited openings for those who had to work their way. She puzzled over the problem until, as had happened before, an incident crystallized her intentions.

When Ruth, a clear-eyed, light-haired girl with a shy manner, finished her Berry classes in home economics with highest grades for the class, she told her teachers she hoped to go to a state university. After some effort Martha managed to make arrangements, and good reports reached her from the college; the girl was making a name for herself. During a vacation, however, Ruth returned to Berry for a visit, and Martha thought she detected a restrained, almost pensive mood.

At first the girl insisted that nothing was wrong, "nothing at all." Martha pressed her, and the story came out: "I've been ashamed, because I just didn't have clothes like those town people." Comforting Ruth, Martha told of her own unhappy days at Madame Le Febvre's school in Baltimore, where she had much the same experience. "As we get older, child, things like that don't make too much difference. But when you're young it hurts terribly not to have what others have."

Soon afterward Martha made her announcement. The next autumn Berry would add a junior college for both men and women, and a few years later the course would become a full four-year one. For these older students the schools continued their industrial-work programs as for the others—two full days of work to four full days of class.

The college was to be coeducational. In the late 1920s and early '30s there was some question about that arrangement, for certain mountain people still did not like their girls "mixin' with the boys." Nevertheless that was the way it would be, and the plan worked. The industrial program also succeeded, though a number of observers doubted that it could. Such long hours, and the demands of farming, dairying, and other operations—wouldn't they interfere with college classwork?

As a matter of fact, Berry students had far less leisure than those at most other colleges; they rose earlier and went to bed at earlier hours. And difficulties about discipline occurred, as some boys found adjustment harder then they expected. A number of the college students rebelled on occasion, and Martha acted sternly in individual cases. More often she called the youth in for talks during which she appealed, offered rewards, or threatened punishment for future violations.

One graduate recalls: "Nobody ever cracked down on me just the way she did. She made me want to cry and run out with my tail between my legs." Another has a different memory: "I felt bad and good at the same time. I was a heel, yes, but there was hope for me if I improved." While a few in such troubles left Berry on the same day that Martha conferred with them, most of them stayed.

Almost always she worked hard to keep the students. A faculty member might storm, call the boy or girl a hopeless violator of basic rules. Martha would intervene and consult the offender. Wouldn't he admit he was wrong? she would ask. Surely he must see that all of them had to make concessions, submit to regulations set up for the general good? Eventually she would consult with the faculty member, and the crisis would be eased.

In scholastic matters Martha tended to greater liberality than her staff. Was one mark more important than a boy's future? When a student had difficulties in a subject she would tell the teacher of the way early staff members like Dr. Cook had sat up with mountain boys to coach them in their deficiencies. "Try a little of that, please, and give this girl some extra attention."

Once a boy with a good record in everything except mathematics seemed about to miss graduation. Martha buzzed for the instructor and protested: "Jake mustn't lose his chance. I know how he's struggled for twelve years for this, and we can't let three points keep him from starting out in life." The mathematics professor sat with Jake every night for two weeks, and Jake got his start. When some objected to the principle of the work program for the college group, Martha stood her ground. "Somebody has to do it. We all work for one another here, and that's the basis of the schools." She remained firm in other respects. Every now and then callers met a student whose abilities or manner made a strong impression—a boy who sang in a deep voice, a girl weaver with a particular skill. The visitor would remark: "Why, he shouldn't have to do labor, with a baritone like that." "This girl ought to be doing nothing but what she does so well." With that a suggestion usually followed: "I'll pay his way." "You just let her go to classes, and I'll take care of the costs."

In each case Martha declined. If the visitor wished to give money for a scholarship, the schools would take it gladly, and that would make it possible for them to take in another boy or girl. But all students had to work. . . . At the same time, as the fame of her movement spread, she had to be hard-willed in another fashion, to make sure that the schools were operated only for those who needed them. The governor of Georgia once indicated that he would like his son to attend, and delicately yet clearly Martha said no. An Eastern industrialist declared that he would give Berry $20,000 if it would take his boy, "because what you do here would mean a lot for him." Although the money was badly needed, he, too, received a refusal.

In these times of increasing honors, Martha remembered a small incident that occurred on a burning summer afternoon. From her window she had watched for days as a dozen boys dug a ditch across the grounds, and finally she went to them. "You've done enough on this job, and I'm going to have you transferred to something a bit easier."

The youths dropped the shovels, looked at one another, and the tallest spoke emphatically. "No'm, we wish you wouldn't. We'd like to finish what we started—*our* ditch." The words reproved her but also made her happy. That proud rejection meant a great deal to her, she said.

At the same time a newcomer to the campus, who had taught for years in California, told her something more about the enlarging "Berry spirit." After his first class at the schools, two students paused at his desk to thank him "for a very interesting lecture." In a thirty-year career, the teacher said, that had never before happened to him!

Eventually Martha stood before Berry's first college graduating class, sixteen young men and women, including one who approached the age of thirty. Years earlier she had completed Berry's high-school course and gone back to the mountains to teach; since then she had returned to the school for college work. Now, her eyes shining, she looked up with the others as Martha gave her good-by talk to this band who were Berry's newest pioneers.

But as always, each advance meant accompanying problems. With every additional student the cost of operation went up. The endowment moneys now provided about $100,000 a year, less than a third of the funds needed to run the schools. In good years, officials might hope to earn another $100,000 by selling craft articles, milk, vegetables, and other produce. Each year Martha Berry had to gather a minimum of $100,000 by her own efforts—or face bankruptcy.

Through the years she said prayers of thanks to the small donors who continued their steady contributions. About 80 per cent of the schools' contributors were individuals who had to save their money to help Berry. And sometimes she saw a marked difference between the spirit of wealthier people and those who went without necessities to assist in Berry's work.

There was, for instance, the incident of the millionaire visitor to a neighboring state and Martha's hopeful meeting with him. Learning that the celebrated man was to be in the vicinity, she made a trip and waited a long time for an appointment. His backing would, of course, mean a great deal to the schools. At last she found her way to his suite and took her place anxiously before him.

For forty-five minutes Martha spoke with her hands folded tensely before her. She told of her long efforts, of the thousands she had trained; of the other thousands, well qualified to attend, who had been on the waiting list for years; of their offers to labor endless hours if only they could be admitted. So little money would provide an education for one of them for a year. . . .

The millionaire listened until she had finished, and then told her it was "one of the most beautiful stories of heroic struggle with poverty that he had ever heard." He was happier to know of it, and hoped God would bless it.

Leaving the suite in dark discouragement, Martha met a woman who, with a younger friend, made "fancy articles," embroidery and the like, and sold them. The two worked steadily and earned only small amounts, Martha gathered. They had heard of her schools and asked questions about them. Then they whispered together and told her they wanted to pledge future contributions of several dollars a year. After a moment's pause Martha accepted. The trip had not been wasted, for she had made two friends for her mountain people. . . .

247

A young girl who had a difficult time conducting a rural school visited the campus. She received a salary of less than $15 a month, and out of it she voluntarily provided supplies, repaired the building, and took care of other costs. Yet she thought so highly of the things she saw at Berry that she forwarded a dollar gold piece. Her grandmother had presented it to her many years before; the "precious souvenir" was all she had, but she felt that the Berry schools needed it more than she did.

One night Martha talked at a dinner about the efforts of her students to rise above their troubles. Later a woman who heard her wrote that the only things of any value which she had were a set of cameos left her in her mother's will. She had just sold them, and was giving the proceeds to provide a year's tuition for two boys.

In a paper box Martha received about $200 in gold—five- and ten-dollar pieces. The donor explained that after her marriage her husband had handed to her, as a sentimental gesture, every such payment in gold by a client. Now she wanted to put the pieces to a good use.

In New England a working woman had selected a new winter coat. Changing her mind, she sent the $50 to Martha, "to help keep one of those boys in school." Similarly the staff heard from a matron who had been working as one of their fellows. While she had served well, her health had been frail, and she had taken a new post with shorter hours. As a New Year's gift she sent $50, her full savings of the past twenty-four months.

A letter came with a $12 check. During her son's short life of eleven years, a woman wrote, he had put his nickels and dimes into a bank. He had hoped eventually to earn enough to go to college. After his death she found she could not give up the bank, until she read something about Berry. Now she would part with it.

And through the years thousands of others managed to send $1 and $2 gifts with regularity. A rough, homemade envelope carried a letter in a feeble hand: "I wish to let you have this dollar as I have been doing for a long time, and pledge myself to do it every Jan. 1 for the rest of my life. I am 94 years old." As Martha Berry once wrote, "We are poor in funds but rich in friends."

A man of whom she had not heard a great deal ran a small factory in Georgia. Paying a visit, he told her quietly: "I believe in what you're doing, Miss Berry, and I'm going to give you $10,000 to help it along."

Delighted, Martha thanked him warmly. At the moment, as always at Berry, such a sum had a dazzling sound. Yet she wondered; the plainly dressed individual seemed hardly able to afford that amount. As weeks passed without further word her doubts increased. She decided to visit him, and found an unpretentious plant, so noisy that they could hardly talk. Though he spoke pleasantly, the manufacturer said no more about the gift. After several more weeks she saw him a second time, and again he did not mention the matter.

Less than a month later Inez handed Martha a newspaper; the man had died suddenly. They stared at each other in harsh discouragement. Had Martha used bad judgment in failing to press him? Then a maiden sister of the manufacturer asked if Martha would call. In a gentle voice the sister explained that he had spoken of his intention to give the money but had neglected to act. Here was a check, a gift from the dead man's estate.

They were, indeed, "rich in friends."

And at Berry the boys could also give. Martha told often of an incident that stirred her. A missionary from India arrived to give a talk, but drew her aside after spending several hours on the campus. The need here was so clear, and so many lived at a level close to bare subsistence, "that I can't make the usual request for funds." Martha stopped him. "We may be poor, but we want to help others as much as we can."

The missionary made his address, though with somewhat less fervor than was customary. Then he saw the boys reach into their pockets for all they had, and one after another went to the supervisor of his work and had him advance other amounts. To pay back the school they would pass up a baseball game and labor through late Saturday afternoon. For these youths the "Berry spirit" was still growing.

CHAPTER XV

MARTHA BERRY'S BOSS

THE YEARS brought changes, good and bad, accidental and inevitable. The strong-minded little Mrs. Berry held tenaciously to life at Oak Hill, a somewhat frightening figure to timid undergraduates, a sympathetic friend to older members of the staff.

Slowly Frances Berry had mellowed in her attitude toward Martha and her schools. She still did not understand everything her daughter did, and she was frequently disconcerted at the sight of boys darting in all directions, of cranes and derricks in the distance, and the behavior of strangers who peered in and asked personal questions. And the way Martha ran all around the country . . . She sighed to those around her.

Incidents such as Martha's unplanned train ride up to New York never ceased to astonish her mother. Mrs. Walter Ladd, the invalid whom she had known for many years, arrived by private train with a party to whom she wished to show Berry. Martha made an immediate impression, and the guests suggested she ride with them to the next station. There, more delighted than ever, they pressed her: Why not be a "sport" and go on to New York? If Martha hesitated, it was for only a moment. She spent a weekend in the East and left behind a band of new Berry partisans.

Nevertheless Mrs. Berry clearly felt pride in her daughter and the things she did. Mrs. Berry would have preferred it if Martha had got herself a good husband and settled down to enjoy her days like her sisters. Still, if this was what she really wanted . . . The dimming eyes followed Martha's movements with an affection that had grown through the long years of their close association.

Toward the girl students Mrs. Berry continued to maintain a mild skepticism. These modern ones talked about work, she said, but they didn't understand what real application was. If she felt well enough to go occasionally to the small Berry camp at Mentone, Alabama, or to the campus, she sniffed a bit at the cooking. "You say you're Southern girls, and you don't even know how to make Southern-fried chicken."

Once Frances Berry became so provoked about the cuisine that she summoned a band of seniors to Oak Hill. "Here, watch." While she herself had not been a great cook, she knew how things should be done, and she would show them. "You must use very little fat with the chicken, and keep a cover on the pot so that the steam stays right in. And for your buttermilk biscuits—you're overworking the dough. Move your hands in and out, just enough, or it will toughen." Thereafter, whatever the quality of chicken and biscuits, Martha's mother was happy in her certainty that she had improved the girls' standards.

Mrs. Berry's lifelong aide, the grim-eyed Aunt Marth Freeman, had changed even more openly in her view of Berry and its works. Now and then she echoed her former complaints: Martha's married sisters had "jes' nat'ral troubles," while Martha had much worse, "troubles de Lord didn' sen'—jes' picked up from ever'where 'roun' 'er." But long ago Aunt

Marth had begun to concede that it "warn't all fool business." Some of the folks over at Berry had sense, and she would not deny it. Looking on at school affairs, she asked questions and made comments, now crisp, now tolerant.

For Martha Berry, Aunt Marth, and the family an unhappy hour came near. In her last months Mrs. Berry accepted the approaching end with an easy philosophy. When someone sent her slippers or a house coat, she told her helpers: "Put them on me right now. Might as well get use out of them while I can." One day she fell, broke her hip but refused to permit an operation. "It would do no good," she said with emphasis, and calmly she awaited the final moments. Most of her other sons and daughters reached Oak Hill before she died, at eighty-eight, in 1926, and a quiet burial followed in the family plot at Rome. Aunt Marth accompanied them, and on the return to the big house there occurred a scene which few would forget.

Martha had often called Aunt Marth, fondly, her "next of kin." Now, as the oldest surviving "member of the family," Aunt Marth stepped forward for a ceremonial comment. She summoned the children of Thomas and Frances Berry and looked earnestly from one to the other. They were middle-aged and grayed or sparse-haired, and most of them had grown boys and girls of their own. But Aunt Marth addressed them: "Ol' Miss dead, and you got to remember never to do nothin' to bring any *dis*grace on de good fam'ly name. You understan'?" Each one nodded to let her know that he recognized and appreciated her concern.

From now on Martha Berry would be head of the Oak Hill ménage, or perhaps Marth Freeman really held that position; many were never certain which it was. Still lean, Aunt Marth had reached an uncertain age. Some thought it was the late eighties, while others insisted she was much older. In any case, delegating only part of her household duties to others, she went spryly about her quarters in the white cottage set close to the main house. Once it had served as the Berry children's classroom, and it retained the early school bell and small chairs around the hearth.

Here Aunt Marth looked after her dogs, of which she always had several flop-eared varieties, her caged birds, and her yard full of turkeys. From her garden and her fowl she continued to earn a small income, which she saved. She had a special liking for turkeys and pride in the management of her flock. She gave the young ones maternal attention, bringing in the fuzzy, shivering newborn from the cold and keeping them in her big woodbox. Berry nieces and nephews who slipped in and tried to hold them received an abrupt warning: "Put one o' yer fingers on 'em, and I knock 'em all off!" If they did not desist, Aunt Marth had a butter paddle to whack about them with a furious energy.

More and more she remained to herself in her spare hours, working with her hands, listening for Martha. Within reach she kept an erratic old country clock with a heavy tick, "louder than I ever heard anywhere," a student recalled. When about to strike it would "wind up like a baseball player and go *bong, bong* like a fire alarm." If the *bong* weakened, Aunt Marth sent the clock away for repairs.

Martha Berry often sat beside Aunt Marth; the two women, more or less alone in the house that had once sheltered so many, came steadily closer. Inez Wooten, a favorite of the older woman, observed that they had a great respect for each other. Each ruled in her own field, and Aunt Marth would still call Martha down if she stepped out of her sphere.

Inez was sometimes shocked when she heard the Negro autocrat issue orders to the head of the school. "Boss, you git right out o' here! When things ready, I tells yer. Now march." At that, without a whimper, Martha marched. And in times of stress Marth Freeman drew on her years of experience to counsel Martha Berry. Once, about to leave for Massachusetts on her everlasting hunt for funds, Martha turned to the house-keeper for sympathy.

"I get so tired of traveling, Aunt Marth," she began. "I'd like to stay here and work at this end of the line. Boston is so far, and it will be cold, and I'll have a hard time explaining things. Don't you think it's time for me to let up a bit?"

Aunt Marth's white-turbaned head rose, and her ginghamed form straightened. "Martha Berry, dat talk don' make no sense. Yer cain't disappoint dem people; yer made a promise and dey wouldn't have much 'pinion o' yo' school ef yer didn't keep it." She paused: "You done toted yerse'f 'roun a long time fer dat school, and yer gittin' some age on yer, dat's a fack. But yer have ter tote yerself aroun' to git *any*whar." Martha nodded and toted herself off.

A year or so later, ready to leave on another long trip, she told Aunt Marth how tense and overwrought she felt. "I just don't know how I'm going to go through it."

"I tells yer what ter do," Aunt Marth replied. "Git down on der floor and roll."

"Roll—on the floor?"

A woman friend who was present was more astonished than Martha herself.

"You heard me, Martha Berry. Git down and roll."

With that the dignified Miss Berry, already in her sixties, lay down on the kitchen floor and turned over and over again. Rising, she wiped her flushed face, straightened her dress, and smiled.

"You feels better?" Aunt Marth asked it triumphantly.

"I certainly do." Martha laughed, and on several occasions thereafter she "got down and rolled" and also recommended the therapy to her friends.

Yet Aunt Marth proved to be one of the few individuals whose skills Martha could not easily adapt for the schools' benefit. Beyond argument, Marth Freeman ranked as one of the superb cooks of the region. Several times Martha persuaded the reluctant mistress of the art to instruct Berry girls in the preparation of a favorite dish—an aromatic meat mixture or a dripping peach pie. But each time Aunt Marth could not or would not impart her full secrets.

Never having learned to read or write, she had no recipes. In any case, she said, she did not bother about remembering exact proportions. Stacking the ingredients around her, she worked quickly, bafflingly with a running description. "Pinch o' dis. Now a middlin' han'ful o' dat. Two specks o' dis-yere." Finally Aunt Marth would fold her arms and survey her young listeners. "I kin tell yer f'om dawn ter dark, but you won' do it. You needs jedgment, an' you ain' got jedgment."

With Mrs. John Eagan, wife of the first president of Berry's board, Aunt Marth was hardly less direct. Tired of hearing her husband sigh happily about Oak Hill's chicken, Mrs. Eagan went to the high priestess for directions. "Yer can come in and watch me if yer wants," Aunt Marth told her, "but it ain' no use, 'cause yer cain't make it. Two things dat yer need yer jes' ain' got. Yer wants to have a whole lot o' yaller-legg-ed chickens a-runnin' aroun' in yer yard, and you ain' got dat in Atlanta. Second thing, you wants to have a lot o' good homemade yaller butter, and you ain' got dat. You ain't never gon' do it, is all." Though she tried, Mrs. Eagan never quite did.

Over the years Martha Berry never left Oak Hill on a trip without a final call on Aunt Marth. On her return she hunted up her adviser-critic-friend to "sit at her feet." Special guests were frequently taken to Aunt Marth, though a certain caution had to be exercised. No matter what the caller's status, if he did not ring true to her, the housekeeper let him and everyone else know it. With the passing years her eyes began to fade, but she could quickly sense the attitude of the overpedantic, the too sophisticated or the slightly condescending and send them rocking on their heels.

Aunt Marth's nose for the fake extended to religious guests

as well. Devout from childhood, she became even more pious with the years. She liked religion, argued it, and wanted to have religious books read to her. Though a Baptist, she had imbibed Berry's nondenominational attitude and welcomed most ministers with a smile. Nevertheless she caught the first signs of pomposity.

One day Martha presented a famous churchman. "Aunt Marth, the bishop gave a remarkable sermon, and you should have heard him. He's over six feet tall and very handsome." As the imposing figure stood before the dark woman, Aunt Marth pointed toward her best chair.

"Set down," she told him. "I don' keer much 'bout 'is importantness an' nothin' 'bout 'is good looks and bishopin'. I wants to axe 'im one simple question. Is yer an hones' to goodness preacher o' de ole fashion' Gospel ter save souls? Ef yer is, dat's all right. Ef yer ain't, den yer kin bishop all over Georgy and Alabamy and de whole United States, but yer won' git nowhars wid yo' bishopin'."

Meekly the bishop replied. "I'll remember that, and try harder than ever to preach the Gospel and save souls." Satisfied, Aunt Marth acknowledged his words.

At first the succession of tributes to Martha Berry appeared to surprise Aunt Marth. "Ever'body hearin' 'bout de boss," she grinned. "All de big folks in Washington, dey fer her, ain' dey?" Now she enjoyed talking to the students about Martha, her work, and theirs. They had to keep their place, of course, and not get too familiar or ask silly questions about ancient days. She turned away from those inclined to regard her as an anachronism or a character.

"Don' wan' no cur'osity seekers comin' roun' me," she grumbled, and her scorn boiled as she imitated the mealymouthed, nosy type. " 'How ol' is *you?*' 'How long *you* been walkin' roun', and who did yer *know?*' Humph, dey don' know sooey!" And, while she might agree to pose with Martha for photographers,

257

she declined most other such invitations. "Don' wan' my pickter taken." After the petitioners left she complained. "Jes' no call fer dat. Don' know dem, and dey don' know me."

One caller who delighted her was Henry Ford, brought to the cottage by Martha and Gordon Keown. They sat together, talking easily of old farming methods, old rural customs which interested the industrialist. By this time her ancient clock had become increasingly dilapidated, and when she told him she had to guess the time because she could not see it he suggested: "It would be fine if you had it strike on the hour and half hour."

Aunt Marth shrugged: "Hit jes' won' strike no more a-tall, and dey tell me dey can't fix up the striker any more." Henry Ford removed the clock from the mantel, took it to his private car, and sent it back some weeks later, adjusted so that its heavy *bong* could be heard twice each hour. Aunt Marth decided to show her appreciation and sent for a photographer. For once she was not camera-shy as she directed him. "I wan' Mr. Ford ter know how I looks wid dat clock all fixed up." Donning a fresh dress and apron, she tied on her best turban and posed with the timepiece in the middle of the table beside her. Gordon Keown dispatched the photograph, and Henry Ford sent thanks.

Yet Martha could sometimes come a cropper with Aunt Marth and the visitors. When a small band arrived, their number included a lady who fancied herself as a teller of "darky tales." Someone concluded that Aunt Marth must be favored with the exercises in dialect, and in this case Martha Berry's judgment failed her.

Bringing the group to Aunt Marth, she smiled brightly, while the housekeeper fixed her dimmed eyes ahead of her and said nothing. The beaming lady told one and cocked her ear for a compliment. Aunt Marth sat staring through her. The performer tried another and another, and a teacher who knew Aunt

258

Marth thought that she grew more furious by the minute, swelling like one of her turkeys.

A final yarn, and the stranger bent forward, inviting comment. She got it. Aunt Marth rose and spoke slowly, emphatically: "I don' like yer stories, and I don' like *you*." With that she walked majestically off like an African monarch.

Only Martha Berry, the witness thought, could have extricated herself from that embarrassment. "She got out of it by saying something about Aunt Marth's age and orneriness, and somehow she smoothed matters over." Later Martha went to Aunt Marth: "You really shouldn't have done that today." Aunt Marth still conceded nothing. "Dat fool, she couldn' tell no story, and you knows it, Martha Berry!" With a smile Martha Berry backed away. Incidents such as these, repeated by those who saw them, gave rise to the saying that Martha had only one boss—Aunt Marth.

The housekeeper frequently urged Martha to find some place in which she could regularly "rest your mind." Like others she heard Martha bemoan the way interruptions came at all hours and wherever she went on the campus. "If I only had a spot where I could think quietly for a few minutes at a time." The words were also caught by alumni, a number of older students, and members of the staff, and one day several of them met.

Someone remembered a point on the top of Lavendar Mountain, the highest spot for hundreds of miles and one that Martha liked a great deal. Why not build a house there with a garden and make a road circle the mountain for an easy approach? They hatched a plot, supposedly a complete secret, and for months the boys dug out stones, built walls, doors, and furniture, while the girls prepared curtains, rugs, and decorations. Martha took pains not to inquire where the files of youths were headed, or why her aides were missing at times.

She seemed completely unsuspecting when invited to "accept a little ride," and asked why they were taking her up the mountain. But when she stopped before the stone building, with its peaked roof outlined against the sky, she was deeply moved. She exclaimed repeatedly as she went over the terraced gardens, stone-bordered paths, and trellised borders. "This is a place," she said, "where I will sun my soul."

From then on Martha rode every few days to the mountaintop to walk over the windy, yellow-splashed plateau. Inside the comfortable house stood a tall stone fireplace about which a crowd could gather. Here she brought guests and staff; now and then for a special campus event she "declared a party," and the seniors or others arrived in a body for picnics among the trees.

On the mountaintop she could stroll by the hour and see the thousands of acres of campus below her. The grounds spread in a pattern of greens and yellows, with scarlet splashes of trees in the fall and the soft shades of flowering bushes in spring. From roofs in every direction rose plumes of smoke, and light glinted over the surface of streams and lakes to the horizon.

In the distance the blue line of Lookout Mountain at Chattanooga lost itself in a haze, and lesser ranges dwindled away at the sides. At the foot of their own Lavendar Mountain lay the buildings of the Mountain School with its rolling campus, the dark tops of Berry's thickly grown forest reserve, and nearby the lines of brown log units, the original girls' school, which Martha thought "sat like brown thrushes in the greenery."

Farther on, among groves of elms and oaks and plantings of dogwood, rose the Georgian chapel and other brick buildings of the college campus, and then the soaring Gothic structures of Henry Ford's quadrangle for the girls. The ever-growing workshops, dairies, brick plant—all or nearly all of Berry was around her. With strong glasses she could make out the boys as they cultivated the fields, the girls as they moved in and out of their quarters.

At sunset suppers on the mountain, both staff and visitors appeared to "loosen up," in the words of one who went there, and talk more easily than at any other place. For hundreds it became a happy, long-remembered spot, where Martha was the most relaxed of all. "You could almost see her stretch out mentally and shed her worries," a staff member says.

But such spells of retirement from activity seldom lasted very long. With Inez, Martha agreed that they would do no work on the mountain, and yet the assistant learned to take along a pad and paper, "as a precaution," to record the new thought, the idea for a fresh project. If one of them really intrigued her, Martha would leave the retreat after an hour or two. "Let's start back and get going on this," she would tell Inez.

Sometimes, pulled between work and a wish to enjoy a rest, she compromised. "We'll walk," she would call out, and stroll down the curving path. Behind her, pencil poised over her pad, Inez would take down the words as they fell. Once she counted twenty letters dictated as they sauntered to the base of the mountain.

The highland area was at its best in the fall, and more and more Martha Berry liked to be there in that season. October 7 brought an annual occasion, Mountain Day. The date was her birthday, but she shifted the emphasis. Years earlier, learning that the staff and students wished to give her a present, she proposed instead a gift for the school—the best birthday remembrance she could think of.

When she heard that all of the students and teachers planned to offer something, she made another suggestion: Let them bring a penny for each year of their lives. Her taste for ceremony helped evolve a touch of pageantry—a table in the center of a broad green woodland, with a flower-bordered basket in which the coins were dropped.

And now Mountain Day observances changed again. Early October usually saw the last good weather before winter, and the occasion became a general holiday and picnic time. Everybody at Berry went to a clearing in the rolling area, most of them on foot along woodland paths and winding roadways, the less hardy in wagons or cars. There, in a clean-swept place beside a cool mountain spring, they gathered around open fires to toast cheese and bacon and other savory food.

Speeches and singing ended in the day's climax, a "grand march" in which hundreds joined. The students passed along first in single file, then by twos, fours, eights, and at the end sixteen abreast, linking hands as they advanced slowly, rhythmically toward the table at which Martha stood with the basket that caught the pennies. Among the marchers were the small pupils in the day classes and, as ever, the Faith Cottagers in their distinctive dress. Finally, as late afternoon came and the distant peaks shone with the final sun, the parties started back toward the campus.

For Inez Wooten an important milestone of her own approached. She had known Will Henry for several years now, and had been attracted by his quiet, gentle manner, his dry humor. He too was deeply interested in the schools, but there were times he wished Inez could stay put for a while. Their courtship seemed largely a matter of broken dates, when Inez took off with Martha at a moment's notice, and with no notice at all to Will. When Will proposed and Inez accepted him, she insisted on keeping the engagement a secret until she found the right moment for telling Miss Berry.

Then one morning, not without misgivings, Inez opened Martha's office door to tell her superior that she was getting married. Inez felt the force of a small explosion, as Martha's face revealed her shock and astonishment. For several seconds she stared in silence at the blushing secretary, and then she spoke slowly: "My child, I can't believe you. Why, it's almost as if the world's coming to an end." Inez was moved and at the same time had a touch of guilt. Obviously Miss Berry had intended to keep her at her side for a long, long time.

She could still think of nothing more to say, but Martha went on more briskly. "Well, you're doing exactly what I planned at your age, and if you've made up your mind you'll do it. Still . . ." She seemed to be feeling her way. "My dear, I've grown to depend on you a great deal. Promise that you'll both stay on for at least a while, and I'll start to look for a substitute."

Inez gave a solemn assurance, and the tension relaxed, although the girl sensed that the older woman was thinking of the subject many times during the weeks that followed. Promptly Martha announced that she would give Inez and Will "the most beautiful wedding ever held in the chapel." Flowers were from her garden, the reception at Oak Hill, the wedding cake by Aunt Marth; the three bridesmaids, sisters of Inez, were all Berry graduates, the groomsmen were all Berry graduates, flower girls and ring bearer children from the campus, Dr. Cook was best man, and Martha was maid of honor.

The marriage, it developed, tied Inez even more closely to Berry. Martha never found a substitute for her as secretary-assistant, and some said, with a smile, that they thought she did not hunt very hard. Even pregnancy and motherhood brought little interruption in Inez' work with Miss Berry. Again and again a message arrived at the Henry house on the campus or Martha arrived in person with a baby sitter snatched up almost at random.

"My dear," she would apologize, "I wouldn't ask this if it weren't important. I need you for just about thirty minutes and I'm sure you won't mind, will you?" Frequently one of the office workers, an elderly spinster who didn't know the first thing about a baby, was drafted as sitter by Miss Berry, and Inez always worried about her ability to handle the young child. Nevertheless she took up her duties, and often they lasted, not thirty minutes, but the rest of the day.

The demands on Inez became more frequent, until Martha announced that she must go North on a vital errand and only Inez could provide the help she had to have. "Oh, but I'm afraid to leave the child with people I don't know," Inez protested. With that Martha remembered something. "You have a sister in Atlanta, don't you?"

"Yes, but Jessie's working full time, in a nice job," Inez explained.

Within the hour Martha had telephoned to the head of the firm which employed Jessie. "This is Martha Berry, calling about something that's important to us," she began, and ended by arranging a week's leave for Jessie. Not long afterward Inez returned to full employment. When little Margaret Henry was about six, a friend called at the house to find Inez gone, and asked: "Child, when do you expect her?"

Margaret knew the answer to that one. "We expect Mama home when we see her coming." And Mama went right on working for Martha and the schools.

CHAPTER XVI

CLOSE TO THE ROCKS

WHEN THE newspapers of October 1929 carried word of stock market trouble in New York, few at Berry took it seriously. Like more learned publications, the school journal made calming references to a "temporary overplus of prosperity" and "simple lack of confidence among businessmen." Matters would soon right themselves, the editor added; Mr. Hoover said so, and so did practically everyone else.

After a time the old mountaineer who ran the campus mill with its great water wheel explained to visitors that he had "heerd a lot of talk about *de*-pression this and *de*-pression that. I kept thinkin' it must be a mighty powerful thing and hoped it wouldn' get down here. Now I fin' out it's nothin' but hard times, and we was raised on 'em!"

Martha Berry also tried to joke. "Nobody has to teach us what a 'slump' is. We've known slumps practically every year since we started here." Yet as 1930 progressed and the nation's economy sank steadily lower, bad news arrived with every mail, with each telephone call. Many of her earliest contributors regretted that, because of "prevailing conditions," they could not continue their help. Pledges received only a few weeks earlier could not be fulfilled; even checks returned unhonored. Brokers and manufacturers had their businesses foreclosed, and the school staff was shocked when a long-time Berry friend, facing bankruptcy, killed himself.

"Everywhere I looked," Martha wrote, "I was told 'We have to economize,' and one of the first economies was in education." But as their donations showed a decline, the demands on the schools increased. Suddenly it seemed that a tide of want was thrusting its victims to the campus.

A girl arrived with an object about the size of a suitcase. "This is Grandmaw's foldin' organ, and before she died she said we must never give it up. But things are pretty bad at home, and the minister said it's all right to trade it to get me to school."

At one of the desks in the central offices a bedraggled boy told how his mother had worked with him in the cotton patch along a rocky hillside. "We bin savin' for this-here day three whole years. I jis' cain't go home and tell Mama it's no use. I want schoolin' bad, but it seems she's even more set on it for me."

A tall boy and a medium-sized one stood before another member of the office staff. "We walked ten miles up the river to git here," the older one said. "This is Bill, my brother. I remember Ma and Pap, but he cain't, so it's like he never had nobody. We been workin' for aunts and uncles might' near as long as we can remember, and we sure do need a heap of larnin'."

A weather-beaten mountaineer approached with two children in overalls. "Sister, please . . . These chillun ain' never had no mother's care, and I ain' much good at tenderin' them. Opal here needs looking after." One, it turned out, was a girl. "Please, they ain' never had a dog's chance."

266

From other rooms came other appeals: "I'm just at the end of my rope, and I don't want these chil'ren growin' like weeds."

"We'll sleep any old place, and we don' eat much 'cause we ain' used to havin' a lot. And we sure are hard workers, I tell you!"

With such words in their ears, a serious-faced Martha Berry and Inez went North at their first opportunity, only to receive another kind of discouragement. While men and women said they would like to contribute, they saw so much suffering all around them that they had first to give at home. "People were interested," Martha noted, "but they often seemed to say, 'Let someone else help.'" And she discovered that a number of individuals had begun to hoard money against worse days which might lie ahead.

All at once Martha Berry sensed that her schools had approached their severest test, a period that would bring them close to wreckage. So, on her fund-raising trips, there was only one thing to do—work harder. From nearly everyone who would assist she could expect less than before; her hope would be to locate more donors, small or large. Tired and aging though she was, she had to get up earlier and continue steadily on and on at her calls.

Inez Henry said that they dispatched so many notes that "we often snatched up every piece of hotel stationery that came to hand, to hold down costs." Whenever possible they used the subway in New York, and Inez "felt happy when somebody invited us to lunch, because that meant we saved just so much more."

One or the other spoke daily—and often several times daily —before clubs or dinner groups. Each evening they added up the amounts they had gathered, and now and then neither could sleep when she thought of the unimpressive totals. They had another reason for insomnia. Berry's auditing department sent figures of daily expenditures—so many thousands to be made up somewhere and somehow. From time to time Martha wearily thrust the sheets away. "Not tonight; they scare me. Last night I dreamed we were drowning in red ink."

In the morning they would drink large cupfuls of tea and dig into their chores. "Every once in a while," Inez recalled, "I'd swallow hard and remember my poor husband and our little girl and ask myself: Was this the end of the school? If Miss Berry thought the same thing, she never let me know it." In the middle of a gloomy morning Martha would jump up. "Nothing can be as bad as it seems. Let's get out and think in the fresh air."

They might walk along Fifth Avenue, look at women's clothes in the windows, and Inez would tell Martha that, depression or no depression, she had never seen prices so ridiculous. "And suddenly she would stop me. She'd had an idea, and we were going back to concentrate on it."

Usually they would finish their trip with enough funds to carry the school through a few more months, and Martha would shrug. "We've done all we can here. Let's get home and find out what's wrong there." But in some cases the margin of solvency was very narrow, and they succeeded only by the generous intercession of someone like Mrs. Hammond or Mrs. Carlisle, those friends of earlier years.

Such strong backers would discover Martha and Inez close to exhaustion, their faces drained by their long effort. There would be a kindly suggestion: Why didn't the two of them go back to their rooms and rest an hour, then come over to dinner? After dark, with the noises of the big city locked out, they would sit together to talk over old days and present ones: what "Prime Minister" Keown had once done to cinch a land deal, the old farmer who had just lost his property and had nowhere to send his five boys. . . . Kind words and encouragement would lessen the nagging worries.

At the end of the evening an envelope would be slipped into Martha's pocket, giving the amount needed for the moment. Several times such a check saved the schools.

Then, returning to Berry, Martha realized the need had grown even more swiftly than she expected. More and more boys and girls could bring no money at all for tuition; at one point 92 per cent provided nothing. Each season witnessed an increase in the number who worked through the summer months to pay their school fee for the rest of the year. (As before, their labor during the term itself took care of their board and maintenance.)

Told that they would have to limit the number of such summer workers, Martha answered emphatically: "That's one thing we can't do. Take them all, and we'll do for them somehow." Otherwise hundreds of students would have dropped out each year.

Most of them now lacked the few dollars that they had previously received from home for clothing and similar necessities. Faculty members brought stories of special hardships, of boys who went about sadly on receipt of bleak messages from home. Many of the youths had cardboard in the soles of their shoes. "Something has to be done to ease things for them," Martha said with a shake of the head. For some years the schools had developed a system by which the students' winter work built up small credits for them at the store; in these depression days the credits were increased.

One morning a boy went to the store. Please, he asked, could he get an advance of five dollars and arrange to do extra work to pay it back? When the store manager asked why he needed the money, the boy looked at the ground and explained: "My ma just died, and we don't have a shroud." He received the five dollars and more. All such additions to the costs, small or large, meant one thing: Martha had to gather more funds.

The hard times dug more deeply at the lives of Berry's mountain neighbors. Every few days additional men and women rode to Oak Hill in wagons and carts. "Miss, I had ter give up my farm." "Miss Marthy, you think you might could take me, the old 'oman, and the boys, and fin' somethin' fer me to do at the school?" Like millions of others, these men sought desperately for work, but there was no work.

Martha stared sadly. She had never known such suffering among the highlanders, and she gave them food and a few dollars if she had money at the house. In a number of cases she went to Rome to ask merchants to provide jobs or perhaps a cabin in the vicinity. Yet in all of the Georgia towns she found soup lines and crowded unemployment offices.

"It ain' money we needs so much. It's food and things to live on." Increasingly she heard the words, and one day she called Gordon Keown, Comptroller Hoge, and one or two other staff men. The schools certainly had no cash, but they raised a large supply of foodstuff. Surely there was work to be done about the campus; why not offer these men a chance to labor, and pay them in produce?

After much effort a project evolved by which the farmers worked like the boys, helping put up small buildings, move supplies, clear roads, grow things, and otherwise benefit the schools. New vegetable gardens and orchards were planted, and the cannery operated overtime to process tons of food. Old cabins on farms that had been absorbed by the campus were provided for some of the families. Men who had managed to retain their teams of horses brought them to Berry and received supplies in return for their work.

Gordon Keown had Berry's magnificent forest reserve on his mind, and he offered a plan of his own. Couldn't these men assist in the development of the pine properties, plant washed-out acres with new growths, thin out areas that were too heavily grown, and otherwise develop the acres of pine? From then on the forest reserve underwent rapid improvement. Here was an investment which would benefit the school for decades to follow, as it created one of the South's great stands of pine.

At the same time the tide of student applicants increased. Tents reappeared on the campus and students were quartered in spare storage rooms, rooms of any kind that could be found.

"But we just don't have places for any more; where will we put them?" her staff demanded. "Hang them on the walls, put them anywhere. Just don't turn them away," Martha answered, and went back to her other concerns.

Throughout the depression she called the students together frequently to buoy their spirits, to tell them some simple truths. "I hope none of you are feeling sorry for yourselves," she said once. "Don't ever forget that it's struggle that makes us. The boys and girls who work the hardest here have been among our best students and our best people when they leave."

She added earnestly: "If we have some who do a bit better than others, it is those who must work for their tuition all through the summer. And if there are some who do still better than those, it may be the ones who work hardest of all because they have a smaller brother or sister or a widowed mother at home. . . ."

Still the schools' funds fell. Martha, Gordon, and others appealed to the boys to use less sugar in their coffee, take no food which they did not finish, turn out any light that they did not need. Fines of five cents were fixed for any who left lights on. Staff members tried substitutes, and Robert C. Alston, chairman of the board, called extra meetings of the trustees to devise further reductions. After a time the school fare dropped to soup, corn bread and vegetables. "Some who knew the situation," Inez Henry remembers, "considered it lucky that they had as much as that."

The applicants beseeched, and Martha continued to accept them. At times her work supervisors reported that they "couldn't use any more boys; there's no more work for them."

"Then make work. That's your job," she snapped in reply. A moment later, softening, she explained: "The thing is to keep people busy, so that they won't rust and feel sorry for themselves." At the same time she wanted the schools to get the benefit of their efforts. With the campus brick plant in operation and a large supply of wood available she suggested: "Let's

271

put up a few bigger buildings. Prices are down, and they should certainly cost less than they did a few years back."

When objections were raised Martha replied: "Well, if furnishings cost too much we'll do without them and get them later." A staff member estimated that one or two structures went up for half the price of the old ones. As a few predicted, the expense of furnishing a badly needed recitation building proved a major obstacle, until their good friend, Mrs. Carlisle, came to the rescue. Asking over the telephone when students would move into the new structure, she learned that it lacked desks and equipment.

"What would they cost?" Mrs. Carlisle asked. Getting the figure, she responded: "Order them today, and I'll send the check." And the official to whom she spoke once more recalled Martha's words; Berry was "rich in friends."

Nevertheless Comptroller Hoge and his assistants had a hard time in balancing reduced revenues with heavier demands. Frequently Mr. Hoge asked creditors to hold off until Martha could make another of her trips. Again he scurried about, trying to anticipate payments due to the schools, in order to meet freight bills or express charges. At times they postponed making single big payments to make many smaller ones "to keep the supplies moving to us."

Friendly merchants agreed to defer bills. With out-of-state firms Berry met charges as soon as possible; with Rome or Atlanta organizations they requested extensions. "They knew we'd always come through, and for months we would live off our good name," says Mr. Hoge.

Yet increasingly often Martha had to ask the faculty to wait a few days or a week for their salaries, while funds were scraped together. One day she told the staff that unless further reductions were made, and at once, she did not know what they would do. She asked the question that most of them feared:

Would they accept a cut in pay? Already Berry salaries were very low, but everyone agreed.

The reduction helped for a time, and then came a new impasse and the need for still another cut. Martha appeared before the faculty, pale and agitated, and Keown, Hoge, and others made talks. They all knew how many teachers were suffering, they said, especially those who had young children or old parents with them. Some were borrowing against their insurance. Yet this month the schools could not meet the payroll. Suppose the staff drew, at least in part, on the school store for canned goods, food, and supplies? They agreed again, and for a time, as one of the teachers remembers, "we managed along somehow."

Overnight Martha fell ill, in a combination of physical exhaustion and nervous tension. The doctor called it, among other things, bronchial pneumonia. Through the bad times she had several other attacks of the same ailment. Anxiously she asked Inez about school affairs, but on doctors' instructions her assistant told her nothing that might disturb her further. "All you have to do is get well."

The students heard rumors of a possible shutdown. On one gray morning Gordon Keown got up somberly in chapel. "This is something I thought I'd never have to say to you," he began, and for a moment his mouth worked soundlessly. Lowering his head, Keown cried before them. A silence fell, and the boys looked at one another. So it must have happened. . . . An alumnus says: "I felt as if the ground had collapsed under us all."

After a moment Keown could resume. For the first time in their history, he declared, a student had been found stealing. The boys let out sighs of relief. The announcement did not make them happy, but at least Berry would not be closing. "Thinking back," the alumnus adds, "I realize I went through a bad few moments; I said to myself, 'Poor Miss Berry, after all she'd done and we'd done . . .'"

Meanwhile the crisis tightened; someone had to perform a new miracle, for the schools lacked funds to buy even essential supplies. At that point another providential inquiry arrived from their friend, Mrs. Carlisle. Having heard unhappy rumors, she called to ask if they were correct. Mr. Hoge talked with her, and once again Mrs. Carlisle saved Berry. A personal check paid bills for two months ahead; Martha recovered and resumed her work.

From then on Martha alternated between optimism and depression, and for a time she went about with set face and lusterless eyes. "I guess I'm losing my grip," she told a business aide. "I'm getting tired of fighting and fighting." Hearing such words, Inez Henry would hastily remind her of the things their graduates were doing, of the school's record, and sometimes she would draw in Aunt Marth as well.

Once Martha remained tensely alone for two or three days at Oak Hill. "I just can't make myself cross the road," she replied to questioners, while letters piled up and decisions awaited her action. Then Alice Barnes, supervisor of the "practice cottage," acted. "All of us felt terrible about it, and I tried to think of something, until I remembered that she liked altheas. I made up a bouquet and took them to her, with good wishes and sympathy. She liked-to cried, but I could see she perked up." Within an hour Martha put on her hat and walked across the campus with the old spring in her step.

In that mood she could chuckle at a comic-tragic episode. A woman who had shown signs of interest arrived to visit Berry for a few days, and Martha and the staff strained with their efforts to impress her. ("I gave up my part of the chicken so that she could have an extra piece," one said later, ruefully.) On the last day the lady discovered two rusty nails near a walk, and let everyone understand that she did not approve of an institution so careless as to lose a pair of nails!

Less critical friends materialized at unexpected moments. News came of a bequest of several thousand dollars from the estate of a woman whose name they could not place. Writing to the executor to express gratitude, Martha inquired about the donor. The reply explained that she had been an invalid in a hospital, and frequently asked the nurse for any available reading matter. One morning the nurse reached into the nearest wastebasket and drew up a copy of Berry's *Southern Highlander* magazine.

The patient went through it from front to back, made inquiries, and called her lawyer to add a codicil to her will. In the 1930s any such gift came as a windfall. "To have someone mention Berry in a will is like having him wave a farewell," Martha wrote, "or invoke a special blessing upon us from heaven."

For some time she had realized that the school publication was a real asset, and soon she evolved a new tactic. Whenever they left the campus, she and Inez took armfuls of the *Highlander*. At business offices Martha would leave one or two, and if a secretary appeared pleasant she was briefed on Berry and handed several more.

Even a visit to the beauty parlor could be turned to good account. In New York, Miss Berry visited the Elizabeth Arden salon for a manicure and also a bit of Berry propaganda. She needed no one to tell her how much talk went on there and how word about the school could be launched in the booths and under drying machines. Making recruits among attendants as well as customers, she delivered a sizable pack of publications and arranged to send them regularly. Whether she knew it or not, Elizabeth Arden was working for the Berry schools.

Martha also carried on her campaign in railway diners, where she deposited copies casually on empty chairs. At her seat she always had a few to present to those whom she drew (also always) into conversation. And the observation car, which some women preferred to leave to the men, impressed her as a good field.

A witness describes the time he watched Martha operate

there. After she had listened for a few minutes to a group of businessmen she interrupted. "I couldn't help hearing your conversation about the stock market, and I thought of my own investments."

"You've lost too, you mean?"

"Oh no. Mine pay 100 per cent, even though they're all in one basket."

Catching the men's attention, Martha went on. "My investments are in boys and girls, and they return a fine human dividend." The Martha Berry charm was working, and the group listened intently. She was given several cards, left the *Highlander* with five men, and eventually received four contributions.

Over a period of years the social restrictions were gradually relaxed. As for the matter of smoking, while many parents wanted a complete ban, high school and college youths were stealing off to smoke in the fields and behind buildings.

Dozens of alumni recall the way Miss Berry quizzed them about the matter. "I told her it should be allowed without any more palavering," one says. Another remembers: "I let her know I thought she was making a mistake, and I reminded her we'd lost several fine students over the point." Martha listened carefully and said nothing. After a time, one boy inquired of her: "How do you feel about it, Miss Berry?" Giving him a wry glance, she answered: "*I'm* asking *you*, young man!"

Eventually she bowed to the times, permitting the use of tobacco for men, but only in certain places. It reminded her, she said, of her problem with one of the earliest students who would chew tobacco in spite of rules and Miss Brewster's threats of expulsion. Miss Berry asked David to see her and asked him how long he had been chewing tobacco. "Well, ma'am, I reckon 'bout ever since I could *chaw*," he replied. "Do you think you could give it up for the sake of your education?" she asked. "Seein' how you believe in me, I reckon I could," he promised.

In another matter Martha herself stepped back from a previous stand. In the 1920s the bobbed-hair fad spread over America, until even the rural Georgia girls began to clip themselves. Traditionalists frowned, and Martha announced that no one at Berry could be bobbed. Women students complained and sought out teachers to argue. Carefully Martha asked dozens of the girls how they felt. She would not discuss her own views; she wanted theirs.

One or two students returned from vacations with short hair, and the issue had to be settled. There were reprimands, threats, tears; and then, on a trip to the East, Martha issued a ruling. She sent a post card to the dean of women: "Let them bob. M.B."

After a few months the schools met a new trial, its "pig crisis." Under recovery legislation of 1933 a processing tax was placed on hogs, and Washington officials ruled that Berry must pay back taxes for some years. The schools insisted that, while their books indicated a profit, it was only a paper one between departments and that it did not earn anything on the animals. But when Martha talked with her board members they saw no course except to pay. "You can't fight Washington."

That was what *they* thought. The schools needed that money badly, and she did not intend to lose it if she could help it. She knew President Franklin D. Roosevelt's mother, an old Berry friend, and a few months earlier the President had received her at Warm Springs, Georgia. Martha judged it unwise to go directly to him; she had another idea. Summoning Inez, she issued crisp directions. "We're leaving on the next train for Washington, and please get the bags ready."

On the way she sat by herself, resting eyes and energies. Arrived at their hotel, she washed her face and told her secretary: "Call Eleanor Roosevelt and say I must talk to her personally on an urgent matter."

Could that be done? Inez doubted it as she spoke to one

secretary, another, and a third. But at last the famous voice echoed over the wire, and Martha darted to the receiver. They made an appointment for an hour later, and the First Lady greeted the Georgians in a friendly manner.

"I'm sorry to trouble a busy woman with a subject like pigs," Martha began with a smile. "But I've brought the Berry pigs to the White House. When I started my schools we had so many razorback hogs running loose in the South that I decided I had to teach my boys to raise better ones. Mrs. Roosevelt, we've thought we were doing a service, supplying food for the boys and educating them and the teachers to improve our pigs."

Martha paused and went to the matter of the new levies. "I don't think the law can mean to charge a school for trying to bring up better boys and better pigs, do you?" Mrs. Roosevelt asked several questions and called up Rexford G. Tugwell, the agricultural official. Martha and Inez went to an office in which they met aides and specialists bearing law books, agricultural records, and documents. Martha had brought her own packet of papers and her own figures. For hours the men put more queries and debated exactly how much sausage and bacon and ham it took to feed Berry mouths.

Not without a sigh, the government finally gave up. Martha had won her point, and she sent thanks to Mrs. Roosevelt, the woman who had helped another woman in a corner. What was it the board had said about not fighting Washington? Going home on the train, she handed out the Berry *Highlander* with a fresh zest.

CHAPTER XVII

"SOMETHING WONDERFUL
AROUND THE CORNER"

BY THE mid-1930s Martha Berry's schools were no longer threatened by disaster. There would be nervous times again, but Martha's equilibrium had been restored, and the years that followed were in some ways her most tranquil, the schools' most productive.

A man who had known her from his boyhood spoke fondly of her and her work in this period: "She had a rare quality, one I've sometimes thought her best—her high-flying enthusiasm. She always believed there was something wonderful around the corner. There often was, if only because she had struggled to put it there. That's what I remember most of all: her gift of optimism and delight at the things that happened, or that she made happen."

She had made a great deal happen. The thirty-thousand-acre campus that had evolved was described increasingly as the world's largest, and the most beautiful in the Western Hemisphere. Thousands who saw its magnificent spread of plains, hills, and valleys never forgot its loveliness. And during her lifetime the school educated about ten thousand mountain people, and eventually more than fifteen thousand.

As economic conditions eased, Martha could turn her full energies back to the creation of building under conditions that might have defeated others—specifically, without funds. John Henry Hammond, husband of her great friend, Emily Vanderbilt Hammond, gave a vigorous description of her operations in such matters.

She would go to New York, have dinner with the Hammonds, and tell blithely of her plans. As she spoke Mrs. Hammond grew buoyant and Martha's own enthusiasm soared higher than ever. "One infected the other," Mr. Hammond said in amusement. "After other guests left, the two of them would have a final chat, and I might sit glancing at a book or a paper in the other corner of the room. I would listen, and sometimes I would stop in horror."

Martha talked warmly of all the fine boys who yearned to enter the schools. "I would hear her bubble: 'We simply must get a new dormitory.' A moment later my wife would answer. 'We really have to do it. Take those new boys, and as soon as you go back tell them to gather the stones, and we'll have the architects draw plans and begin work in a few weeks.' Mrs. Hammond went on to say she'd call the Berry Pilgrimage association and have a meeting to start hunting for funds."

At this point Mr. Hammond would approach the excited pair. "Look, this is all very nice, but I'm one of those shortsighted businessman-lawyers. You just don't do things like that. You have to get the money first and *then* talk about drawings and stones!" He shook his head. "Well, they would stop —for about sixty seconds—and my wife would look up and tell me patiently: " 'We'll find a way, as we've always done. Have you no faith?' "

" 'Not that kind,' I'd say. I don't suppose they even heard

me, because they went right on as they intended, the cart a mile before the horse. I'd groan, and members of the board would grumble. Still, a year or so later the building would be complete, the money would be in hand, and everything would have worked out." In time, when Martha and his wife put their heads together, John Henry Hammond learned to leave the girls alone.

One of the trustees worried a great deal more. He was Walter Ladd, husband of the invalid who had developed a remarkable interest in Berry after the death of her young nurse. Both the Ladds occasionally felt disturbed about Martha's insistence on taking in students before she had funds to maintain them. Once or twice they had spoken of the subject to Martha and to an old friend of all of them, the bright-spirited Mrs. Augusta Hope.

Now Mr. Ladd went to Mrs. Ladd and Mrs. Ladd went to Mrs. Hope. The latter was due to visit Berry before long, and Mr. Ladd asked her to carry a message: If Miss Berry wished to continue to receive the Ladds' support, she must really change her methods. The sanguine Mrs. Hope sailed in and explained Mr. Ladd's view. Martha sat serenely quiet until the caller finished, and then nodded. "My dear Mrs. Hope, I can understand his feeling, and I always like to hear what people think about the schools. But will you please tell Mr. and Mrs. Ladd that I will keep on opening the gates wider for boys and girls who need it so desperately"—she nodded no less serenely than before—"even if I must lose the backing of some of my best friends."

Returning North, Mrs. Hope repeated these words and added: "I've gone to Martha Berry for the last time with such a message. She was so direct and so simple and dedicated when she told me that—why, I just wept and apologized. The next time you have word of that kind, you'll have to give it to her yourself!" With this Mrs. Hope wept a second time; Mrs. Ladd shed a tear of her own, gave her husband a dressing down, and that ended the opposition. Mr. Ladd stayed on the board, continued to provide funds and, when he died, left a bequest to Berry.

Another board member raised a question when he heard that Martha had accepted a contribution from a gilded Easterner with certain sporting connections. Martha cocked her head and mused a moment. "So that's where he gets his money. You know, I wonder if any of us can be sure just where ours came from." The gray eyes twinkled: "Well, we're going to put his to a good use—and redeem it for him!"

The trustee realized that Martha had been far from repelled by his information. If it affected her in any way, it made her more curious than ever about the donor. "As much as anything else," the board member said with a smile, "she felt an unending interest in human beings as human beings."

The mid-thirties brought a form of recognition that meant a great deal to Martha Berry, an invitation to address the Southern Association of Colleges and Secondary Schools at a meeting in Nashville. "I'm as scared as I'm delighted," she informed Inez and Dean Cook, while she fretted over what she should say. "I've always just stood up and told stories. Before all those learned folk that won't be enough."

After her friends offered suggestions, Martha made a careful outline, dictated paragraphs, revised them, junked the whole and started over again. Rereading the finished product, she laughed ironically: "It sounds so big and dignified—nobody'll think it's me at all, and that may be just as well." As she, Inez, and Dr. Cook drove to Nashville, her doubts still nagged at her. "We're so young in the college department. We have to put our best foot forward, don't we?"

They arrived in a rush of dust and a rash of nervousness. Delayed by automobile trouble, they reached the hall only a few minutes ahead of time, and Martha stepped directly to the platform. The academic audience applauded with restraint. As Inez watched anxiously, Martha's eyes passed over her notes, and then she put them quickly down. In the flash of an instant her judgment must have told her that the educational jargon was not her style.

"I'm like Br'er Rabbit today," Martha began. "I'm just in from the cabbage patch." As she explained her fears, she heard chuckles which became roars, and Inez sensed that precisely the right note had been struck. Improvising as she continued, Martha presented a plain tale of her experiences, the lives of the mountain people, the way she tried to train and teach the young. Cutting through the formality of the occasion, she made a great impression.

On the way home she said she hoped the experience had taught her what she herself often told the mountain girls. "Be yourself; if you're a cabbage, don't try to turn into a rose." Relaxing in the car, she promised that she would "keep right on being a cabbage."

That same year, on another off-campus trip, Martha figured in an incident of which the staff did not learn until later. Bates College of Lewiston, Maine, invited her to receive an honorary degree. When one of the college officials met her at the railroad station, he took her to his car and went back for her baggage. On his return he saw an unshaven, disreputable figure at the car window. As the man moved away, the official asked if he had been annoying her.

"Oh no," Martha replied. "I've just been speaking to him."

Something in the way the man walked off made the college man persist. "He was begging?"

"Well, I did give him some money." After a moment Martha laughed. "I'll tell you about it. He came up, pulled out a gun, and told me to hand him my purse. I asked what he wanted the money for, and exactly how much he needed. We talked a little, and I told him that he could surely handle his troubles without a gun; it wasn't necessary. Then we went over his problems, and I gave him the amount he mentioned."

The astonished college official assured friends that, as he

stared, Martha showed no sign of shock or fright or resentment of the man's act. Instead he read a simple curiosity about human motives and a compassionate understanding.

Still another visit during this period gave a warming proof that Berry's work was making itself felt. One of the first graduates of the college department had been Carrie, a girl who finished the high school many years earlier, then returned for further training. With her diploma, achieved after such long struggle, Carrie had found her way as a teacher to a place where schools had always been scarce, which had no community organization, no district nurse, no hospital or similar facilities.

At that first Berry college commencement, Carrie had heard Martha urge the students to "work for a higher Master and higher pay than your salary checks." She heeded the advice. Her pay was small, hours long, the people almost destitute and victims of numerous prejudices. The shabby one-room school had no desks or stove. Carrie gave part of her salary to buy a heater and, remembering Martha's own story of the early times at Possum Trot church, promoted a "community working." Walls and roof were repaired, doorsteps straightened, and shrubbery planted, and then Carrie herself refurnished the interior.

Invited to the school for graduation, Martha discovered her former student finishing a table. Laying her hammer aside to greet Miss Berry, Carrie explained: "The school needed furniture, and so I made these things. I learned at Berry to take what I had and make what I need." When Martha smiled in satisfaction, Carrie quoted her familiar saying: "Put your brains into your fingers and your fingers into your work."

The little school was to hold its ceremony that night, and as the children began to appear Martha noticed how clean they were. Most of the small girls had neatly laundered white dresses. Again Carrie had recalled her Berry days; since the families could not provide costumes, the teacher had found flour sacks for conversion to the purpose.

284

Carrie told Martha that the region's prejudices included strong resistance to medical treatment. "That boy"—she indicated a lad of twelve—"had influenza, and just as he was able to walk again he stepped on a rusty nail. When I saw how infected it had become I begged his mother to let a doctor look at him. She said no doctor would have a chance to cut off her child's leg."

Carrie went to the house, made hot poultices, and sat up at night to do what she could. For a time she continued desperately to urge the parents to call a doctor, and then she herself went to a medical man, got advice, and administered treatment without letting the family know its source. Meanwhile the girl kept the school running every day, spending the evenings with her patient.

"We pulled through," she finished. "I did it because I thought of the story you used to tell about the boy who had gone to Berry in the early days and developed measles and pneumonia. I remembered the way the doctor called it smallpox and everybody got so scared you had to isolate the boy in the log cabin and nurse him yourself."

The school bell was ringing for the night's graduation. Carrie would be her own master of ceremonies, and Martha chief speaker and guest of honor. As the parents told her later how their children were receiving an education which most of them had never known, Martha nodded happily. Berry's shadow was reaching farther and farther. . . .

The time had arrived for another rest. She was sixty-eight now, and had been working for years without a letup, and one day the doctor spoke to her sister, Mrs. Campbell. Martha, he said, needed a real vacation. Mrs. Campbell spoke to her husband, who was then chairman of the board, conferred with one or two of the staff, then brought an ultimatum to Martha: She was going back to Europe, and the Campbells were going to take care of the expense.

"I have nothing to say about it?" Martha smiled wearily. "You do not," her sister replied with emphasis, and so it was arranged. As plans evolved she received word that she would be presented at the Court of St. James's. The thought amused her; her ancestors had left England to get away from kings and queens, and here she would be, bowing before them. Still, the presentation might draw notice to the schools, and anything that did that had its value. . . .

Martha again had doctors' orders not to talk of the schools, not to think of them; and as before, she had not sat for five minutes on deck when she drew the passenger beside her into conversation about international affairs. Within another few minutes she had the subject, of course, around to the schools. During the weeks that followed, Martha established new beachheads of friendship with people from all over America, from four or five European countries, received funds and pledges. "And it's all been very restful," she insisted.

In London she prepared for her court presentation. At an establishment which traditionally provided costumes for such events, she explained that she ran a school and had limited funds. When an attendant suggested a silver lace dress, she hesitated. It was very expensive, and yet she could wear it again for Berry affairs. Her family sometimes lectured her about her costume, she declared; it could be "my 'wedding dress,' when I give my girls away in marriage."

The three feathers also seemed costly. Nevertheless, she had to take them, although, she said, "I can't think what I shall do with these white feathers in Georgia." Then came the last detail, a soft blue velvet train, trimmed in silver. As it was draped behind her, she asked the price. "Three hundred dollars? I'll have to go without the train."

The attendant looked startled. "Miss Berry, you have to wear a train when you're presented." He had heard of American oddities, but this was the strangest of all.

Martha turned to him: "I could keep several boys in my

schools for a year for what it would cost me to wear the train for one evening. Right now I have one who wants to be a surgeon; he has the surgeon's fine hands, and I've watched him work for years . . . No, it would be sinful to spend so much."

"Madam, you don't understand. You simply cannot appear at court without a train."

"Then I shall have to send my regrets to the King and Queen."

The attendant stared at her in dumfounded silence; as Martha said later, she could feel the British Empire tremble. After a moment he spoke: "Madam, one doesn't send regrets to the court."

Sensing the near calamity, the manager appeared, only to be scandalized in turn. Such an episode had never arisen in the history of the establishment.

A new thought occurred to Martha. "Could I rent the train?"

"Miss Berry, we do not rent trains. People are so pleased at a presentation that they keep the whole costume and hand it down from generation to generation. Their children and grandchildren . . ."

Martha drew on her coat. "I have thousands of 'children' and nobody has counted how many 'grandchildren.' I wouldn't know how to divide the train among them. If you'll consider renting it, will you advise me at my hotel?"

Eventually she was informed that the organization held a long meeting on the impasse. Miss Berry must never tell others of this decision, because it would set a difficult precedent; but rules had been waived and she might rent the train. Some months later her gown and feathers went into a case at the school—without the traditional train.

Refreshed, her energies revived, Martha returned home and, as usual, found new demands, new campus emergencies. Almost at once she came upon a case that challenged her ability to move swiftly, using "both hands and both feet," while violating a rule or two to get results.

Her anger and also her compassion were stirred when she discovered that a nearby tenant family was in a serious situation after managing to send its two daughters to the school. The girls needed money for uniforms, shoes, and other clothes; while others might have considered the amounts small, they were beyond the family's available means. The mother, determined that they would not drop out of school, had skipped meals, eaten almost nothing for days at a time, until she collapsed.

When she learned what had happened, Martha Berry exploded into action. With a doctor and two faculty wives, she went to the home, taking foods, money, and blankets. She demanded that everything necessary be done to bring the mountain mother back to health, by special diet and constant attention. This became the responsibility of the two faculty wives as much as of the doctor. Daily the young wives went with the doctor, preparing the food, giving it to the patient with a spoon, making certain that the rest of the family understood the doctor's instructions, that the younger children received care. The mother slowly recovered, and Martha found work for the father.

Not long afterward she came upon a tragically malnourished baby. Within an hour or two she had a doctor on the job to prescribe treatment. Already the mountain mother had accepted the prospect of losing the boy, but Martha quieted her. "Stop it. We're going to save him, and then you're going to take better care of him!"

The doctor was decidedly pessimistic, but Martha became adamant. "He's going to live. If you can't manage it, get somebody who will." For weeks she rode back and forth to the cabin, almost dragging the doctor with her. "How do we know what we'd lose—a genius, a great man?" she demanded. Her eyes were searching, then as always, for that "other Lincoln." And the child did live.

At other times, however, she admitted that she missed chances to act. On a trip to Chattanooga she once stopped at a filling station where she heard of a transient family with a "stricken" child down the road. Her curiosity stirred; she had herself driven there and saw a little girl who had once been badly scalded, the tissues of her legs damaged so badly that she could only crawl. Martha talked for some time to the parents before she had to leave for important appointments in the Tennessee city.

Meetings and other duties in Chattanooga kept her for ten days. When she returned to the farm she learned that the family had just moved in search of other work; no one had any knowledge of its whereabouts. For months Martha made inquiries without success, and the child's fate disturbed her greatly. "You see, Inez, there's always time to do the real things. Nothing that took us to Chattanooga could have been more important than saving that child. We lost our chance, and it ought to teach us a lesson."

Martha concentrated again with fresh fervor upon her effort to bring the Berry campus to fuller beauty. Remembering the softly rolling countryside of England and southern Europe, she labored to reproduce something of such scenes. As chief bargainer, Gordon Keown received assignments to buy a particularly fine tree that Martha thought would dominate a hill, or an impressive bush which caught her eye. The country people snickered at the thought of transplanting things like that; nevertheless she paid cash, and most of them took it. She sent out groups of boys on two-day trips, as far as fifty miles each way. They would uproot and pack the grown trees, protecting the roots as they loaded them on trucks and brought them back.

At times even the canny "Prime Minister" Keown had a comeuppance, as in the case of an elderly farm woman who had nurtured one of the finest boxwoods that Martha ever saw. When Gordon wanted to make the purchase the mountain wife shook her head. "No, sir, I flat couldn't sell hit. Got the first cuttin' fifty year' ago in my bride days. But I'll let you have a nice cuttin' and Miss Marthy can put 'em out like I do."

Gravely Gordon accepted the slips. Alone again with a student, he broke into a laugh. "Anybody who knew Martha Berry could imagine *her* waitin' fifty years for a boxwood or anything else!"

Students chortled over the story of a freshman who glanced out of his dormitory window at the sweeping grounds and felt an older boy nudge him. "Look good at that road, son," he was advised. "It may not be there tomorrow. Martha Berry came poking around today."

When a party of important visitors were reported on the way to Berry but still forty-eight hours away, Martha stared reflectively at the front of a new building. "It doesn't look really well, does it?" she asked, and her soft, low voice became still softer and lower. "There ought to be a nice line of trees and shrubs. Let's put them in."

That night scores of youths worked for hours, digging, lifting, planting by flashlight. By the time their callers arrived, three oaks and many plants grew as solidly as if they had been in place for years, with beds of fully blooming lilies around them.

Whatever changes occurred on the campus, her rule was that they must spare the better trees. A new road would have to skirt them; if an important building went up and a good tree stood on the site, the tree must be transplanted with care. During one of Martha's absences, a student ran in to Inez Henry. "Some electric workers are here to run a line, and they're a-slayin' them dogwoods left and right. Come quick and save 'em!" Inez intervened promptly.

"Put our best foot forward, and keep it there," Martha often repeated, and she meant it. As she went about the campus her eye caught a shutter that hung slightly awry, a board placed against the back of a building, or a slate out of place. A few minutes later the grounds superintendent was called on the telephone, or a messenger sent for him. Would the superintendent see that the condition was righted that morning? If the afternoon found it unrighted, the superintendent received a second and more vigorous message. Suppose a visitor saw such disorder?

Frequently, as she was driven over the grounds, she called to her student-chauffeur. "Wait. Somebody threw a piece of paper over there." She herself would often be out of the car before the driver, picking up the offending paper. Whenever she went in or out of a building, her eyes roved left and right, hunting for bits of litter. Walking about the campus with a guest, Martha sometimes motioned to a helper to draw the visitor into conversation; then inconspicuously she would snatch up a wad of paper and return with a look of satisfaction. The child of a staff member, on a vacation, once asked: "Papa, can I throw this gum wrapper away, or will Miss Berry have to pick it up?"

No clothing was allowed to hang out of dormitory windows, and no personal belongings could sit on window sills. Martha wanted no "back yards" at Berry, no places where clotheslines flapped and garbage cans piled up. Laundry was done indoors, and everything connected with garbage stayed well out of view. One hard-working staff member had a habit of resting for an hour or so in a porch rocker. "My dear, that wouldn't look good to friends of the schools," Martha said seriously. "Suppose they thought you just didn't have things to do? You understand, don't you?"

An hour later, to make sure that the girl had understood, Martha sent a truck to pick up the rocker. Before dark she called to take the girl for a ride, during which she made graceful amends. But the rocker did not go back.

At such times Martha had what a Berry staff member called an "eagle look" in her eyes. "She was a small eagle, but still an

291

eagle. When Miss Berry came in, she would smile and chat with us in the dining room, compliment this and that. But me, I always watched those eyes, darting around, missing nothing. If they fixed for a moment on something, I knew I would hear about it before long, and I went to work to correct matters then and there."

In putting those best feet forward, some of the Berry people almost lost their balance. Faculty wives groaned over sudden assignments which they had never anticipated. Martha had once been surprised when, looking out of her window, she beheld fifteen or twenty of the wives talking together after a social function of their own. "What *are* those women doing?" she asked. The sight acted as a spur; if the ladies had time to stand around, they might be using it to help Berry. Soon they were doing just that.

Martha studied the particular skills of most of the staff wives. Mrs. Clifton Russell had an easy charm, a gift for conversation. Mrs. Hoge, trained in home economics, could organize a meal or a reception in ten minutes. Each woman, her special ability well catalogued in Martha's mind, was put to work. Mrs. Green's telephone would ring. "My dear, I have forty guests on their way, a bit unexpectedly. Could you handle a little tea for me, with some of those cakes you do so well? Oh, two hundred will be enough—with icing."

A faculty wife promptly learned that domestic duties came second. If she had a particular knack, she might find herself summoned to display it at a reception, a formal dinner, or during an automobile ride; or she would be called on five-minute notice to the mountaintop house for a conference with a guest. "Miss Martha has the car waiting outside, and we're due up there right now." When the husband and children arrived for supper they would fix their own. One daughter of such a family said, "I grew up on notes left by my mother: 'M.B. *sent for me. Find eggs and bacon in the box.*'"

For these wives, as for everyone else, desperate developments called for desperate measures. With a garden expert coming to visit, jonquils once became a necessity. But Martha discovered that neither her garden nor the school nursery had any. Closing her eyes, she recalled that some faculty members had fine plantings of the yellow flowers. Time was short, and they could not appeal or confer; she ordered a raid. The jonquil growers returned to find their beds stripped. Yet they understood; "at Berry you always understood."

A leading industrialist and potential benefactor loomed unexpectedly on the Georgia horizon. On his arrival he smiled as he saw himself in a handsome frame on the walls of a main Berry building. A little later the tycoon beamed when he made out a similar likeness in a dormitory. That night he glowed with happiness over a third picture in his guest cottage. He never knew that Martha, having only one picture of him, had stationed boys to move it from place to place, within minutes of his arrival.

Out of such activities arose a Berry joke. While several youths worked on the campus, one supposedly looked up and cried: "Do something quick, fellows, even if it's wrong! Martha Berry's coming." Yet she insisted, she said, not on labor for its own sake, but intelligence in work. Walking along one bright morning, she stopped before a student setting bulbs at the edge of a path.

"What are you doing?" she asked.

"Just planting, ma'am." The boy smiled.

"Planting what?"

"Don't know, Miss Berry."

"You don't know what they'll be when they come up in the spring?"

"No'm."

"Well, if I were you, I'd stop right now and find out what they're going to be. That way you'll do a better job." She watched while he went to the supervisor to get the information. At Berry, not only must everybody be going somewhere; he also had to know where he was headed.

CHAPTER XVIII

SO LITTLE TIME,
SO MUCH TO DO . . .

FOR YEARS she had fought a series of ailments, a slow weakening of the flesh. Now, as Martha Berry passed seventy, the effort grew harder, the spirit less buoyant. When the doctors diagnosed a heart condition and high blood pressure, she agreed to rest more often, and for the most part she complied—until "something important turned up." Then she forgot caution, marshaled forces, rang bells to summon her staff, called Inez, and rode forth.

She returned, as a rule, more tired than ever, and the struggle to recover took longer each time. Geddins Cannon, Berry graduate who chauffeured her in the 1930s, took her frequently, with or without Inez, on five- and six-day automobile trips to Tennessee, North Carolina, and other nearby areas. Although such excursions were intended as part work, part holiday, in many cases they became all work and no rest.

Now and then she would go early to bed in some hotel, only

to find it impossible to relax. Ged Cannon would hear a knock and Martha would announce: "Geddins, I just can't sleep, and I think we ought to get on to the next place." She had already packed, and Ged would start out with her a few minutes later. They might ride a hundred miles, arriving past midnight. On the way, half exhausted, Martha nodded in the back seat and Ged avoided jolts or sudden turns. Even at the second stop, however, she might lie awake for hours before falling into a restless slumber.

Back at Oak Hill she was uncomfortable in the evenings. When she picked up books or magazines, her eyes gave her trouble. She arranged to have a student read to her for hours, and she would doze off; but soon she stirred again, called to the girl, and sometimes would lie for five or six hours, seeking desperately to rid herself of her tensions.

When the doctor recommended a "Mediterranean cruise" Martha refused. "My days of long travel are over. Still, I'll compromise with you." She was especially fond of one of the Berry lakes and had a student row her back and forth in the afternoons. "This is my Mediterranean cruise," she laughed.

Inez Henry and others tried to relieve her of as much paper work as possible. Even then her sight bothered her, and after much persuasion she agreed to see an eye specialist. He told Martha what she had feared; she had cataracts and in time must have an operation. Nevertheless she declined to slow down or take precautions. "While I stayed as close behind her as I could," Inez says, "she would dart ahead, jump into an elevator, and look over at me with a smile. Sometimes she fell, picked herself up, and went right on."

Eventually the operation appeared imperative. A long period of uncertainty preceded and followed it; even with thick glasses, Martha had to squint and guess at faces or sights. Inez would stand at her side, whispering: "Mrs. Alston is coming over." "Here's Mr. Wyatt, and Mrs. Inman." Firmly Martha advised her secretary, her family and staff: "Now don't tell people. I'm not headed for the scrap heap and they'll misunderstand. I have so little time and so much to do. . . ."

It was her only reference to the possibility that she might have to give up her work. One faculty member said privately: "Maybe she can't see so well, but she spotted a run in my stocking at ten yards."

The year 1939 brought the crest of her long wave of recognition. A series of honors was climaxed by one of the highest professional rewards she would receive. The National Institute of Social Sciences gave her its gold medal, with her friend Mrs. Hammond making the presentation. Previous medals had gone to Madame Curie, Andrew Carnegie, Charles Evans Hughes, and Presidents Taft, Hoover, and Coolidge. Before a formal audience on the Starlight Roof of the Waldorf-Astoria, Martha told of that first trip to New York for her schools, when she knew only two people in the city.

"We walk from one place to another on the friendships we have made," she said. "And it is wonderful to be allowed to work; it is one of God's greatest gifts. It is a privilege to work for boys and girls that you believe in; it keeps you going through all kinds of hardships. . . ."

Back home again, Martha had near her an astonishing model of fortitude. Aunt Marth was now somewhere above a hundred years old, almost completely without sight but in many ways as salty and independent as she had been at eighty or sixty or forty. She always chuckled when one of the staff members arrived with his wife, who was somewhat plump. "Come in," she would call to the wife. "I knows *you*; yer always blots out the sun in the door!" Aunt Marth knew others by their step, and these, too, she welcomed.

While she wanted no one to lead her around, she accepted invitations to attend Berry commencements or special events, where she occupied an honored place. Hearing that people were contributing to Berry funds, she sent word frequently that she,

296

too, wanted to give five or ten dollars from her small bank account.

Martha decided to present a radio to Aunt Marth, and dispatched Ged Cannon with it. "What you got?" Aunt Marth demanded. "Radio? Git it right out o' here. Won' have it in my house!" Well briefed for this reaction, Ged said he could not return to the store that day. "Well," Aunt Marth murmured, "leave the fool thing." Ged turned it on before departing. When he went back several days later she scowled at him: "What you wan' now? You let my radio be." Aunt Marth had found a major joy, for two of her main interests—religion and baseball—were broadcast almost every day.

She had always liked the sport, and now she became an even more energetic fan, following teams through the season, memorizing batting averages, and arguing over ratings with student callers. And radio made her faith more vivid than ever. Learning when hymns, sermons, and obituary news came on, she waited through the day for these special hours. If a caller arrived at the same time she raised her hand: "Jes' wait a little and den we kin talk. I got to know what happen' and also git the 'rangement for de funerals, 'cause dey ain' gonna pernounce it but once." She astonished one of Martha's Philadelphia guests, who mentioned that he had passed a bad accident on the road a short time earlier and wondered if any one had died. Aunt Marth gave a prompt résumé: "Two kilt, five hurt, one real bad," and proceeded to add full details.

When Homer Rodheaver and his sister, the "gospel singers," stopped at the schools, Aunt Marth greeted them warmly. "I heerd you a hun'red times on de air." A few minutes later the callers knelt at each side of her chair, and as they sang "The Touch of His Hand on Mine," tears fell from the sightless eyes. "I'm waitin' patient now," she told them. "My hand is in de hand o' de Lawd."

When Martha presented twenty-five-year service pins to the staff, Aunt Marth was included among the five or six recipients. Facing the audience, she said with feeling: "I guess I been workin' seventy-five years 'stead o' twenty-five, but I sure appreciate dis pin, and may de good Lord bless ever'body and keep dis school a-goin' on wid de good work." And she raised her hands as if she were pronouncing a benediction.

For Martha Berry herself one last tribute awaited. In spring of 1940 the Variety Clubs of America, an organization of the nation's theater men, voted her its award as the American who did more than any other for humanity in that year. (Editors chose her by a large margin over Secretary Cordell Hull, J. Edgar Hoover, and Herbert Hoover.) A plaque carried with it a thousand dollars for her favorite charity. "I won't have trouble deciding on *that*," she smiled. The banquet for 1500 people was to be in Dallas, but Martha's physician shook his head; the strain of such a talk and the long trip would be far too much for her.

Secretly Martha planned defiance. Ged drove her to Atlanta, where she took off by plane in a storm. "I thought it was the last of her," Ged says. Arriving in Texas, Martha met, instead of the anticipated quiet reception, a roaring airport crowd, lines of cars to take her in a street parade, and an orator with a ten-gallon hat, which the seventy-two-year-old Martha promptly put on her head.

As newspapers reported, when the frail little woman entered the banquet hall, producers and exhibitors rose in a shouting welcome. Representatives of Gracie Allen and Joan Davis led their stars out by a side way to make new entrances with less competition.

While Martha hesitated this time, it was for only a few seconds. Soon she spoke easily, masterfully. "My doctor told me I couldn't make a long train trip, but he didn't say I couldn't fly. He told me I couldn't make a speech but he didn't say I couldn't talk." She proceeded to take the show from the professionals.

Once more at Berry, she settled down again. "I know I'm

living on borrowed time," she said casually. "Still I feel fairly young, and I'm going to keep going as long as I can." She joked about age: "These bodies of ours are only something God's given us to tote ourselves around in; it's the spirit that counts. I used to look in the mirror and be horrified when I saw wrinkles, and after I found how white my hair was turning I was very disturbed. As I've grown older, though, I'm grateful that a wisp of hair still sticks to my head. And these eyes and thick glasses . . . They're the price we pay for living a long time. The more handicapped I get the harder I have to work."

In these days Martha grew disturbed when a number of faculty members urged that Berry alter its methods and its work program. At times some argued that the school should shift with shifting times to a liberal arts plan, or one tending in that direction. At one point a group of teachers conferred and sent a young staff member to present its views.

Martha received him on a pleasant afternoon. (She had learned in advance of his purpose.) Her greeting was charm itself. "It's such a fine day, let's go into the garden. I always think best when I walk among the flowers." There, as they went about the sunny paths, Martha listened for a while, then looked over her glasses.

"It's interesting to know what the new faculty is thinking, and I appreciate your coming to tell me," she said. "But you go back and tell the new faculty"—she repeated the last phrase with only a slight emphasis—"that I founded the schools to be *different*, to fill a need for a special kind of student, and we've carried on this way for quite a few years. We're going to keep Berry *as* Berry, and will you please tell the new faculty that if they don't like it that way, they will have to 'faculty' somewhere else?"

Though spoken quietly, the words were hard ones, and the crestfallen teacher left after a moment. For the rest of her days Martha frequently urged those around her "not to change the schools."

Steadily her health declined. She went to the hospital for an operation and stayed for months, carrying on many of her duties from her bed. Allowed to return to Oak Hill, she walked slowly about the campus, followed by a student or staff member who kept her within sight. An aide watched her one afternoon as she stepped into the little log cabin near the big house, where she had sat reading that day when the mountain boys looked in. She let her hands run over the old melodeon and sang softly to herself. It had been more than forty years ago, the incident which changed her life. So much had happened since then, in so many places. Friend after friend, co-workers, and helpers had gone, while she remained. . . .

The severest blow at this time was the sudden death of her brother-in-law, John Bulow Campbell. During the long years he had served as trustee and then as chairman of the board, Martha had come to depend on him more and more. As her health failed, she thought that he would look after the schools when she was gone. And now he was gone before her.

Once more the doctors examined her and now they told her she would have to go to Atlanta for extended treatment. Agreeing, she left the house on an August morning of 1941, pale and trembling slightly, with Inez, Ged Cannon and Ruth Hart, a Berry graduate. She had a call to make at Aunt Marth's cottage. The blind woman looked up intently, and as the others listened, these two who had been so close spoke briefly and did not conceal their emotions.

"Aunt Marth, I'm going again. They say I'm not well but I can still use my mind." Martha gave her old friend a fond look. "You've set me a good example, the way you've never complained."

Aunt Marth shrugged and smiled: "You just work yourself down, and you better git some rest and sorta git prop' up 'fore you kin do mo'." They laughed shakily together, and Martha went outside. "Let me see the garden once more," she told Inez. About Oak Hill's terraces, between flowering summer bushes and pools and lines of roses, she made a slow progress, Inez supporting her, Ged following with a chair. Every few minutes she swayed and Ged pushed the chair into place behind her. She touched a rose, plucked a piece of lemon verbena to take with her, and they led her to the car.

A minute or two later Martha asked Ged to stop the machine for a moment. She wanted to look again at the Sunday-school log cabin, out of which her schools had grown. Then she motioned: "All right. To Atlanta, and make it fast." Even to get to a hospital she intended to lose no time on the road.

Soon after her arrival Martha told Inez: "I have a promise from Dr. Sauls that I can go home again, at least once. He'll let me know in time." But the days at St. Joseph's Hospital became weeks, the weeks months. For hours she lay listless, spent, yet few days passed when she did not work for the school, dictating replies to mail, asking questions, receiving reports. Inez and Ged made the two-hour drive daily from Berry, bringing correspondence and papers for transacting school business.

On Inez' arrival each morning Martha whispered to the nurse: "Another pillow, my dear, and push me up." She listened, murmured replies to letters, began memoranda to the staff. Sometimes her voice faded in the middle of a sentence and her eyes would close. Recovering, she would indicate a word or two, and Inez would take over the reply from there.

And always she asked questions: "Who's been on the campus?" "What's Leila Carlisle doing, and how are the Fords?" "You're sure we've thanked Emily Hammond, Inez?" "Remind the board I want Mrs. Ford to have a degree, and Leila Carlisle, too."

Repeatedly she asked about Aunt Marth. "You're sure she's well?" As she wrote Alice Barnes: "I am so glad to know that you are looking after Aunt Marth; that means so much to me." (Little did she realize that Aunt Marth, although sightless, would survive her by nine years.) When she learned that a

Berry graduate was soon to be married, she appealed to Inez: "Keep it all bright and don't let my sickness make any change. Get the flowers from Oak Hill and decorate the chapel, will you? Do the honors and have the reception on the mountain-top. And one of Alice's fine cakes, please, and have *his* family stay at the guest cottage. And, oh, Inez, take Irene shopping in Atlanta."

Martha's sisters and brothers called, and so did staff members, "Prime Minister" Keown, Dr. Cook, Comptroller Hoge, and many others. With them all she passed over questions about her illness, joked with them and the doctors. Just as she had taken over the Plaza dining room, observation cars, and steamship decks, she attracted hospital workers and patients. Nuns stopped in daily, fellow sufferers pushed their way in wheel chairs to her room, and children clustered about her bed.

Receiving jelly and small cakes from the campus, she sent them to the other hospital rooms: "From the Berry schools, you know." Old habits were hard to break; and in any case—she smiled as she asked it—why shouldn't she go on trying to make friends for the work? The Berry staff tried to hit on presents that she could not give away, but most of the things that came to her ended in other hands.

When October 7—her birthday and the great campus observance of Mountain Day—came near, doctors rejected the notion that she be allowed to go back. She told them she wanted above all to be there on this occasion, when the hundreds of students and alumni sang and picnicked and marched along the slope of Lavendar Mountain. Couldn't she be bundled up, then brought right back to the hospital? The doctors were emphatic in their refusal.

Nodding, Martha told Inez: "Then you must have it exactly as usual. Make it a gay day, please, a happy time. Not one gift for me, and nobody here—everybody at the school. You understand?"

Inez and the staff understood, but this time she, Gordon, Dr.

Cook, and several others arranged to ignore Martha's wishes. The birthday was her seventy-fifth, obviously a major event. Arrangements went forward for the campus observance, but also for a surprise call at the hospital. The girls prepared a three-tiered cake in pastel shades with seventy-five candles and a basket to be filled with food that Martha loved—a small broiled chicken, a boiled custard.

Students and staff contributed $75, to be given to her for school purposes; many of the girls worked overtime to earn nickels and quarters and converted them into silver dollars which they cleaned and polished. And alumni conceived a special presentation. For years Martha had talked of her hope that someday Berry would have chimes for the chapel. The graduates raised the money and arranged with a music company of Atlanta, which was located a few blocks from the hospital, to set up an amplifying system so that the chimes might be heard in Martha's room.

Before noon on October 7, 1941, Inez and others stood quietly in the hospital hallway. Word had spread, and doctors, nurses, and patients filled the narrow passage outside her room. At twelve o'clock the chimes rang forth; after a moment of silence Martha cried out. "They're playing Berry songs, and it must be coming from the schools!"

The Berry party entered, and the alumni president made his speech about the chimes. They cut the big cake and Martha offered slices to everyone. Then Inez produced a wide mountain basket, filled to the top with birthday letters, telegrams, and cards. She read aloud the first one and Martha, half blind, reached out to touch it lovingly and thrust it under her pillow.

The secretary read a second message, and Martha whispered: "I must have that one too." After Inez went through several more Martha murmured: "Don't take any away; I'd like all of them here." Inez read for an hour and a half, and Martha held each one for a moment before Inez placed it on the pillow, on the chair beside her, the radiator and the other chairs, until the room seemed covered with them.

They were from elderly women and from young boys, from mountain parents who printed their words on brown paper, from couples in Chicago and San Francisco and Pittsburgh. Did Miss Martha remember the morning she found the girl working on a farm . . . ? Did she know that the former Berry couple were doing well in the East . . . ? A boy recalled his years at Berry; a day never passed that he did not think of them and of her.

When Inez finished, Martha's face glowed. "This is the happiest day of my life." After a moment she stirred: "But you and Geddins must go quickly and get back for Mountain Day. I can see them marching up the slope, and hear the band playing 'Onward, Christian Soldiers.'" It was the music which always climaxed the event. "Tell them all how wonderful they've made me feel, and, please, don't let them be sad." Her voice failing, she gently motioned them away. Inez and Ged sped back to Berry and arrived as the students were marching, sixteen abreast in the grand finale, while the band beat out the rhythm of "Onward, Christian Soldiers." . . .

Two months after Martha's birthday, America and the Berry schools entered a new era. For long months England had fought the rising tide of world fascism, and Martha had winced as she heard of German and Italian successes against the democracies. Then on December 7 of 1941 the Japanese attack on Pearl Harbor brought American entry into the war, and promptly Berry men were enlisting or being called to service. Most war news was withheld from her, as well as word of the difficulties that arose on the campus.

In this war, infinitely more terrible than the one of 1918, Berry became almost empty of young men. In the college barely fifty were left, all or most of whom were classified as 4-F. The high school boys were also being taken, or preparing to leave at any time. How was the great farm and industrial machine to keep going? The dean of women called together the girls and told them that if a number volunteered they might somehow run the place, or most of its essential sections. She warned that the summer ahead would be long and hot, and that they would have to work from before dawn until after dark. She had hoped to get a dozen volunteers, but more than a hundred stepped forward.

From then on the Berry girls did much of the planting and harvesting of crops, the repairing of buildings, feeding of cattle, stoking of furnaces, cleaning of the vast campus in groups that went tirelessly from section to section, assignment to assignment. Henry Ford sent down new tractors, some of them improved models, with a representative to teach their use. The girls operated them without trouble, drove campus cars, and did other mechanical work. It turned out, one or two Berry officials said, that they kept the machines in better condition than did the boys.

The news from abroad was grim. "Missing in action . . ." "Bravery beyond the line of duty . . ." One Berry man who died was a youth whom Martha had watched grow from a baby; she had taken him his first warm clothes. After his mother and father died he lived on the school grounds as a boy and finished his education there. Another victim had entered at thirty as a high school student, graduated with honors, and become a Berry college freshman. He had hoped to be a minister.

There was also the "gate boy," who kept the visitors' register. When he was not greeting and directing callers he had used his penknife to carve small wooden figures for the school, and when he left for the service he had completed more than 300. Near the place in which his friends displayed the carvings the Berry service flag hung, with long lines of blue stars and gold ones in the center. In the gate boy's case as in others, before his blue star could be added word arrived that it must be changed to gold.

Berry men died in the Italian landings, during the bloody Battle of the Bulge, on the Bataan death march. As in World War I letters told of the way Berry training helped them in service. Headlines described an incident in which a youth had his plane shot down over the North Sea. With quick wit and self-control, the boy tied together the remnants, pulled wounded companions aboard the improvised raft, and kept it afloat for a day and night until a friendly submarine picked them up. Inez spotted him—a former student whom Martha had taught to "put his brains into his fingers and his fingers into his work."

For Martha herself the shadows were closing in. By early 1942 she had lost a great deal of weight, and her pale skin seemed transparent. Now and then she lay for hours, eyes closed, fighting the pain. The doctors now said there was nothing further they could do, and she accepted the verdict calmly.

She reminded Inez of the doctor's promise that she would go home at least once again. "But, my dear, Dr. Sauls has waited a little too long, I think. Still, we can't have everything, can we? The Lord has been good to me, as good as I've let Him be." Speaking with difficulty, her assistant tried to remind her of all that she had done, of the accomplishments that she would leave behind. Martha smiled. "Inez, I could have done more, a great deal more, and it's my fault that I haven't."

That did not mean that she would not work, or try to work, up to the final hour. She sent messages, letters of inquiry, letters of thanks for continuing gifts. Several times she called for John Sibley, the Atlanta lawyer who was the new chairman of the board, to talk over events and programs at the school. One day she remarked calmly to him: "My fear isn't death, but that people, perhaps well-meaning ones, may try to make just another school out of Berry. I'd rather see the doors close."

Her brother Tom visited her regularly until he died suddenly on a trip to Florida. On the doctors' orders her associates kept the news from her, yet she sensed the loss. "What's happened to Tom? You're hiding something, and I wish you'd just tell me." Then and on other occasions she had hours of great sadness, but they ended in new optimism and a spurt of labor. Once again there was so little time and so much to do. . . . She joked with the doctors, with her family, with the few callers allowed to her. Her good friend, Dr. Louie Newton of a leading Baptist church of Atlanta, wrote in a newspaper: "Miss Berry, yonder in her hospital room, doomed to die, nearly blind, her body racked with pain, is happier with God and her memories than any person walking the streets of this city."

Nevertheless her energies flagged, and the last hour was very near. On February 26, midnight was to bring Atlanta's first complete war black-out. After dark Inez sat beside the bed, holding the soft, frail hand. Martha said little; a word or two, and she turned her head and lay silent for a long time. At a signal all of Atlanta's lights went quickly out. A few minutes later the white hand fell open. Inez Henry wept, and rose to give the news to those who waited in a score of places.

At dawn the Mount Berry chapel tower began to toll out, and students looked at one another and halted to ask the question. The bell, which had rung through the years for religious services, weddings, commencements, pealed seventy-five times, each toll slower, sadder, as a gray morning started. And mile after mile the word traveled—to the coves and valleys and mountains in the distance.

EPILOGUE

"But to Minister"

"BUT TO MINISTER"

IN EARLY AFTERNOON of the same day, as the sunlight sifted through the campus trees, all work stopped at Berry, and the old "Gates of Opportunity" opened to receive Martha Berry. Speaking in hushed tones, the students lined up on both sides of the road along the curving route to the original log-cabin chapel, named for her friend Captain Barnwell. Martha had wanted her body placed within the walls that would remind the students of the schools' first days.

Many times the boys and girls had waited here to greet school guests; today there were solemn, thoughtful faces instead of smiling ones. A number of men in service had ridden over hastily and stood at the gateway in army, navy and air force uniform. At Atlanta others had asked to be allowed to accompany the procession to the grounds. Then the dark car approached. A salute followed, and as the cortege entered the campus the students marched behind the bier to the rustic structure.

Seniors carried in the bronze casket to place it between iron candlesticks wrought by the boys, with long lighted tapers. A girl in a crisp chambray dress draped Martha's Doctor of Humanities hood over the casket; the students sang a hymn, and one of the boys led a brief prayer. Slowly they marched by, and the seniors began the watch, two for each hour.

At Oak Hill, sightless Aunt Marth Freeman accepted her friend's death with the philosophy of a lifetime.

"De Lawd knows best. I'se prayed fer de Boss and I thanks 'Im dat all wuz well wid her. De rest of yer will have ter pull you'selves togedder. Ain't no time ter be goin' ter pieces; jes' time ter go ter work."

Men and women arrived from all over the South, and friends from Rome, alumni from Georgia and Tennessee and other states, families from the hills and coves. And millions of words, hundreds of pictures appeared in the newspapers.

The Atlanta *Constitution* declared: "No woman of our time, has achieved more in life than did Martha Berry." Another said: "Her monument will not be the brick and stone and wood and land of the Berry schools, but the light that she lit in the minds. . . ." The New York *Herald Tribune* thought that she left "a record of usefulness which has few equals in American history." The authoritative *Survey* magazine called her story "one of the epics of American social history."

Others remembered that Berry boys had achieved notable positions among the nation's professional men, as doctors, college presidents, teachers, among farm and industrial and labor leaders; and that schools modeled on Martha's methods had opened in England and the continent, in the Scandinavian countries, in India. One journal put it simply: "She dies—her work lives." And one man said, summarizing her life, "Martha Berry always believed that everybody was somebody."

About midnight, Inez Henry returned to the chapel, thinking that the crowds would have left. They still came, whites and Negroes, Protestants and Catholics and Jews. Inez stood watching, hearing snatches of comment as they passed before the thin figure dressed in a soft robe of purple velvet, with a bunch of violets from her garden close to her heart. After another hour or so the place quieted, and in the candlelight stood a newly arrived guard, a pair of seniors. One of them Martha had watched in his cradle, the other during his formative years at Berry. She was to be spared the knowledge that within a few months both would be held in Nazi prison camps.

Through the next day new throngs passed the bier, and hundreds stayed for the late-afternoon services in the big Berry chapel, which was filled, with many others waiting outside. She had asked that there be no sermon, only a few favorite hymns and prayers, the reading of Scripture. Again the students lined the walk and seniors carried the casket, covered with roses and Easter lilies, to the burial spot on the chapel hill, under a pecan tree that she had admired.

Some had spoken of placing her grave at the front of the chapel, until she had said she wished it at the side in a less public spot. "The band plays right in front," she had said with a smile, "and if I'm resting there some boy mightn't blow the horn quite as loud as he should."

Now the family gathered about the grave, with members of the board and staff. In the forefront stood a circle of children from the Possum Trot vicinity, with several that Martha had cared for as babies. The benediction was pronounced, and as the throng moved back a girl of six went up to place a bunch of wild flowers beside an elaborate spray of orchids. She was crying.

Slowly the crowds left, and in the dusk Inez returned to offer her private prayer. Standing beneath the sheltering tree, she heard footsteps, and looked up to see Henry Ford, who had attended the services with his wife. He had come to the grave for his own last meditation, and together he and Inez went away.

When the students and staff got up the next morning they found the campus covered with a snow which turned the grave into a pale mound. Slowly the snow melted and the flowers came back into view, preserved against the softening white background.

313

And soon a plain tombstone was placed there, bearing only Martha Berry's name, birth and death dates, and the words on which she had based her rich life: "Not to Be Ministered Unto, but to Minister."

ACKNOWLEDGMENTS

Over a period of years many people have assisted in the research for this first full-length biography of Martha Berry, providing recollections and impressions of her, letters and cards, copies of her remarks, and printed data.

The main sources, however, have been the words and writings of Miss Berry herself. For more than forty years she sent out thousands of communications, formal or informal; made hundreds of addresses; wrote magazine and newspaper articles, including a few summaries of her purposes for books. In her own vivid words she told hundreds of people of her experiences and the details of her work.

Another primary source has been a large though scattered volume of Miss Berry's notes and notebooks. Her personal books, scrapbooks, and related material, bearing her own comments and notes, have been of unique assistance.

During most of their history the Berry schools have drawn marked attention in Georgia, in other parts of the South, and in the United States. As a consequence countless magazine and news-

ACKNOWLEDGMENTS

paper accounts give details of the institutions' growth and difficulties over the years. The schools' own extensive collection of scrapbooks, programs, messages in connection with special events, etc., has been of inestimable help.

This is not an authorized biography, but members of the Berry family and the staff of her schools have been generous in answering questions, giving impressions, and offering suggestions.

Mrs. J. Bulow Campbell of Atlanta and Mrs. Alexander Bonnyman of Knoxville, sisters of Miss Berry, have devoted hours to interviews and checking of facts. Mrs. Bonnyman made one or two trips to Atlanta, during which she discussed subjects relating to the founder of the schools, and also provided a volume of written data. Mrs. Richard W. Courts of Atlanta, niece of Miss Berry, also a trustee of the Berry Schools, aided greatly. Mr. and Mrs. Thomas Berry, Miss Berry's nephew and his wife, and Mrs. Thomas Berry, widow of her brother, all of Rome, Ga. were helpful.

Mr. William McChesney Martin, Washington, D.C., chairman of the board of trustees, talked over his own recollections of Miss Berry. Mr. G. L. Westcott, Dalton, Georgia, member of the board, provided a large set of letters, as well as his own vivid memories. Mrs. John J. Eagan of Atlanta, widow of the first chairman of the board, gave generously of her time.

Thanks are due to Mr. John A. Sibley of Atlanta, former board chairman, who contributed a number of sharp incidents of her career, and to other board members, including Dr. Philip Weltner, Dr. Harmon Caldwell, Mr. Robert F. Maddox, Mr. E. E. Moise, the late Mr. George Winship, and Mr. R. W. Woodruff of Atlanta; the late Dr. James G. K. McClure of Asheville; and Mr. Nelson Macy, Jr., of New York. Mr. Macy added a number of anecdotes of his aunt, Mrs. Kate Macy Ladd.

Mrs. John Henry Hammond of New York, long-time friend of Miss Berry, gave a series of interviews and also provided much written matter and many suggestions. Mrs. G. L. Carlisle of Norfolk, Conn., made herself available for many questions about her own close observations of Miss Berry. Mrs. Ripley Hitchcock of Greenwich, Conn. interrupted other activities to answer many queries. Mrs. E. J. Bellinger of Mayville, N.Y. gave much help.

Mr. Harvey Roberts of Montezuma, Ga., former Berry staff member, gave up other work to assist in handling Berry documents, in seeking Berry school friends in the area, and in answering written queries.

Members and former members of the Berry staff and their wives provided a wide range of Miss Berry's letters and memoranda, notations, and recollections. Among them were Dean S. H. Cook, Mr. and Mrs. Walter A. Johnson, Dr. and Mrs. G. L. Green, Mr. and Mrs. Geddins Cannon, Mr. and Mrs. E. H. Hoge, Mrs. M. C. Ewing, and Miss Alice Barnes. Dr. Green provided a set of extensive memoranda; Dr. Cook permitted consultation of his own Berry data, and Miss Barnes was particularly helpful in sharing letters, pictures, and her own memories of her long-time friend. Mrs. Ralph Farmer assisted in copying material and letters. Mrs. D. C. Sullivan gave much help, as did Mr. Arthur Beaird and Mr. Winifred Moore.

Other staff members who helped were Mr. and Mrs. Paul King, Mr. F. C. Moon, Mr. Thomas Taylor, Mr. Nathan Perry, Mr. Horace Fletcher. Miss Florrie Jackson, librarian of the Berry schools, gave swift help in locating out-of-print items and other data, and Mrs. J. L. Henderson, librarian of the Rome, Ga., library, aided in locating related material.

In Rome, Mr. Hugh Keown, son of the late Mr. Gordon Keown, drew on his lifetime of residence on or near the campus, and Mr. C. J. Wyatt remembered Berry stories, as did Mrs. Turner McCall, and Dr. R. C. Gresham.

Judge Eugene Gunby of Atlanta arranged a surrey ride during which he described vividly his many similar jaunts at Martha Berry's side, when she was seeking students in the mountain areas. Mrs. Frank Inman, early friend of the schools, drew on her fund of memories, as did Mr. and Mrs. Clifton Russell, Sr., and others of their family, long-time residents of the campus.

Mr. W. C. Henson of Cartersville, Ga., pioneer graduate of the schools, in interviews and letters helped recreate the original Berry atmosphere. Mr. Milton L. Fleetwood, president and editor of the Tribune Publishing Company of Cartersville, granted interviews and consulted his files.

Mrs. T. E. Wright, Mr. and Mrs. Hal Smith, Mr. Fain Ingrim of Chattanooga, and Mrs. E. K. Jones of Ringgold, Ga. helped arrange consultations and correspondence in their area. In New York, Mr. and Mrs. Hayes Overcash and Mr. and Mrs. J. D. Driggers were especially co-operative, as was Mrs. Sadie Summerall Nagel.

Mr. W. A. Dobson, regional executive of the Boy Scouts of America, Atlanta, gave interviews and correspondence. Mr. John C. Warr, general manager of the Georgia Baptist Children's home, Hapeville, Georgia, gave similar aid, with Mr. Clarence Walker and Mr. Johnson Head of Atlanta. Dr. Louie Newton of the Druid Hills Baptist Church, Atlanta, provided reminiscences, articles, and talks about Miss Berry.

Appreciation is also due Mrs. Robert C. Alston, Atlanta, whose late husband was for many years chairman of the Berry Board; Mrs. Laurance Rockefeller, New York; Mrs. Medora Perkerson, Atlanta; Mrs. W. W. Martins, Gulfport; Miss Julia Wooten, Atlanta; Mrs. E. W. Register, Macon.

To Mrs. Florence Kane Reynolds, Mrs. W. J. Kane, and Miss Anna Marie Kane of New Orleans.

To Miss Mavis McIntosh, Mr. James Gilvarry, Mr. Austin Wilder, and Mr. Alton S. Wolfert of New York.

To the late Mr. William W. Phillips of Rome, pioneer pupil of the schools; Mr. S. D. Moxley of Birmingham; Dr. John N. Ware of Rome; Mrs. Howard Frost of Los Angeles; Mrs. Helen Wilmerding of New York; Mrs. Merrill Parrish Hudson of Memphis.

To Mr. John Hall Jacobs, librarian of the New Orleans Public Library, and Mr. George King Logan, assistant librarian; to Dr. Garland Taylor, librarian of the Howard-Tilton Library of Tulane University; Mr. James W. Dyson, librarian of Loyola University; Miss Ruth Renaud, Miss Margaret Rucket, Miss Gladys Peyronnin, Miss Lily Mouton, Miss Marion Mason, Mrs. Alice V. Westfeldt, Mrs. Ellen Tilger, and Mrs. Bernice Zibilich of the New Orleans

Public Library; Mr. Robert Greenwood, Miss Martha Ann Peters, Mrs. Clayre Barr Lewis, Mrs. Evangeline Thurber, Mrs. Dorothy Lawton, and Mrs. Beatricia Ford, members or former members of the Howard-Tilton Library staff.

To Mr. Jesse Cunningham, librarian, Cossitt Library, Memphis; Mrs. Marie Bankhead Owen, Department of Archives and History, state of Alabama, Montgomery; Mr. Dan S. Robison, state librarian and archivist, and Mrs. Gertrude Morton Parsley, reference librarian, Nashville; Miss Martha L. Ellison, head of reference department, Lawson McGhee Library, Knoxville.

Over a period of years Mr. Ralph McGill of the Atlanta *Constitution* has written numerous articles on Miss Berry and her work. Mr. James Saxon Childers of the Atlanta *Journal* wrote a recent and perceptive article about her in *Reader's Digest*.

Other treatments of Miss Berry and her work have appeared under the signatures of Miss Celestine Sibley, Mr. Harold Martin, Miss Margaret Shannon, Mr. Ernest Rodgers, Mr. Harry Stillwell Edwards, Dr. Raimundo de Ovies, and others of Atlanta.

For the past fifty years numerous and lengthy magazine studies have appeared. Among the most helpful have been those of Mr. John Mathews in *Everybody's Magazine*, Dr. Albert Shaw in *Review of Reviews*, Mr. Harvey Roberts in the *Georgia Review*, Mr. Herman Hagedorn in *Outlook*, Mr. Fred K. Hoehler in *American Forests*, Miss Alice Booth in *Good Housekeeping*, Mr. Charles H. Dickey in the *Christian Herald*, Mr. Raymond Leslie Goldman in the *The Shrine Magazine*, Miss Genevieve Parkhurst in the *Pictorial Review*, Miss Faith Boyce in *The Woman Citizen*, and Martha Berry's accounts in *World's Work*, *Survey*, and other sources.

Additional accounts in pamphlets and other special publications have been presented by Mr. Frazier Hunt, Mr. Russell Sheppard, Lexie Dean Robinson, Mrs. John Henry Hammond, the Rev. Mr. Samuel H. Shoemaker. Use has been made of numerous other articles from the Atlanta *Journal* and *Constitution*, New York *Times*, New York *Herald Tribune*, the old New York *Herald*, Washington *Post*, Louisville *Courier Journal*, *Christian Science*

ACKNOWLEDGMENTS

Monitor, Quincy *Patriot-Ledger*, New Haven *Sunday-Register*, Rome *News-Tribune*, Boston *Herald*, Indianapolis *Times*, the former *Literary Digest*, *Time*, *Life*, *Newsweek*, *Chattanooga Times*, *Chattanooga News-Free Press*.

Especially helpful have been the *Southern Highlander*, *Mt. Berry News*, and *Berry Alumni Quarterly*.

Tracy Byers's "Sunday Lady of Possum Trot," published in 1932, when Miss Berry was alive, was also of assistance.

Of highest value have been the authoritative recollections of the late Miss Elizabeth Brewster and Miss Alice Wingo, and others of the staff.

Miss Zella Armstrong of Chattanooga suggested several important sources, and Bob Meyer of Festival Information Service, Mrs. Fidelia Anding of the Anding Bookstore, New Orleans, and Bill Fountain of the Fountain Library, Columbus, Ohio, assisted in locating various references and out-of-print items.

Thanks are due to Mr. Erwin A. Holt for his help in so many ways, and especially for furnishing copies of letters to him from Miss Berry, for answering questions, and for providing copies of the old *Southern Highlander* and other publications.

Thanks to Mr. W. T. Henry, Mr. and Mrs. Thomas Jones for their patient and understanding co-operation.

WITHDRAWN